Profound Effect

VICTORIA AND JOHN STEWART

Tellwell Talent

www.tellwell.ca

ISBN

978-0-2288-0956-2 (Hardcover)

978-0-2288-0957-9 (Paperback)

978-0-2288-0958-6 (eBook)

Acknowledgements

We would like to express our immense gratitude to the loving intelligence that has shared with us over all these years ... a kind of wisdom one can only dream about.

Table of Contents

In Summary

Today we have something new beginning to form around our thoughts about life, and it begins with this one single question:

"Can we, the human race, have a more successful and a more loving society to live in and be fulfilled in?"

This now is the question that is paramount to all of us here, and we must share immense concern about this. We must begin to think into this question as though it was everything to the world's future, for otherwise what will become of us all if we do nothing? There can be no doubt that today human civilization is looking back at itself wondering where we next need to be heading and what we should be doing in order for us to become the true living saviours of this planet.

It is now at this most critical point in modern history that this book is aimed at the human populace and how we can learn en masse to shift the human consciousness—to reshape its internal thinking powers such that we no longer will require fear, strife, famine, and disease. No longer will we have the need for greed to overtake the human mindset. Nor will we require wars and conflicts to resolve disputes throughout the globe once we re-examine the growth of human civilization to date and then imagine a new world to come.

It will be a different world and a better world, one that will bring an untold bounty of true happiness and joy everywhere without the fear creeping in that might otherwise compromise these most amazing new beginnings on the planet.

So the bigger question now is how one can even begin to imagine a world population doing that in the first place if they cannot feel free enough in their own minds to go there—to a place in this reality that shows such promise and intrigue. This book will deliver that greater understanding to you now.

I am a simple soul walking down the road of life with the sun on my back and the wind in my face, and I have this feeling that something good is just around the next bend in the road. And that's why I keep walking …

CHAPTER 1

THE SEARCH

Today we are two simple people who only want to know more about this life. We want to understand what it can be and become to a world of men, women, and children who only want to know they are going to be okay and that their lives here have meaning and worth. For some time now, this notion has been the catalyst beneath our thoughts in our search to find the ultimate truth of all truths about this life—that somehow, some way, there must be more to come to this world than what we see here today.

It was roughly twenty-one years ago when this all began for us. We were on vacation at the time on the west coast of Canada, contemplating our next move in life. This was our way of escaping the survival needs of our everyday lives so that we could take the time to reflect and think more clearly about our future together. Standing near the water's edge watching our children play, it came to us both at almost exactly the same moment that something needed to change for us, but not for any single reason you might imagine. It wasn't that we were in great distress about our lives in general. In fact, we were in a place that gave us much in terms of the value this life has to give. But still there were challenges we faced—the same kind of challenges people face all around the globe today. Like many others, we too felt the uncertainty of what life would bring to us in our future. Would there, for example, be enough money to look after the needs of our family? Would our children be healthy and happy?

Furthermore, we didn't feel at ease with what was going on in the world in general. There were concerns throughout the planet—big concerns that seemed almost surreal in nature, and we didn't know how to make peace with these in our minds. There seemed to be no clear way out from beneath them. People everywhere seemed on edge about their lives, not knowing whether they were going to sink or swim, and that just drove us crazy thinking about what this world of ours was going to be like in the future.

We were in the middle stages of raising our two boys. Our oldest was ten at the time and his younger brother was seven. When we looked into their eyes, we saw such vitality and promise for their future, and that got us to thinking that there had to be something better for them in this world than what we saw. This life that showed so much promise seemed so unstable and so out of sync with how one might otherwise want things to be. It gave us no guarantee for our future, and that to us just wasn't good enough. We wanted more, and so we set out on a pathway to "moreness." We said to ourselves, let's at least try to find a way to make life work better for these two young boys of ours and then bring that to their lives.

And so the journey began for us, just like that. We made a decision to find the answers we needed from life, and then we went searching for those answers in a place where most don't seem to go today—into the inner depths of the human mind. We began with the assumption that there must be more to life than what meets the eye, or to put it another way, there must be an intelligence beneath this world of parts far greater than our own. This was something we felt to be true, yet still we didn't know for certain. Still we didn't have a full understanding of what set of rules this life was based upon. In our minds, there surely had to be something more concrete to go on in life than just a hope and a prayer, and that was what plagued us. That is what drove our passion to know more and to begin an exploration—a journey of discovery—to determine whether, in fact, we were alone … or not!

We said to ourselves that if it is true that a greater intelligence does exist to this world, then we must somehow find a way to move straight toward the kind of knowing that only a much higher power could have. But to do that, we had to first eliminate the thought that we could not enter our own brainwaves, our own thought structures, and there learn to communicate with a source of wisdom far greater than our own. To our way of thinking, it had to come down to this in the end—this rather obscure way to think into a space of the mind to ask certain key questions and somehow begin to hear critical responses back.

Now many would say that we must have been out of our minds to believe that we could indulge in a two-way communication with a source far more influential than anything our brains could ever muster up, but in fact that is exactly what happened. This dialoguing system actually took place. Why that was, we can't really say for certain. Perhaps it was because we had this overwhelming need to actually hear something back in response to all the many questions we were asking. And so the answers came to us slowly and more and more precisely with time. It wasn't that we could actually hear the words; rather they flowed into our minds just like a river of knowledge, one after the next ... as though it was meant to be this way all along.

The truth is that when we first began, we never really expected to find what we were looking for. We didn't suspect we would actually come across such an amazing source of knowledge that some would call "the higher self" while others might call it God. Nor did we think we would find all the answers we were searching for. Those answers, it seemed, were just waiting to come to the surface of our awareness by way of our own willingness to hear them. They delivered an understanding about life that was extraordinary. At first we couldn't even believe what we were hearing—this myriad of love-filled notions delivered to us with unending exuberance and passion, all with the aim to try to bring this planet out from beneath its turmoil.

It was as if a new perspective had been dropped into our laps, as if all of a sudden the mysteries of life were being revealed to us through this loving connection, this untapped capacity of the human mind. We were learning the reason for our existence and how this world now could be reworked to be so much better in a multitude of ways. Of course, at first we couldn't comprehend how this could be true. But on the other hand, we could not deny that the messages were exquisitely expressed. They were delivered with such conviction, such certainty, and such care for all of us on the planet that we couldn't turn away from them. We just had to know more.

So we moved more and more questions into the discussions, and each time we did that it became increasingly apparent to us that these were extraordinary, compelling stories about the world we were hearing. These were not your everyday spiritual delivery systems illuminating their truths through a script written hundreds of years ago. No, this was unlike anything we had heard before. It was a new storyline about how the world could be different now—how it could move to a new position of strength that no one today can even imagine. And it all came by way of a new amazing truth about the undefined, unrealized potential of love in us all and how it now can be utilized by people across the globe in many different predicaments, to bring to their lives what they now need and fully require in order to be saved.

There was a problem for us, however, in that there seemed to be a weakness in this theory that was being laid out to us about how all of life could change for the better. Its vital link—its connection to all of us—appeared to exist only through love, and historically love as a positive force in the world seemed to be woefully inadequate given the ways people were choosing to live with one another. All across the globe, people were fighting the fights, you might say, against life and against one another, and in that fight there was only so much room for love to thrive. For so many of us on this planet, life seemed to be such a struggle just to get by to that next day, and from what we could see, the values of love had done little to rescue the human populous from that struggle. Love didn't seem to have a strong enough influence to change this world for the better.

But this is exactly what this loving god-like intelligence was now showing us—that the world is missing something and we must now fix it. We must begin to understand our lives from an entirely new perspective, and it must be done soon we were told, for time is not on our side. Time is our enemy here, and so we must act quickly in order to manoeuvre past all the many concerns that are out there in life today, so that they do not become unmanageable and *beyond our abilities to fix them*.

Of course to us, this kind of dialogue seemed rather surreal, but nonetheless we pushed forward to pursue this line of thinking. We opened to this connection for many years, and we took the time to learn more about the ins and outs of how the powers of love within us all could work in the world to change everything. At the time, it was perplexing to us how love could now be the answer to all of our prayers, as we were being told. But with time, as our conversations continued with this loving advisor, it all became more clear, so much so we could no longer ignore the obvious fact before us—that this was the miracle we were searching for. This was the way out from every dilemma the world was in today.

In our minds, these words were the most powerful words and the most compelling words this planet could ever live by because they delivered what, to us, was the real story about how this world of parts is actually run—which is by one consistent driver and that is love in one form or another. In life, everything it seems hinges on this one central theme—that love is the presence and the influence inside it all—in every event and every possibility ever lived or imagined.

And that brought to us a kind of hope for the world we had never known before. From that point on, we never looked back again. We began to think differently about life in the future. We began to imagine a world of parts that could somehow now come together as we were being told, all with the same aim in mind—to rescue this world of people from their pain and suffering and bring this planet back to health again but in a most sensible and sustainable way, a way that would serve to energize the base of human understanding about love like never before.

Then finally one day we were told most emphatically that this style of communication we were engaging in should be revealed to the world at large because, in the end, if people could take hold of this in their own lives, everything would change. This planet would be saved from ultimate calamity and we would have everything we needed to address all forms of human discontent, so that we together as one nation of people could begin to turn this ship forward once and for all, never to get off course again.

And so we just had to do this. We had to write this book and present to you with the greatest humility, these messages of hope that have been passed on to us over all these many years. After all, we had nothing to lose by trying. In our minds, there were no other answers for this life now becoming better and outlasting all the negatives out there today. People were in pain on so many levels, and in our minds this needed to stop. These messages just had to be shared.

So with this in mind, we have included in these pages certain passages given to us by what we believe to be a loving God. However, because the word "God" has had many different meanings attached to it in this world, we will refer to this higher intelligence within us all as "*Love*." We wanted to express these portions of the book to you this way so you could feel their authenticity and get a sense of how the words were being delivered to us so eloquently and with such concern for our overall well-being as a nation of men, women, and children. To us, these messages were truly magical and ... intoxicating. To you, well, that will be up to you to decide what importance they will bring to your life. But regardless of what you decide, the burning question will still remain: What will happen to us all if we do nothing now and these messages prove to be true?

Message:

There are over seven billion of you in the world today, and every one of you feels life in a different way and therefore has a different understanding of what it means to you. You each have a different truth to live by. But the question this book addresses is whether there can be a bigger truth to believe in that will bring more certainty to your lives here on this planet and guarantee you a future you will all want to be in.

In these pages to follow, I have given you messages of hope that are all about the vitality of a world that now is in need of your combined help, to flow new love where today, sadly, it does not exist. And if you can turn your heads in this direction, then you will have this one last chance to make life better and to rebuild what has for centuries now been a mistaken identity of the world's greatest power and influence over this planet. Finally, the love that has been hidden deep within the pure essence of each and every last one of you will be brought to the surface of your awareness because this is what you, the human race, are wanting now at some level of your consciousness.

Yes, you in fact are the lucky ones who have chosen to come at this particular moment in human history to play the biggest role in what this change will be. You are the ones who will determine the fate of this planet. This now is your destiny to grab hold of and run with. But you will not be alone with this because I have a plan to help you, a plan that is going to change the living dynamic relationship you now have … to me. It is a plan that will serve to break you apart from the misguided belief systems of your past that have led you to this untenable position the world now finds itself in. And finally, this plan will allow you to feel the pure strength of who you really are to this planet. It will help you to understand the purpose of your life and how now you can play this most critical role in making the shift in human consciousness that is required of you. Without that shift, this world will not continue to survive and prosper. It is failing on almost every front now, and it needs you to change this because only you can do this. You are the ones who have what it will take to make the shift into a remarkable new beginning for each of your lives.

To date, this life has been adjusted and made to feel better and flow better because of me, through this connective space we have together. Yet for the most part, this has been at best a temporary fix because I would not allow for my presence to be known, if only through your imagination of me there. This then has made the connection between you and me feel less important to you … less meaningful … less engaging and therefore more tenuous in many ways.

The connection we did have, however, was there for the most part to make certain you did not let go of your life too soon and forget why you came to this life in the first place. I was there constantly nudging you along, trying to show you the way toward certainty in your life, but all the while there was little to no certainty of my connection to you in your mind. There was only uncertainty and confusion at best. Yet still, the strength of our connection, although buried deep within your mind, was conveyed to you through those feelings of love you carried for your life. This was the one reason why you all came to be here in the first place. It resided in your need to feel more love in your existence, and this was the place to find that expansion. This was the place you could come to ... and create that opportunity.

So why now is a change in this dynamic relationship between you and me required? The answer is that the world is in pain right now in almost every aspect of your lives together. This world is just not working to the benefit of the whole of life any longer, and so we must find a way to correct all the injustices that have occurred over all these many centuries and then live in that newness.

And understand this too: this planet knows who you have been trying to be over all these many years and it, this earth, wants for you to remain. It wants all of you to find the centre of your truth about this life—why you are here and the ultimate purpose for your existence. However, if you are to continue moving in the direction you are moving today, I am afraid this planet will no longer be able to sustain you here. The reason I say this with such conviction and concern for you, the human race, is because I know we only have a limited time frame to get things right, and no matter how hard you may try to correct this world of parts on your own, you will never get there without me in your minds. This is just too overly complex an issue for you to completely grasp what this is ... alone.

Now you must begin to understand this world from an entirely new perspective because in every lifestyle and in every home, there is concern—be it money issues or lifelong commitments gone bad or one of the thousands upon billions of other concerns that are out there today. You all have them, and you all are moving to correct them in whatever fashion suits the day. The problem is, however, that many if not most of these concerns have resulted in negative effects being levelled at the planet's health. Adjustments in methods of agriculture, for example, have manifested a profession that has taken away from the planet's vital nutrients rather than propagating a nurturing and positive effect. As well, billions of lives are at risk of extinction if they do nothing about the deterioration of the world water supplies. Clearly most of you have been looking the other way when it comes to these concerning situations. Your minds have not held the energy of care that will be required now in order to correct what this is. And now, there can be no clear direction to move along unless you and I come together and open up the portals of opposition to all of these negative consequences being levelled at this planet.

Today I can feel that the people of this world now want this shift to begin, and they do not want to move in the opposite direction to this any longer. But know this: you will need me to make these movements now fully sustainable. You will need to think into new directions of health for this planet, and then take those assertions—those movements—and shift into action together with me. On every level of human behaviour patterning, this earth—your earth—needs your help and commitment to this cause. And most importantly, there is a need for you to make your connections to me now ... *PERMANENT.*

So what does this mean to have this connection between you and me now opened to in a more vibrant and energetic way? Well, it means I want to show you your world in ways that you can only dream about today, and I know this will take time. But when the true vitality of this movement is flung into action and the world can finally see and feel what this can be, then suddenly you will be awakened to a life that will be in perpetuity ... a truly magical space to live in. And this new spirit connection to me will have taken you all there, to that next logical step in your evolvement as a species. You will begin to feel differently and think differently but in a good way and in ways that today you simply do not have.

From where I sit, I can see that this planet now desperately needs my loving assistance but in a much more profound and consequential way than ever was there for you in the past. This is the most important objective of the twenty-first century—to unearth a mountain of controversy felt everywhere on the planet today and then turn it all into positive, progressive constructs that will serve to change what this life is and make it better in all aspects of human life.

This is what will be your saving grace and the world's new dimension of truth to live by in order that we make the necessary adjustments to correct what this world has become. And if and when you all want this change to begin, it will unleash a magnificent tapestry of vital and earth changing movements around the world so that no aspect of human life will be left behind. Everything will be on the chopping blocks of life to be eliminated by you if they do not show promise and if they are not doing what they have to do in order to bring this world back to order again—back to a state of being that will be staggeringly good for you, the citizens of this planet. A *profound effect* will be felt everywhere around the globe, and your world—your loving world—will thank you for it because you will be the ones who do this. You will be the true saviours of this world of ours.

CHAPTER 2

THE OPENING

In this world of great complexity and disarray, there are billions of people, it seems, who have nowhere else to go to make sense of this world we now are living in, except to turn inward to their own minds. Today for so many people, the world feels more and more like a place that can do nothing to make certain of our lives going forward. More times than not, life just does not work out as we had hoped or planned it to be. And so we are left to wonder what can be done when everywhere you look bad things are happening, lives are lost over senseless actions, and people are giving up and leaving this place of life because they think they have nowhere else to turn.

In recent times, we have been pushing forward in our discussions with *Love* to try to bring clarity to all of this ourselves. In fact, the focus of our discussions has been moving further and further into a place of deep and relentless concern for the planet and all of her inhabitants. *Love* would say to us, "What the world is in need of now is a new beginning state of existence—a fresh start at life as you know it to be because nothing today is working the way it now must work in order to rescue this world from its plight. And now we are in a hurry to arrest the negative charges that have for centuries been levelled at this planet so that they do not do any further harm and so they do not threaten the existence of life itself."

With this in mind, we now present to you a message from *Love* about the state of the world today.

MESSAGE:

What this world is in need of today is nothing more and nothing less than a miracle of gargantuan proportions—a miracle that will once and for all eliminate human suffering and pain and move this planet to a new position of strength in love. This is what your world needs here and now, and yet to date that miracle has not arrived on the scene. You, the human race, still do not know how to make this miracle your newest reality.

It seems to elude you here because you think such a cure-all dream for the world could never be achieved. After all, life shows this to you each and every day. It places all kinds of obstacles in your path and presents you with many a dilemma too big to solve, it seems. And so you are left to think there is just too much standing in your way to even consider that change on such a grand scale is even possible.

But here is the real question. Is it really such a wild assertion to think there might just be something that could come along now to readjust life and make it better for people all around the world? If you can even think this for a moment, then why can it not be a possibility? After all, you went to the moon and back, and a hundred years before that, people would have thought you were out of your mind to even suggest such a thing.

Well, in this same vein, this elusive miracle the world needs today is within your grasp, and all you have to do to set it in motion is begin to imagine it. Imagine a new life possibility for this planet that will evoke change in monumental ways— ways that will give to the human populace an opportunity to experience life in its fullest and grandest form. And this is something that has never existed within your modern society with all its many concerns and earthly dilemmas.

But now with the awareness of this untapped driver of love within you all, you can begin to free your minds to think about life in a much broader and clearer sense, and in doing so, you can change the rules you live by forever. You can eliminate the pain and suffering of people all around the world once and for all, never to look back again and never to turn away from a feeling in you all that says … now we are finally on the right track. Now we have a way to move past all the dismay of this place of life because now we have a loving force within us that we can count on to take us to new heights of success. With this one single driver, we can change this planet's trajectory in a magnificent and courageous new way.

For the human race, this could be your new starting position. This could be the magical new beginning space within your collective minds that will bring a new awareness of the many possibilities that life could now offer you. These possibilities, these magical new positions of strength, are what I will reveal in the messages of this book, the messages about you that have been missing since the beginning. Those mysteries now can come out from the darkness to give everyone this chance to live life as it was always meant to be lived—with a keen eye toward everything good rather than the opposite to that.

After all, you weren't born to be held down to a world of struggle and dismay. No, you came here to feel every bit of goodness that life could offer, and this is something you fully understood and lived by in the very beginning of your lives as young children. For most of you at least, that goodness factor was felt deep and wide in those early years. It gave to you a freedom about your lives that was everything to your way of thinking, and you used that freedom to play at life without restraint. There was no dream too big or too elusive to become your next big adventure because life, to you, was this wonderful, magical place that made it all happen.

With time, however, those simple truths of life became clouded, and so life did begin to change for you, much the same way it changed for all the many generations that came before you. Those hopes and dreams you once lived with became somewhat dashed by the very life that brought them here in the first place, and so your lives didn't seem to hold the same promise you once knew when you were young. Of course, life still was a good place to be in for the most part, but it wasn't always good because it didn't always have a way to make things right. Oftentimes it couldn't give you what you wanted and needed the most, and as that was, life became a need state of existence, which in turn changed everything.

Today human need has overtaken the human psyche. Need has become the single most misused concept known to humankind, and through it there has developed throughout the world a greed mentality, which still to this day has not been resolved in any meaningful way. Nonetheless, this is the reality you now have learned to live with. You live in need of all the things that life denies you, be it a simple glass of water or a solution to global warming. The needs are varied and they are everywhere, and because of this, a feeling has been fostered in the world at large today that is neither free of spirit nor free of mind. This feeling is imbued with thoughts that are negative and full of resentment and disdain for this world you now live in, and as a result you can see in people everywhere this mistrust of a life that no longer seems to be a friend one can count on.

You all know this to be true because today if you look around the globe of life, you will see people who do not feel safe, supported, and loved the way they would want to be. Millions live in desperation and abject poverty with no clear understanding of how to break free of their present-day dilemmas. For these ones, life feels unpredictable and most uncertain. It seems to have no order to it, no peace, and no contentment. Many are living on the edge of extinction every day of their lives. Even their most basic of needs cannot be met.

Furthermore, there is injustice everywhere. Bad things happen to good people for no apparent reason every single day. You have to wonder why some would even want to go on amid all the tyrannies that are out there. Many of you would say to me, "What kind of place is this anyway? Why would we choose to come here to this life, if in fact life is even a choice? This place is not a safe place at all. It is a place where anything could go wrong at any time, and then all might be lost."

Life has been this way since the beginning. There are always these negative influences that come into the picture of your lives—the ever-changing daily events that seem more often than not to affect your living styles adversely. It's everything from rain on your wedding day to flood, famine, and mistreatment by your fellow man, and all in all these tell the tale of a life over which you have no control, it seems. It is a life that has the power to take away your joy in the blink of an eye, and over many centuries, despite your need to have it all be different, nothing has really changed in this regard. The world is still a precarious place to be in, and you still have no idea as to the true cause and effect of things. You feel vulnerable to a life that doesn't seem to care if you are happy or sad … or whether you live or you die.

It's no wonder human survival has become *THE* paramount theme of the human race and the single most compelling reason why the lives of so many feel so difficult to be in. In fact, you don't go anywhere today where survival isn't on virtually everyone's mind in some form or another. It exists everywhere and without restraint, and for most of you the message is clear. It says that if this world will not guarantee you a place here, then you must fight for that right. You must take life into your own hands. And if that means you must compete with every man, woman, and child and every other living thing on the planet for the limited goodness that does exist here, then that is how it must be. If you must sacrifice the needs of another in order to save yourselves, then that is what you must do because, well, life made it that way. It placed you in this tenuous situation right from the moment you were born. And now you must ask why that is. Why is it that you who want so much more for your lives and you who dream such lofty dreams should be held back by a life that seems to have an agenda all its own?

This is, indeed, the human dilemma you all face today, and as yet you haven't figured out how to get out of it. It's something like the feeling of being stuck inside a box with no way out into that bigger, freer, and more amazing space you all dream about—beyond the box. So here you sit feeling great pain about the fact that the world as you know it to be, just isn't big enough to satisfy your growing needs to survive and prosper.

Today you see this kind of pain everywhere. Where there are people in need of more, there is pain—emotional pain and physical pain—and I'm sure you all will agree this doesn't feel correct. It doesn't seem right that life should be like this. Somehow there must be a way to make your lives better. There must be room for more to come, and by that I don't mean just inconsequential things either. I mean things of the heart and things that will forever hold great meaning for your lives— things like trust, love, sincerity, the values of giving and sharing, and the beginning of a new life movement for you when life otherwise could have looked so bleak. These are all out there to be had, and yet today these rich values are sadly lacking much of the time. As such, the world seems to be spiralling downward with no true way to climb back up. Those avenues of mindful thinking that would have brought you to a much better position in life seem to have been closing down for some time now.

It's as if there is a missing piece to the puzzle of life you haven't found yet—a missing link that would now make sense of everything and give you a way to be here in life that is magnificent in how it brings a true happiness to everything you do. That link still is missing though you've looked everywhere to find it. You've searched high and you've searched low. You have scoured every frontier on the planet and you have even looked into space. You've delved into the annals of history and you've asked every wise man on every mountaintop and still you are a world in crisis. Still you are a world in need of more to come to your lives here, and so far nothing has come along to set you free of that need. Nothing has released you from your pain and taken away the uncertainty about what is next to come. And this is why today you are still this world of people waiting for a miracle to happen … and wondering if that miracle will ever come.

But now what I have to share with you is a new pathway into your future, and it comes by way of a new story about life on this planet—about who you are and why you are here. And I can tell you it is not at all about making the best of a bad situation. No, this is a very different kind of story that will give you a way to see life not as a place that was meant to limit you or harm you in any way, but rather as a place that would take you on an ever-widening journey of discovery that would forever build your love for everything that exists here.

Now how can this even happen? Well, to that I say, this will begin with a feeling in you after you have read these words, a feeling that will start you off thinking, now this is different. This is a feeling that doesn't seem to match anything I've felt before and I want to know more. I want to understand this mystery of life that seems to have the answers to all our questions and an understanding of the underlying causes of our concerns.

You may think this is just too compelling a story for you to let go of and simply dismiss offhandedly because … what if it were true? What if the human race could suddenly change the way they think and the way they live life on this planet in a gargantuan manner using love—but love with a much bigger connotation to it than what now exists? And if this were true, wouldn't you want to be part of it? Wouldn't you want to play a role in this new movement to unearth a mountain of discontent throughout the world … and begin the push to start over?

love

CHAPTER 3

THE MORENESS

People now understand that the world needs to change, but what force throughout humanity will take you there, into a future that now seems so unclear and full of unpredictability?

This is the question you all want to know about. You all are on edge about this question, and so what must you do? How can you make a world full of people become something new when, in point of fact, they cannot feel the freedom to make that change happen, nor do they in some cases even want the change in the first place?

So here lies the real truth. If you, the human race, are to survive and make certain strides to change this planet's trajectory, then you have to do something. You have to take this time now to make this difference to your lives, and you must do this with all the vigour and enthusiasm you can muster, so that you can be better now … so that you can be different … and most of all, so that you can have a life to live in that builds from within each of you, that precious love you all need to feel.

After all, that's why you're here, isn't it—to feel that wonderful love of life? Surely you all can agree there is nothing else quite like that feeling. It's something that develops early in your lives, and with time you come to appreciate it as the main reason for living and the most important thing you possess in life. And every one of you wants to feel it. Every one of you needs to feel it, for otherwise you would not even exist. You would have no reason ... to take one more breath!

So to say that this is now what we can utilize to unearth this new movement of earthly passion toward a world in need of more is an understatement to say the least.

love

Love—the Quintessential Element ...

MESSAGE:

The one true passion of the human race ... is to know love in its fullness. The love is at the root of everything you think about and everything you do. It is there in your thoughts when you feel excitement about your lives, and when you feel resentment or dismay, you also have a thought about love—the love that is missing from the equation of life. Either way, it seems, you're trying to find your way to it because it is everything to you. It is a beingness in you all that you cannot deny. You cannot let go of it.

For most of you here on this planet, however, you tend to think of love as just a human emotion that comes and goes with the changing events of time, but in truth it is so much more than that. It is the quintessential feeling of the universe, there with you from the very beginning of your lives for a purpose that cannot even be quantified. It simply is too vast and too complex a notion to think about in any singular, definable way.

While some would say that its significance is small in the overall outcomes of life, in truth, it is the end-all and the be-all of life. It is, in fact, the only thing of equal importance to life itself because it is the driving force that makes this world run. It is the spark that ignites the engines of life for every one of you here. It's what makes you get up every morning. It's the reason you think about tomorrow. It is why you are ... *ALIVE*, and as that is, this is where we need to begin our dialogue here. It all begins with love, this simple yet profound little feeling of life that is everything to you. You all want it. You all crave it. You're even willing to fight for it because it is the only thing that makes you feel good about the fact that ... you exist.

Now you may say that for you and others like you, love is not at all the thing that drives your life because your days are consumed with other more important things—like making certain you have everything you need to survive and get by to the next day. Love, therefore, is an incidental part of what goes on here for you. It's something more like a luxury that feels good when you take the time to feel it, but it can come and go from your life with little consequence.

For all of you who feel this way, think now why you do the things you do. Why do you get out of bed in the morning, and why do you try to survive to that next day? Is it just for survival's sake, or is there something else driving you—some other reason for you to participate every day in this game of life?

I ask you, what makes you all feel good if not love? Does there exist anything outside of this feeling that makes you even want to be alive? From where I sit, there is not a person on this earth who can live without this precious feeling of goodness because this is what gives all of you a purpose for being here. The love is what grounds you here. It's what gives you the will to continue living. And this is most important to understand because it takes will to get up each day and participate in this life experience. When people lose this will, they die, plain and simple. They let go of the need to even be here, and the reason is this:

Life exists only because there is love.

Where there is love of life, there is a will to exist and a will to feel life as it is but with an overwhelming desire to have more of it each and every day. You live life because you have a love of it, and without that aspect to you, nothing would make sense. But once you begin to realize this, once you come to understand that love is your game and this is why you are here, then you can begin the process of learning what it means to have this love-filled existence. You can understand more about why that feeling seems to drive you … why it seems to be so important to you … and most of all why it exists in you in the first place.

love

If you think about it, there is no other reason for any of us to lift one finger or make one move other than to feel something good about that movement. Without that inner goodness factor to inspire us, we wouldn't try to do anything or be anything. We would have no reason to change or to grow or even to move one muscle. Quite simply, we would stop dead in our tracks, and there would be only stagnation—a space that allows for little to no love to exist in.

Just imagine a world without love. There would be no appreciation for anything that exists. There would be no love of another, no passion for any experience of life. You would not feel the pull to follow a dream because the love would be absent from that dream. You would not appreciate the simple things in life—like the sun on your face, the laughter of a child, or the simple fun of meeting someone new. These things would bring no joy to you nor would they have any meaning. You would not even hold your own child dear to your heart nor would their love for you even exist. In point of fact, neither one of you would care at all about the other or anyone else for that matter because in a world without love, compassion would be nonexistent. You would feel no connection to anyone or anything. You would feel separate and apart from life and without the need to see, hear, touch, or taste anything. The outer form of life would be there, but you would feel no pull to engage with it in any way because there would be no inner feeling about it all.

Yes, without love, life would certainly be a dull and dismal place to be in—a meaningless existence, something like a dead zone where no one even had the will to go on. And the simple fact is that without that will to keep going, we all would have come and gone in the blink of an eye. Our history together would have been short, indeed, and without any true purpose. But instead life has continued because we had a way to feel its richness. We had a way to understand its value because we had love and that feeling told us everything. Through love, we could connect to our world. We could understand that life ... had worth!

This is why, for centuries, we kept walking down this road of life. Love gave us that reason to keep going through wars, famine, and unspeakable hardship of every kind. In the course of our history together, we faced many a bad turn of events that could have ended the lives we had, but we didn't let that happen. We simply were too much in love with this notion of life, and we didn't want to let go of it, no matter what it threw our way. We kept on going, searching and searching for every bit of goodness life could give us ... just so we could love our world all the more. Always there was this loving strength behind these explorations of life, and always there was this hope there would be something more to come—something new that would make our lives here feel ... even more worthwhile.

The Miracle of Human Life ...

To date the human journey has been a remarkable one. It is small in the eyes of a universe, but from a human perspective it's big in so many ways. So much has changed for us. We've taken the goodness factor here and made it bigger for many people on the planet. We've raised the bar of our love by way of the thoughts we placed in our brains about how life could be better in that next moment of time—and then we created that. Just think: from the time of the earliest man or woman who produced that most amazing spark of fire to warm themselves to the present-day man or woman who uses that same spark to transport themselves across space, we have come a long way on so many fronts. We've explored every frontier on the globe. We've brought in scientific and technological advances that have radically changed the way we live on this planet. We are thinking in more complex ways. We have greater physical capacities. We are even living longer as a testament to the "moreness" of the human race.

Yes, the bar of our lives has been constantly moving for the betterment of humankind herself, as long as we had love there in our brains to make that happen. And looking back on it all today, surely we all can agree that it has been nothing short of amazing how we've transformed ourselves every inch of the way into something different from who we were centuries ago, decades ago, years ago, and yes, even minutes ago.

MESSAGE:

You, the human race, are constantly changing. You are constantly evolving without even recognizing how remarkable it is to become something different in that very next moment of time. This is the miracle of human life, and it is a miracle of gargantuan proportions you live out in your everyday, ordinary lives—without even giving it a second thought!

Think of this: there exists no other life form on this planet that lives life like you do. There is nothing else that has such a capacity for change and growth or the will to even be these things. The nature of life for the sparrow, the ant, the hippopotamus, and all other animal life forms you see around you has remained virtually the same since your arrival to this world. They are still being an ant, a sparrow, or a hippopotamus, and they are doing the same things they have always done with the aim to propagate and survive. They don't seek to change the world around them, nor do they try to become anything different from what they have always been unless the world changes around them, and then they make the necessary adjustments.

The trees and the plants are the same. They are quite content just to be as they are unless you, the human race, decide you need them to be different—and then they willingly, without any reservation and with the utmost of concern for you, become that. They allow you to make that change. They live freely and they die freely in peace about who they are to this place. They accept everything in life as it is, and they live in harmony with all that exists and all that takes place here, regardless of how that might look. Their desire is simply to feel the true joy of being in these lives they have as a loving part of the magnificent whole of life, and they want nothing more than this.

But you are different! You are always on the hunt for something more. You want to feel the excitement of a life on the rise—a life that can become something new every step of the way, and the miracle is that you have a way to make that happen. You no sooner think that next amazing thought, and then presto ... you are that. That reality becomes your next newest reality because you make it so. This is the magnificence of you. You are different. You are ... amazing. You are the movers and shakers of life's grandest dreams. You are the makers of destiny, and you have come here to be part of this life structure, not just to reside within it to feel its majesty like the other life forms, but rather to be here with the express intention to expand its very essence.

Yes, you are the ones who have come to this world to give it finally—a purpose! You are here to take over the reins of what has been lovingly put into place for you, so that you of your own free will could make it all into something better, richer, and more impactful as it relates to the meaning of love in your lives. For many thousands of years, this is what you've been doing, but now it can be different. Now you can feel a much greater ease to this process because now you can eliminate the struggles and frustrations with a new understanding that you do, in fact, hold the key to all life's bigger possibilities. And now you can use this key to unlock the door into a future that will bring a much needed certainty to your minds and an excitement to your hearts that you will not have felt before. You can do this because you are the ones with the will and the power to imagine things, direct things, shift things, and manoeuvre things. You were born of that power. You are the power that can begin to make something more of this place, something much more.

You, in fact, were constructed to do this, to be these vehicles of change because you have within you the quintessential driving force of change … and that is love. It is the motivator of all motivators that not only inspires you to make something more of yourselves but also gives you the means to actually become that "moreness" without you even being aware of how that exactly takes place.

love

Now, to us, this notion about love was an altogether new way of thinking that was extremely intriguing. It gave us an entirely new feeling about our lives, and we wanted to know more about how this loving aspect of our humanness might work to our advantage. And so through further discussions, we learned about how this intelligent nature works from within us, not as an idle bystander in our lives but rather as a central player in everything we do. And this understanding, we believe, is essential at this critical time in modern history.

MESSAGE:

Think of me as an active participant in your life's actions like none other, with the ability to take you places you cannot even imagine. I can tear down the walls of normality in front of you and open up the gateways of "moreness" when you need that, and nothing else in life can do that for you. I am the only one with such influence over this world of yours.

I can take your life as it sits today and change it into something new tomorrow. I can eliminate your pain, your sorrow, your anger, and your frustration and bring a new vitality to your life. I can do all these things for you and more because my creative powers within you supersede everything. My influence over life is truly magical and all-encompassing. There is nothing that can take away my ability to manifest new life for you, and now it's time you understood this. It's time you came to know what I am all about and why I exist inside you because this is the miracle you all have been looking for. And that, to me, means everything right now. There can be nothing more important than this ... nothing!

love

Love tells us that to date the human race still knows very little about how this most important aspect of our humanness actually does work and how it plays such a vital role in our lives. It seems we have only just begun to scratch the surface of its most amazing influence, and that is truly a tragedy, we feel, because in our minds this *Love* is the key to our survival now. It is the quintessential element of our lives with the ability to transform our world from the inside out. As it lovingly conveyed to us through our discussions, it can take one person, one family, one community, or even one entire planet in peril and change it into something completely different in our favour. It can do this because it—your *Love*—holds the key to life's moreness. It can give you an understanding of what must be done in the world right now to fix things on every level of our human existence—and not just a few things, either. We are talking about *all* things because within the very essence of *Love* are the answers we have been searching for since time began—answers that have remained buried beneath a sea of human controversy we couldn't escape from.

This is why for so long now this precious *Love* has lurked in the background to our lives, waiting in silence to be recognized and brought forth in its fullness to the surface of human awareness. It has remained a hidden treasure to the world so that when the time was right, when the world was truly ready and willing to become something completely new, it would unleash its magnificent truths upon humanity so that every person without exception could become something far greater than any human life has ever been before. And now *Love* has revealed that the time is here. The time has come for a new truth to be told about a living organism of love that is a very real component of the human anatomy—a part more real than the body you walk in and the brain you think with. It is an intelligence you possess, separate from your brain, that now is ready and willing to play a new and vital role in our human evolution.

As described to us, it is the hidden aspect of our physiology that exists within us in much the same way as a core exists to an apple. The core brings to the life of an apple a magical formula for its success, which is to say it brings to its fibre a way to get bigger and more robust in the course of its lifetime. This is much the same way the core of *Love* works from within the human anatomy. It builds from within each of us of our own will, to then create outwardly the very fibre of our changing lives, always with the highest intention and always with an eye toward expansion of life in the most meaningful ways. This is what *Love* is to you, we are told. This is what it can do. It is the force from within that drives life forward when nothing else can. It is always there by your side, ready to turn on a dime and make your life better just because it can and just because it exists in you to do exactly that.

Yes, to us, it is so much more than just a good feeling. We have come to understand it as an indelible part of our humanness, one that plays a critical role in our everyday lives in the way it opens a person up to certain thought structures that will make them feel good about every decisive move they will make, if they listen. It can do this because it has an intelligence in and of itself, an intelligence beyond what you could even imagine. It is a part of you that can be opened to and used by you, if you wish, to engage in a two-way communication process of thinking that will move you toward expression after expression of goodness—all of which will serve to make your life better each and every day you are alive.

This is the sole reason for *Love* to exist in you, we are told. This is its one purpose. And it has the greatest will and determination to help you succeed at this. It is there to you in every instance of your time to help you see the light at the end of every proverbial tunnel, and your task is simply to grab hold of that light and fly into everything good but with a zest and a passion that wasn't there in you just seconds before.

A greater ally you could not have in life. To us, there is simply nothing quite like it. Its motivations are so pure toward each human life. It wants for only one thing, and that is to feel its true value to you as it places one creation after another before your eyes, all with the aim to bring to your life the richness of a feeling in love that will only get bigger throughout the course of time. It wants for nothing else but this. It has no other agenda except to explore the outer limits of this amazing space of life ... with you in hand.

The Other Half of You ...

MESSAGE:

Today it is an anomaly to think how people feel so alone in their strife and their struggle when you consider that they have me right there within them to call upon. I am the other half of who you are. I am the invisible half and yet the very proactive half that lives together with you in all your humanness to form this amazing duo that can do anything ... *THAT CAN REBUILD LIFE ITSELF* when there is an awareness of this magnificent connection between us. Indeed, it is remarkable what can happen when you and I come together, each with our own unique task but united as one loving unit for the sole purpose to make something more of ourselves—something more than what would exist if we were separate, alone, and unaware of this amazing life potential we have together.

The truth is that I need you and you need me in order to live a life successfully. We cannot do this alone, either one of us. Alone, we have nothing ... no way to proceed ... nowhere to go ... no means to be more. Without one another, we are lost. Without one another, we would not even have come to this life because this most precious life would then be without its purpose—its purpose to have this connection and then to build from it, a love for this place of life. Yes, we are everything to one another. Together, we are the very fibre that makes life itself ... exist!

love

These words, to us, are no small deal at all. We believe their meaning is most profound because they speak to the *purpose of all life,* and it is simply this: a growth into love that will go on forever, pushing the limits of human possibility toward all things good—unless of course we, the human race, decide to turn our backs on this and move the other way. What a noble cause this is. We can think of no greater a purpose to have bestowed upon humanity than this—no finer a mission. In our minds, we are all lucky beyond words to have the chance to fulfill such a destiny at this point in our evolution.

We do understand, however, that it might be a difficult thing for people to feel the truth of this at first, given that life for so many people is challenging at best. To some, this growth into love doesn't feel like an attainable thing amid their struggles. They can barely even feel that love inside of them, let alone feel it grow. But know that while the beginnings of this process of discovery may be difficult to be with, once you have established a true base of knowledge about how this *Love* works inside you, there will be nothing that can stand in the way of its potential. This *Love,* we believe, is simply too extraordinary to resist once its power and influence are understood.

MESSAGE:

To date it could be said that humanity at large hasn't yet felt the intensity of love they might otherwise have felt, given all the concerns that surround your lives today, but the reason is not what you might think. It's not because you weren't good enough or because you didn't deserve a better life, no, not at all. It's not even because you didn't have the power or the means to make it all different—because you did. The reason is simply that there was not the awareness in you all about how love plays such a vital role in the building block processes of life or, in other words, the expansionary processes. This is why you, the human race, have been rather stalled in your overall human development. It's as if you're still in the starting blocks of life, poised and ready to burst forth and run the race of a lifetime, but you just can't figure out how to get out of those darn starting blocks.

Yes, in a nutshell, you could say that you've come up short on this planet when it comes to your understanding of this life. And you know this to be true because you can feel that your connections to me and my love seem somehow less than what they should have been, given the immense human needs that are out there today. And why is this, you will ask. Well, until now, there has been no way to get yourselves out beyond the limits of this creative space you think of as life, with all its concerns and limitations, and this is why you haven't been able to strengthen and build your connections to my love far beyond where they sit today.

You are still here in this box of life such as it is because neither the logic of your brains nor the magnitude of love in your hearts has given rise to any sort of concrete solution as to how to live a more joyful and love-filled existence successfully and without the attachments of pain and misery. This doesn't mean, however, that you haven't done well to this point to attain what magnitude you have attained so far. Over the course of time, you have felt a greater source of love to some degree. But what these messages are saying to you is that there is room now to *SUPER EXPAND* life through what I would like to call a new *SUPER GROWTH MECHANISM.*

And this is where science and philosophy will come together to explain the mysteries of how the universe works, which all come down to one simple premise, and it is this: all of life exists because of a connection in love. That connection is what holds all of what you see as a universe together as one living, breathing, pulsating organism. Every particle of existence, every atom, and every molecule has arrived to feel love—the love of another. The love is the attraction between all things. It's what makes one atom want to join together with another atom to be as one in a new formation. It's what makes you want to be with your wife or your husband, your sister or your brother. It is what makes you want to breathe in the air around you.

The number of these connections is endless throughout the world, and they all have one thing in common: they all have love at their base. Love is the glue that connects all the parts of life, and without it everything would fall apart into separateness and disarray. So if you want to re-energize this life and build it into something much bigger and richer in its feeling, then you are going to have to understand what love is all about. You are going to have to understand this mystery that can now be revealed to be what is needed to change everything—this amazing new force within humanity called love that boosts you up and builds in you a feeling that you can do anything inside its ever-widening value system.

Once you begin to feel the significance of all of this and the strength of this within your lives, it will seem as if suddenly there was this extraordinary new friend together with you—the friend who can take away the fears in you that would otherwise stop your march into the freedoms you so desperately need and deserve. I will be this friend to you. I will move away any limitations that would stand in the way of your new life to come, if you choose to open to me now.

Then what you will see is a new and most powerful force of influence emerging out of the depths of normality in your lives, to bring to this planet a new kind of life that will feel good and correct on all fronts. Why? Because finally it will be a life that doesn't hold you back from everything good that a life can be—which means that things that once restrained you will no longer be a restraint but rather an opportunity, as in the case where you meet someone new. You will no longer be in a place of concern and mistrust but rather a place of intrigue that sets you up for the excitement of what is next to come for you in your lives together.

It will be a life on the rise that flourishes and builds in every sense. It will bring a bounty of goodness all aimed at the betterment of everyone here.

love

We want to tell you all at this juncture that we found these words to be true in our own lives as we progressed into this dynamic relationship with this inner nature of *Love*. Life opened up to us, and we began to feel this immense new strength come over our lives, so much so that we never wanted to be without this friend again. In our minds this *Love* was the key not only to our own lives but also to the survival of the world as a whole. We believed that if there was a way to change this planet's trajectory and make life better for everyone, this was it for sure. This was the way to find a new centre to all the discontent out there in the world today.

And over time, our understanding of this became more and more complete as we pushed forward with this inner exploration into life itself. We developed a kind of synchronicity with this loving nature and its ways of thinking, and that brought us to a whole new level of understanding we could never have achieved on our own. Everything in life became clearer as to its purpose, and that was truly ground breaking. It was as if we had stumbled onto some sort of benevolent gift that was popping into our brains, new ways to think about the world's earthly concerns.

We found ourselves seeing everything differently. Our thoughts about life in general were growing stronger. We were thinking in more worldly terms, feeling the pains of this world of people and in turn wanting to help relieve them of their pain, using *Love* as the way to do this. Each night we would turn to the news to think about how this inner intelligence we were tapping into could now be utilized in meaningful ways to arrest the injustices of life we saw everywhere. We were thinking deeply into a space of pure love trying to see, for example, how global warming could be solved; how a life in complete and utter misery could be made better; or how a person with nowhere to turn could suddenly make their way past all the roadblocks they were facing and then move to a better life.

Amazingly, this connection we were opening up to was only too willing to show us the way into that understanding, with the idea that we were doing this not just to be self-serving but rather to become engaged to the world this way, using *Love* as the central theme of our lives. And never were we to stop doing this. Never were we to become complacent toward this style of thinking, for in truth this was the answer to the world's concerns now—and not just a few of them—but all of them! As *Love* conveyed to us many times over, the world needs this now more than ever before.

MESSAGE:

It is my wish that all of you now can begin to feel my presence and explore my inner workings within you so that you do not miss this opportunity—this great human potential sitting there together with you all, just waiting for you to give the signal that you are ready now. You are ready to move mountains of discontent throughout this planet and begin the slow process of change for the better in all aspects of your lives together.

And I tell you this: you all will have a role to play here because, in truth, you all have come here to be a part of this new amazing life potential, and it would just be a matter of time before you would come to realize this. Every one of you, no matter who you are and no matter what circumstance might befit your lives, is an important piece of the magnificent whole of life, and as such the part you each will play will be immense beyond measure. All you have to do is fully open to this now—nothing more and nothing less. You just allow that your lives can change for the better by learning more about what it means to flow love together with me, and then let that love—your love—do the rest for you. And because this kind of connection between us will be nothing like what you have had to this point, life will most definitely change for you and change on a much grander scale than you have felt before. So to that I say, get ready for these changes to come, for they are now what the world is in desperate need of.

Let's begin right here and now with each of you taking the time to think about why I exist inside you as an intrinsic part of you ... why I am so important to your lives ... and why you need me now to survive! Let's take the time to examine how I actually work in your ordinary, everyday lives, and most important of all you will want to understand "the why" behind the life I create before your eyes each day because "the why of it all" is the key here. This is where the story of you begins to make sense. It's where you will come to understand that those inner stirrings of love, those yearnings you felt in your past, were me there trying to show you a new way to think and a new way to move so that your lives would feel more to the point of why you are here—which is to be constantly on the move looking for more of the magic behind life itself, the magic that exists inside the love that is so very important for humanity to understand now and be with in its fullest form.

So don't turn away from these pages just yet because in these pages is a way into a better future for you all. In these pages is a way to unwind the past and explain the truth of all life—which means to say that the world in all its human controversy will be reduced down to one thought, just one simple thought that says this: you have one single reason for being here today, and it is to build those feelings of love you have for this life and then live inside the excitement of those feelings. If you can do this now, if this can now become your newest reality, then you all will be forever embraced in the richness of a true state of mind that will give back to you constantly and without equivocation ... your world in its true majesty.

love

CHAPTER 4

THE CONNECTION

MESSAGE:

When Life Was Simple

Remember when you were young and your life felt so free in that you could imagine yourself to be anything you wanted to be. You were free to think in ways that did not limit your movements ... that did not constrain your thoughts ... that did not let your mind think anything else but to love who you were becoming.

It was a precious time for you back then. You were always thinking about what next to do and how to play at life with all the gusto and zeal you could muster. It was your way of just being a kid. Everything was about playing a game, and nothing else even mattered. For you, the world and all of its parts were there to do one thing, and that was to bring a true happiness to your life. It was as if you were travelling along a high road toward everything good, and so you remember those days most fondly.

Today you wonder if that could be your life again. What if you could feel the pure freedom and exhilaration that you felt when you were young? Most don't even try to think this way or even give this a second thought, but today you should. Today you must try to understand the importance of this because back then when you felt the sheer excitement of who you were becoming, you held the key to life in your hands. And do you know why I say this? It is because nothing was more important to you as a young child than being engaged to life with a style of thinking that moved mountains there for you each and every day.

That's just how it was for you back then. Life was all about being a kid, thinking about nothing else but a perfect space to live in. That was all you needed—a perfect space within your mind where you could understand life and live in it, loving every minute of what it was giving back to you.

love

The Why of it All ...

MESSAGE:

Everything that is life today, everything that is your world ... exists to be love, plain and simple. Love is the why of it all, and every day the world in all its glory awakens to feel itself as this love in every blade of grass, every tree, every stone, and every creature great and small. As the day begins, all of life swings into motion. It becomes enlivened to its purpose. Every molecule moves and vibrates as if to say it is alive to a world of goodness ... alive to the excitement of becoming something new.

This is your world, and it's an amazing place to be in because it always holds the promise of a new beginning in love. That promise never goes away. It never dies off, even in those places that have known only darkness for eons and eons of time. Even there in that darkness, there is this opportunity to feel love. Why? Because love exists everywhere. It even exists between the cracks of a person's mind where the energy seems lost and the fortunes of life seem to have fallen away.

Today, everywhere, this promise of love is waiting to come alive to everyone in ways never seen or felt before—ways that will push the limits of human possibility well beyond all limits of time and space as you know them to be. And the truth is that you need this now because to date those limits you have lived within have had a much too burdensome and negative effect on people's lives. Those limits need to be adjusted somehow to allow for more to come into this world, so that people everywhere will finally have a place to go inside their minds to settle the discontent, manage the anger, and take away the pains of life.

love

Of course, it isn't the norm today to think of life as this space of unlimited promise. Right now, that thought of a life with unlimited possibility seems so far away from our brains, and yet it feels so good to think it might just be true because if it were true, then everything would change. It would change because we would have the power then to rescue humanity from the insufferable pain that is felt everywhere and on all fronts. That pain wouldn't even have to be there anymore because *pain is nothing more than a feeling of being stuck in a dilemma without a way out … without the hope that it all could be changed.*

All pain, be it physical or emotional, is about this we are told, and you see this everywhere today. There are people stuck inside of every imaginable dilemma without the means to break free. There are unresolved conflicts. There are needs of every kind that go unfulfilled each and every day, and there is frustration and resentment about that fact. There is pain. It's everything from low self-esteem to incurable disease and a lack of the most vital resources on the planet, and to date we haven't felt the freedom to change all of this. We haven't found a way to set our brains free of every last limiting circumstance—to think in ways that will bring resolve to everything we do rather than dismay and discontent.

MESSAGE:

You know that who I am to this world is a solver of concerns first and foremost, and when you think of me this way, the essence of pain in a person's life takes on a whole new meaning. Why? Because then you have a way out from all your pain … using me to get you there. To put it in another way, you suffer in the pains of life because you are unaware that I exist to help all of you. You suffer because you have no idea that the pain is only a by-product of an old style of thinking about your life, and as that is, you don't believe you can release the pain. You are, therefore, made to feel helpless, alone, and afraid.

Constantly in this world, you are reminded that you cannot solve pain, be it a common cold or the pain you feel when a loved one dies. It all cannot be solved, you think, by merely thinking the opposite to that. It just is what life has made it to be, and you must live with the pain and resist nothing in this regard.

Now some would say that all kinds of so-called "pains of life" can and do get relief from artificial means, but this has caused all number of misguided events to occur including death from drug overdose. This is why it is important now to understand that people are in pain because of one simple fact. They do not know who I am to this world … yet. But as soon as they can feel what it means to live a life with me as it is written about in these pages, then the whole of life—the whole of their lives—will forevermore become free from pain.

This is what I can do for this world of yours, and this is how I will start to work inside each of your lives. I will take hold of your human psyche and turn it into a progressive state of influence, which means I will adjust your thinking styles to consciously re-remember who I am to this planet. I will connect the dots about the life you can have and the reasons why you are living here now in self-doubt … about everything. Then for those of you in pain today, your charge of life will not be about pain any longer.

Just imagine life for a queen and her king living well in the past and then think of what their thoughts would have been inside their so-called gifted life. Their thoughts were of pain, of course. Why? Because with their fame came an enormous responsibility to get things right in their world. Their lives were completely immersed in the task of solving the pains of life they felt and saw everywhere within their kingdom. Now is this a life anyone would want or choose given the enormous responsibilities they would have to undergo? People were suffering all around them, and they had no clear direction to move into where they could successfully solve the pains that seemed to be so prevalent everywhere.

While I was there with them in this reality, I let them choose their fate because they themselves were to be the creators of their own destiny. This is my promise to you the human race. You are in charge of your life. You set the path you next want to walk along, and I simply allow for this to become your next newest reality because you choose that and because that is the only thing in that moment of time that makes sense to you. And no matter what that might look like and no matter how hard that premise of life may seem to you, realize that this is your plight. This is your destiny to choose.

So in our story as time went on, this queen and her king moved in whatever direction they determined to be correct. As well, they turned inward to pray to a god in their times of need to help them maintain the strength they would require to face their immense storehouse of so-called "pains of life" and relieve them as best they could. Unfortunately, in many cases their ever-present thinking patterns were not aligned to mine. Instead of making life better and building in their minds a picture of how life could be more constructive, more progressive, and more to the point of why they were here in this life, they moved to the opposite side of things. They utilized misguided principles built out of their past that took them down a myriad of rabbit holes of further concern, and these in turn created an endless stream of pains that they themselves did not need or want.

Despite my constant subtle urgings to come and play on the other side of the life they were creating and make their connection to me more vibrant and active, they moved away from me. As a result, danger ensued, all remained lost, and their pains of life just kept on coming. Nothing was successfully accomplished. It was as if they had a fishing rod with no line or bait on the end of that rod, and so life became even more difficult, more intense, and not at all connective to me like it could have been. This, you see, is how humankind in the past has missed the point of why they were even here in this life.

So you will ask why this happened. Why did this queen and her king not listen to those ever-present urgings that I placed before them back then to go a different way instead? What held them back from this, you would ask, and how did they not find their way to me when, in point of fact, this was the purpose for life itself—to be together with me and do good things in this world?

Well, the answer to this is really quite simple. People need to know I do exist, and if they have any doubt about this in any way, shape, or form then they will choose the route that they, in their own minds, think is correct. They will act in any way they please because they know no other way … because they do not feel me … and because their will to just live on as they are is greater than their need for this loving connection to me to be made stronger. So even though I was there to this queen and her king in their greatest times of need to help them see life differently, they chose to go it another way in many cases, and that is why wars broke out, famine ensued, and disease of any number of causes occurred throughout history, just to state a few examples. The pains of life just kept coming over and over, again and again throughout all these many centuries past.

This was life as it was back then, and it would continue until this very day when you the reader would choose to open this book and learn more about what it means to live a life with me. In an incredible twist of fate, what you are reading about right here and now would have changed everything back then for the queen and her king—if only they had known what it means to hold a love for this world that only a god could know. What I wanted most of all was for them to turn inward to me, but not to pray. Instead I would have asked them to join forces with me at the onset of their pain—to shift and build their reality to fit a new modality that would have corrected the injustices of the past and turned this world into a place of pure love instead. With me, they would have had a way to see life through a different lens, one that would have eliminated all the pains of life and made their lives work in a more masterful way that they in turn could have shown to the children to come as … the only way to make this life actually work.

Now, what does this show us? Well as it turned out, in many ways this was a lesson about tolerance of life as it was in the past rather than a lesson in how to solve the pains of life. In the past, it was all about surviving to the next day and not about turning to a love that could have made life work on a much higher level. Don't misunderstand me here. There was most definitely a connection to me there in that past. Everything in life is connected to me, in fact. It's just that when it came to the strength of that connection, it was weakened by misguided principles, and so in the end, people were without a true guidance vehicle there to speak of. It was as if they were a fish out of water with no true way to breathe.

But now this is all to be different. Now people can have a way to look past all the pain and move into a position of strength that will resurrect in each of them a renewed passion to eliminate the pain. With me, all things now are possible and most importantly, new and refined to their purpose to become a bigger love in the making of such a thing. Today there are millions of you in complete and utter peril who need this clarity in order to make certain that no further pains of life befit you. Yes, these are the days unlike the past where we will be progressively searching for new and wonderful solutions to every kind of pain that exists in life today. And we will find these solutions now because I will be there with you, leading your minds into the newest inventions throughout the world that will be truly groundbreaking in every way.

My mind now is eager to get started with all of this, and all I need is your eternal blessing that … you want this to happen. And then I will be there for you, just as I am here to you right now as you are reading these words. I will correct what has been missing in this world … and I will never let you down.

love

Today we believe these words from *Love* are important to hear because, as we now understand it, the ways we are thinking about our lives are actually quite harmful. Most of us are not thinking about a way to build life and take away the pain that exists everywhere. Instead much of the time we are thinking in endless directions of sameness that never seem to relieve the human discontent. In fact, we are told that those everyday thinking patterns are the very reason why we feel such discontent in the first place. We call this *stagnant thinking*—those thoughts that wind aimlessly down an endless path of nothingness only to end up with us wondering why we went this way in the first place.

This is how it often works in this world today. People take their minds down a rabbit hole of discontent, thinking this way and that, only to say in the end that they did it wrong, and they wish they could have this one last chance to do it all over again; but this time in a better way that would intensify their positive feelings of life instead of taking away their excitement for it. This happens all the time when people choose to move through life without the certainty that *Love* could otherwise bring to them—the certainty that they are in fact stepping in the right direction in the first place. And the inevitable result is that life doesn't play out the way they wanted, and so they move on to another adventure only to find that this one too has trouble, and on and on it goes. The magic of how life otherwise could have played itself out is lost forever, it seems.

We are told that the minds of billions of people have gone now to a place of deep uncertainty with no true way to think beyond their dilemmas. To so many of us on this planet, life seems unpredictable and outside of our control. It's something like climbing a rather treacherous mountain where every step takes concerted effort and concentration. The challenges that come along the way can be great. There are so many obstacles that could stop a person and take a person down in one fell swoop, and so one must step carefully using every ounce of ingenuity to stay safe and out of harm's way. After all, we are just these simple human beings, it seems, with only our own hands and our own brains to keep life on track and to keep us moving forward in the face of everything that might confront us.

This has been life in the past and this is life still today. But maybe now it can be different. Maybe now we can consider a new truth to live by that says we have more going for us than just our bodies and our brains to help us succeed at everything good. And as *Love* has explained many times, that truth about you, you won't find anywhere except inside love. You won't find it in any other feeling of life. You won't find it in the world around you. You won't even find it in the logic of your own brain because that logic is derived from a myriad of information compiled from your past. But the real truth about you is much bigger than your past—infinitely bigger. It's something that can only be felt deep inside a person's *Love* aspect, that intelligent field of influence within us all. That's where the truth makes itself known by way of a feeling of goodness you can't mistake. There is simply no denying its authenticity because it is the only thing in life that tells you there is always more of you to discover and more of the world to build upon in the true ever-expanding nature of humankind itself.

Today we both can attest to this because we have begun to feel the significance of this human potential in our own lives. In the course of just a few years, we have created much positive change that has elevated our feelings about life to new heights, all because we took the time to explore more of this hidden nature inside us—this inner intelligence of *Love*. We wanted to understand whether this intriguing aspect of our humanness had any real substance to it. Was there any truth to the feelings it conveyed? Did it have a way to actually make life better? Those were the big questions that needed to be answered. So at sacrifice to an otherwise busy lifestyle working and raising a family, we continued our exploration into the truth of this life. We delved deep into a very new space within our own minds to find answers people have been searching for, for centuries now—answers as to why life was as it was in the past and how now it could be better and more fulfilling for every person on the planet, bar none.

Now some would call this just a form of meditation, but to us it was uniquely different. It was more like an inquisition of sorts whereupon we stumbled onto a sort of fact-finding machine in our minds that was helping us understand the reason for everything in this world. And when it did that for us, we were ecstatic. We were on fire with the idea that we were not alone in life any longer because now we had this loving friend together with us, opening up its wisdom like it was a flower suddenly blooming with all the vitality of nature at its finest. And with this new aspect of our being working in the background of our lives, life progressed more easily and more creatively. We didn't feel so uncertain of what was going to happen to us in the future because what we came to believe through our connections to *Love* was that we would always have a way to set things right with our world. We would have a way to move past any encumbrances or limitations, knowing that this intelligence of *Love* is always there with us and is a much more powerful ally than we ever could have imagined.

It is, to us, the friend the world has needed all along, the friend that lies beneath our skin and underneath our human psyche as the all-knowing truth that says *we do not do this thing called life alone.* We are connected at the hip with this internal *Love* mechanism—this hidden aspect to our lives that is as necessary to our human anatomy as an arm, a leg, or even a brain. It fills all those spaces within us and more. It lives inside every molecule and every particle of life, and just like all of these very visible parts of our human physiology, it lives to play an active role each day in the success of our lives as human beings—only in the case of *Love*, the role to be played is immense beyond measure. Every moment of life depends upon this *Love* and is determined by it because what it does for you and everyone else is to open up a space of possibility for you to live inside of … right from the moment you are born.

The Space of Love ...

Today we both think about *Love* as a space that you open up to, a space of pure potential and a space of goodness and mercy into which your life enters at birth and through which it proceeds. And here is the amazing part. That loving space that is your life can be made bigger— through the human will to make it so. This, to us, is the majesty of life itself. It can become something new in an instant, and *Love* is the nucleus, the catalyst if you wish, through which that change begins. It is the connective force that opens life up to you, so you can reach your highest potential in every moment, given you want that to take place.

You can think of it as the connective link that makes way for your overall growth by bringing new life possibilities to you at any time and in any place, if that is what you want and need. *Love* can do this for you because it houses inside its intelligence every human possibility that ever was imagined or will be. That's what makes it so extraordinary. That's what makes it different from other kinds of love spoken of or written about in the pages of history. Those familiar expressions that speak of love are what some would say are just emotions or an innate feeling of goodness.

We, on the other hand, are speaking about a creative nature in humanity with unlimited powers of influence, meaning there are no borders to its thinking. There are no possibilities it does not contain. It can make your life into anything it needs to be given the proper timing and order to things and given that your will is there to be this. And what an incredibly powerful statement this is because it means that *YOU WILL ALWAYS HAVE A WAY TO BE MORE TO YOUR WORLD*. This is what this infinite nature of *Love* represents to you—a way to be more and a way to be engaged with life that is forever progressive, prosperous, and limitless in its delivery system. And once a person comes to know and understand this, they will begin to live their life differently. They will carry a feeling that says there can be no challenge too big for me to conquer and no value in life that my *Love* cannot bring to me. This *Love* is simply too big to fail, too powerful not to succeed at whatever it is you need it to be.

In our minds, there has never been such a compelling story about the immense powers of *Love*, about the infinite nature of *Love*, and about the true character of how it will be there with you and for you … in every moment of your life.

MESSAGE:

Think of me like this: I exist as a part of you—like an empty shell of human possibility that wants you to come along and bring me to life. I sit ready and waiting for you to engage with me, to open to my majesty and to create from within the pureness of my love, with your own brainpower. And you, on the other hand, are the willing participant of life who has come with a true need and desire to build your connections to my wonderful love—to think your way into my space of possibility and to become that space in totality through the miracle of life itself.

love

It is extraordinary to think that just by virtue of this *Love* being an intrinsic part of us, we have an instrument of change through which life can get infinitely bigger and richer in a multitude of ways. For us, this is so much more profound than how we first thought about love, as a feeling of passion and excitement. Now we know it is there within us to be fully engaged with us in every moment of our lives and in all sorts of measures—all of which revolve around one main theme, and that is *to turn us into something new!*

Yes, the newness of us is what *Love* is all about! *It is our connective link to an infinite field of energy,* if you wish, into which all of life can now proceed given that there is a willingness and a determination to do that. It's something like hooking yourself up to a hidden source through which you come to be … life in a fuller form. And that, by the way, is why we exist here each day, we are told. This is why *Love* exists. It is the fundamental element of our lives, the real live piece of us that can reshape, rebuild, and revitalize life in all aspects of human experience—which means without exception, we all can recreate the life we have into something new. It's just a matter of learning how to activate this living potential inside us, so that we can develop a synchronicity with it that is yet to be developed in modern society. Then we can be as one together within this new physiological framework, to therefore reclaim our freedom to be more to this world at every turn—and to hold a love for it in our hearts that will never move away from us again.

MESSAGE:

When you and I work together as a unit of oneness, life becomes a much easier place to be in and a much more certain place, as well. It's just like when you're playing a game of chance, but instead of rolling the dice with concern you might roll an incorrect measure, you will be playing with exacting certainty—winning with every chance you take. The foibles of life will start to dissipate, and the never-ending tedium of daily struggles will become a thing of the past. Life will seem quite extraordinary. It will bring a new delight to you each and every day. You will feel differently and play at life differently, just as though you were a swan who knows no way to live other than to be magnificent in every sense of the word. Life will hold a true magical bounty for you, rather than drudgery and misgivings.

This is what I can do for you and more. I can make things right with your world, whatever that might need to be in any one moment of time. I always am a willing participant in whatever it is you next wish to play at. Always my aim is to help you feel the richness of a life that is everything you need it to be, and I know exactly how to make that happen because I am a part of you and I know you like none other. I understand what you are needing before you even need it. I understand how you think and I know who you are trying to become in every single moment of your time here. I understand why you've lived the experiences you've lived. I can tell you why you've been angry or why you've been sad. I can tell you what your greatest fear is and where your deepest passion lies. I can tell you the truth about every event in your life and how it all was there for you ... *TO LOVE*.

And regardless of who you needed to be and what you chose to do inside those events that came your way, I only wanted to live life with you and through you—no matter what that life needed to be, regardless of what belief system or philosophy you held. The point was that we were together, exploring new dimensions of human possibility. We were together recreating life over and over again ... into something new.

This is what you would call the evolutionary process of you, and it is not without purpose. It is most precise in nature. It always is what it needs to be for any given moment of your time, and as such I hold no judgment as to how that all takes shape for you. I never look down upon your life no matter how you may choose to live it because I understand the process through which you grow. I feel the truth of who you are and who you are becoming, and I therefore accept everything that takes place for you—and that includes even the misguided behaviours of the past that have led you down all kinds of pathways of dismay. Even these, I know have had their purpose to help you eventually see the light of day.

Never do I want to interfere with your free will to choose your course of action or adjust your lifestyle. I only want to guide you down a path rich with reward. I never want to hurt you or take you down in any way, no matter who you are or what you've done because my purpose is not to tear you down but rather to build you up from the inside out, no matter where you sit in life. Always I see you as a perfect truth about a human love potential on the move that has made its way thus far in life and will come to know more and more of its own truth and its own magnificence in its own time and in its own perfect way. And there are no exceptions here.

In my eyes everything in life has its own perfection. Every moment is a perfect truth about the magnitude you all wanted to be and were willing to be as time progressed. Every bit of what transpired was purposeful to the world. The growth you had, the failures you endured, and the overall feelings you felt along the way all served to propel you to the next logical step in your overall evolution. And the way you did this was by using love as the singular statement about why you did what you did and how that could be used to inspire you to move again to the next step and the next step after that. None of it was outside of your purpose, though you didn't realize it at the time. It all was there as your way of unfolding the truth of all truths about the power of a human force of love that is without limits to its greatness ... in you.

love

And now, if you wish, this extraordinary intelligence that resides at the very core of you can come to the surface of your awareness too. It can help you to see your life through a rose coloured lens, just like it did for us. It will make all things known to you and help you to understand the why of everything, so you can love this life all the more. Then it will turn and show you how to change it all—to make it even better. It will open up a new pathway for you to walk down by giving you a new perspective that says, there is always room for a better life to come in this place of miracles because, in truth, nothing is here to stop you. Nothing is standing in the way of your life becoming something new, and once you come to realize this, nothing in your world will be misconstrued in your mind to be less than what it really is.

You may say, however, that it is preposterous to even think that there exists such a part of us as this extraordinary potential we are describing. You might ask why you don't feel this, if it really does exist as we are saying here. And furthermore, why is it you don't have the answers you've needed? Why do you feel so alone in your times of trouble?

The answer, as explained to us, is this: we have needed time to unfold the ultimate truth of who we are. We have needed these many centuries in order to grow and unveil step by step the magnitude of this *Love* potential we are, so that no part of it would be missed ... none of it would go unnoticed by the human populous. That's why in the beginning nothing was clear to us. We couldn't feel the enormity of where we were heading. That truth was hidden from us, so we could grow into that understanding slowly and ever so deliberately—through the wonderful process of life. And guess what? It's been working ... somewhat.

A Greater Truth ...

Over many centuries we, the human race, have slowly come to feel a greater truth about who we are. We have discovered that we are something different than first thought and something much greater than the earliest woman or man could even have imagined. In fact, if that first human being were to stand face-to-face with us here today, they would not even believe we were of the same species, the changes we have undergone have been so remarkable.

MESSAGE:

It is through the gradual progression of life that the truth of one's own existence becomes clear. Think of this: if you had first arrived to this world with the full knowing that you are this infinite creative potential that can reinvent life at every turn and in any direction you please, it would have been difficult to take your experience forward in any meaningful way. Why? Because you would be without a road map to follow. There would be no starting position to build from and no reference point to measure your progress into love. And thus, there would be no basis for love becoming anything more meaningful to your lives.

Consider how far the human race has come to this point and how all of that has given you a clearer sense of what it means to be a human being walking the planet today. You all can feel the significance of the changes humanity has undergone through the course of your history because you have embodied those changes—changes that made way for those creative steps to take place that would move you up the evolutionary ladder of success. But without this gradual climb, your understanding of life and your appreciation for who you are would have been much more difficult to come to.

If, for example, you had arrived on the scene just as you are here today, without the knowledge of your history as a human race, you would have no basis for understanding why you are as you are in this moment with your present-day physical and intellectual attributes. You would not feel what a miracle it is to become all of that with each new breath. You would simply be all of what took centuries to unfold and not give it a second thought, not truly understand how amazing it is to be all of those things. And thus your energies of love would not have been on the move. They would not have made their mark on you through time with the same impact that they did.

Think about this because to understand this is to understand why in the past there was needed this most gradual opening to every love-filled experience there ever was. It all was there for you to feel this most profound progression into self-knowing. Every moment of it was needed to bring you to that point in time whereupon your next new reality could be delivered to you, but in a way that would widen the scope of your thinking and move you to a new understanding of who you next wanted to be.

It all has been an earthly design perfectly contrived and developed to bring to you a powerful new awareness of why you have life. Every moment of it was very precise and most deliberate in its cause. None of it came by chance, no, not at all. Life is more than just a series of coincidences coming together at a particular time and in a particular space; and it's more than just a manifestation of human thought energies that are without any true purpose and without the correct order and timing to things. Life is not just about a law of attraction arbitrarily summoned, as some would think. Rather life in each moment is connected in purpose. One moment leads to the next and then to the next in a most precise way. It all exists to deliver to humanity an exact moment in historical timing that will allow for the greatest expansion to love needed in that instant, if the opportunity is seized by you.

Each event in your life, therefore, has a much deeper meaning than you think, no matter how it may be delivered. Every circumstance is there to lead you to a new measure of love in one form or another, and what that all looks like outwardly doesn't even really matter. You can fashion your life to be anything you need it to be. It doesn't matter whether you move this way or that or whether you hold this particular passion or something different. It doesn't matter how much money you make or how many things you accomplish in a day. It's all about the value felt there inside those experiences, the inner value of love. This is the most important thing to be gained, and in every moment of every day, life is bringing you opportunities to open up to that love—to understand it, to feel it, to fuel it, and to rebuild it into something miraculous. And it works in the most amazing ways to do that, ways that the human mind cannot always grasp and so often misinterprets.

Today, however, you all must be much clearer as to how life works on this planet. You must understand this stuff like no one has understood it before, and here's why: the generations who came before you didn't need to know. They were all about a progression to life that did not move past any milestone too far out there in terms of their style of living. Their lives were simple enough that they would progress slowly and without the need to feel that anything more was required of them.

But now life is to be different. The margins for error on your part are small because the concerns of this planet as a whole are far greater than they were in the past. As such you do not share the same needs and wants as those who came before you. Now your progression into love needs to move at a much faster rate and with a will in people that will far surpass anything that has come before this time.

love

A Change to Come ...

MESSAGE:

Today you have assembled here on this planet, almost eight billion of you, to witness these most extraordinary changing times whereby the human race comes to know a much greater purpose for their lives. Yes, today is the day you all are to be awakened to the "why of it all," to therefore understand how this precious connection to the human love capacity in all of you can move your lives to the next logical step in your overall human evolution.

This is big news for you to consider if life is going to change in monumental ways that will reshape the face of the planet and build in people a resolve to learn more about how they now can fix what is broken—broken lives, broken thoughts, broken everything when it comes to the love of a life or lack thereof. Today you all need to consider the ways you are thinking and the ways you are acting out those thoughts. This is your Achilles' heel, and millions of people now seem to be on hold in this regard because they have no way to understand what it means to be alive to a world of love.

It's understandable because, until now, not nearly enough has been said about the true strength of this living potential that you are. The meaning of what this love is to your lives has been mired in controversy that has left no true path to move down. You can see this inside of all the concerns of life today. But now your pathway can be straight and this connection to me the most important connection you will ever come to know about.

This connection will in and of itself create new life for you on this planet because finally everyone will be on the same page, living life for the same purpose—the same noble purpose—and that is to unwind the perfect truth about a perfect love that exists inside it all.

love

Today the perfection that *Love* speaks of clearly still eludes us, and we all know this to be true because all those working parts of life haven't really come together successfully and harmoniously the way we would want them to. As a result, for so many people on this planet life has felt rather tedious and dull and not at all a sacred space to be cherished and worshipped. In fact, for some people, life has been a living hell, plain and simple, and not at all a place that felt like love from the moment they were born.

We understand why people feel this way, and our compassion for them is huge. But know that in their feelings, there is purpose. In their pain, there is a way out of a thought that says there can be nothing more to their lives here amid these miseries. Today this is where the minds of so many rest right now, it seems, in a place that has no hope of being anything other than painful and discouraging. This is a space of the mind that exists outside the greater influences of love and outside of human freedom. It speaks to a way of living that is the furthest thing from who we all have come here to be. And now life is trying to bring this message forward to those who suffer, by way of the pain they feel right here and now.

MESSAGE:

For those of you in pain today, know that there truly is room to move. There is a way out for you, out of the living hell that is your world today. You have simply become stuck inside a process of life that was put in place to keep you moving up the evolutionary ladder and not to stop you or hinder you in any way. While it is understandable that you have come to this position of lost hope given the history of your world events, know that this is tantamount to throwing away your last paddle in the boat of life. So if you choose to go in this direction, there is little chance of your life becoming anything more for you than what it is today ... unless, that is, a greater truth now comes to bear.

So think now of this pain that you feel as just a stepping stone to help you find your way back to a bigger truth about your life that will take that pain away. You were never meant to stay there in that place of misery, which only seems to bring more misery. Life can be more, and now it is waiting for you to give the signal that *YOU ARE READY TO BECOME SOMEONE ENTIRELY NEW*. And to begin, all you have to do is ask yourself these questions: Are you ready to see life in a new way? Are you willing to become someone new? Or do you believe that life as it now stands is everything that a life can be for you from this point on?

It is my hope that you do want more for your life on this planet because to my way of thinking, there is so much more to come for you. In the short time you, the human race, have been here on this earth, you have only just begun to unearth the treasures of this place. You have only begun to feel the magnificent potential here. This is why I say to you that this search for love must continue. The search for everything good must go into the unknown darkness of life to come. That's where those possibilities, those amazing opportunities, still lie hidden in isolation from you, only to be discovered at some future moment in time for you to feel their utter amazement and their mystery.

It's all there waiting for you now, but only if you, the human race, can begin to work with me in an entirely new way—with a deeper understanding of the magnificent process of life I am telling you about. This is where you next need to go— inside the magic, inside the truth of how life and all its parts really do work. And there you will finally understand what has never really been clear before this time—that your salvation lies within your minds, inside that loving space that holds your thoughts, your very next thoughts of life to come. That's where your future sits and that's where the masterful powers of love exist to you ... and for you ... and no place else.

love

CHAPTER 5

THE MOUNTAIN CLIMBER

MESSAGE:

A Story about Hope

When we were children we knew a man who loved to tell stories. He would say to us all, "Would you like to hear the story of how I climbed a mountain?" And we would say, "Yes, yes, tell us your story!"

So then he would begin to speak to us about all his exploits up there on the mountain and how he would climb without the aid of a rope or any other kind of device that would have otherwise made his task much easier. This was done, he said, out of sheer excitement of trying to scale the mountain with nothing more than his own inner motivations.

We would laugh, and then he would go on to say how those days on the mountain were the days that gave him more satisfaction than anything else in his life— just to breathe in the air and take in the rich smells of the forest. He loved the trees, he would tell us, and at times he would stop to sit among them. He would take a break for a moment and turn his gaze to the top of the mountain, just to see where he next was headed. This gave him the will to go on, he would tell us, and we would ask, "What does that mean to have a will to go on?"

"It means," he would say, "that when you have a deep, burning desire and a passion to achieve something, you will let nothing stand in your way. You will take charge of life with determination and love of the task you are venturing into, and in that way you are reshaping and rebuilding your life. And most of all you are learning what it means to love your life for what it's sharing with you and giving back to you each day, so that when all is said and done, you feel complete. You have a true contentment about it all because you have come to know a truth that you could not deny, the truth of how you just love to feel the love of this life." For our friend, that was everything, no matter how high the mountain, no matter how big the obstacle, he climbed anyway because he wanted to feel ... more love.

Now back when we were kids we didn't understand the full meaning of what he was saying, nor did we even care at the time because, well, we just loved our friend. We loved everything he did and everything he said because through his stories he conveyed to us a feeling about life that was extraordinary and unmatched. Indeed, nothing seemed to be more important to him than the rich feelings through which he portrayed his life.

The story would go on, and he would say to us, "Shall I continue up the mountain and tell you all what I came upon?" And this was the part we all loved the most because we wanted to know what magic might be there atop that mountain. We hoped someday we would see it too and be the magnificence that he was. In our minds, it was a miracle just to be a climber, and we wanted that too. We wanted to feel the same excitement coursing through our veins, and we wanted the same inner strength our friend had—the strength to keep our brains pointed in the direction of hope for what is next to come ... in the story of life's biggest dreams.

Now many years have passed since those wonderful times we spent together with our friend, but to this day we still think of him fondly. In our eyes, he was a magnificent passenger of this earth and a giver of hope eternal, and never will we forget what he described as the true joys of his life on the mountain. They were extraordinary to hear about. They made an indelible imprint on our brains because they opened us up to a feeling about life that began with excitement and anticipation and ended with an eye toward everything we could be in our future—that most tantalizing new future born just of our own feeling of it. It was a future that somehow would give us everything, if we just learned how to take on his position of strength—if we simply began each day with the mind-set he had, which was of unparalleled truth about the love aspects of his life.

You see, in so many ways the lives we lead on this planet today seem … *HOPELESS*, but what he shared with us through his wonderful stories was incredibly … *HOPEFUL*. To us as children, it felt as though we had been gifted something extraordinary. It was a new way to live our lives that we, at the time, did not understand completely. But there he was anyway in all his glory just opening up that door for us to feel the secret he had found—so it could be ours too if we simply learned to love life as he did there … on the side of the mountain.

love

CHAPTER 6

THE CLIMB

M ESSAGE:

A Tale of Three Minds ...

There once was a man in my life I admired greatly. He and I would drive home from work together on certain occasions, and once in a while we would share a meal together. I enjoyed his company immensely because he was the kind of guy who knew where he was going in life. He always seemed so certain of everything. Life came easily to him, I thought, and that was extremely inspirational for me.

But then one day he opened up to me. He told me he felt rather alone, vulnerable, and uncertain about his next move in life. He said that the world no longer seemed to hold the promise it once did and that he couldn't feel the same excitement and enthusiasm he once had for his life.

The dilemma he had concerned a certain person in his life who had been stricken with an incurable disease that he did not have any answers to. He was, you could say, without words to give to his dearest friend, and that is what plagued him. That is what took this man to a most uncertain place in his mind when in his past everything was certain—everything was complete to his way of thinking. But now his mind had nowhere to go, and this clearly had caught my friend off guard. As well, it was a shock to me to see him in this state because, to me, he was the master. He was the man I looked up to and the man I admired the most. But not now! This was not the same man I once knew, and in that moment we both knew it.

But then something happened that neither of us expected. The answer to his seemingly unanswerable dilemma came almost simultaneously to us both. Right then and there out of nowhere, we felt the pull of what was needed, and neither of us could really explain why that happened. It was as if there was a third person, a divine influence there within our combined brainpowers, moving us at almost exactly the same moment to a place of utter certainty in our minds.

Now I know this seems to happen to many others too, but on this particular occasion, neither of us could deny that the feelings we had that day were different from any in our past. We could actually sense that we were not alone in our quandary of life and that another source of wisdom was present to us, arresting our concerns and moving us to a place of complete knowing of what was needed in the situation at hand. And though we were not certain what this unseen help was or why it was there with us in that moment, we both embraced it nonetheless.

We opened up to this new understanding of what life could become for us both right then and there, and that is when everything changed for us … in an instant! All of a sudden, we could feel our concern for this dying man changing into something of a blessing because what we began to feel there in that very moment of time was a new beginning for this man's life; and this meant that his struggles and pain would soon come to an end and his life's existence would no longer limit his growth into love. Moreover, we could sense that through his passing there would come to him a certain peace about his life and as well a new pathway to move along that would bring him into a new alignment of love, which he wanted to experience anyway. This to us meant everything, just to know that this was not the end to his life but the beginning of a new journey for him.

And so it was for the two of us that life changed from that day forward. We continued to live our lives as we always had lived them but now with the knowing that what we both had received that day was a benevolent gift of sorts—a gift that gave us a kind of understanding of life we didn't have before. It was as if, all of a sudden, we had a new starting position to begin with, and we were on the hunt to learn more about what this would mean for us. We wanted to bring this new discovery of ours front and centre to our lives because, after all, if this internal pull was real to our minds once, it most certainly could be real again. And what an amazing opportunity that would be, we thought, to have this source of knowledge available to us that was profoundly moving, extremely intriguing, and so incredibly powerful in its wisdom. It made everything feel different.

love

Love Will Prevail ...

Today you can see people all around the globe who think this life is a rather unworkable, uncaring, and unconquerable space on so many fronts. For some, in fact, they feel it has defeated them completely. They will say this world, as it sits, has no way to progress into a better space. They will say there are just too many things beyond their control and too much they would have to overcome in order for this place of life to feel like a safe place and a good place for all. People everywhere will tell you that no matter how hard they try to make it all different, life doesn't really change. The world stays a dangerous place just like it's always been because, well, some things just can't be turned around, it seems.

MESSAGE:

The ultimate truth about the human race is that you are here in life to overcome every obstacle by unveiling the sweetest truth about the power of a human love in each of you that can and will prevail over all else. Life, in fact, gives itself willingly to you in all its many forms just so you can do this—so you can transform life with all its limitations into a magical tapestry of events, all there to create a greater and greater fulfillment for the human race as a whole and for as long as you are willing participants in that process.

Now how is that for a statement about life? Isn't that the kind of life you would want to see and feel … and be a living part of? After all, you didn't come here to this most vital space to be defeated. No, you came here to succeed at everything good, and succeed you will once you get back on track again and become energized to a process of life that was lovingly put in place to help you in the face of any obstacle. But to do that, you must first understand this one important truth that my friend the mountain climber lived by and truly understood … that *LIFE BEGINS INSIDE YOU FIRST!* It begins within your own brainpowers with this most amazing connection to my love—right there in your physiology.

love

The Pull of Love ...

For the most part, people today tend to think of life as something quite separate and apart from them, meaning that it exists of its own volition—its own will—and we all just jump into it. We move around inside that life as it twists and turns to the beat of its own drum. We observe it, analyze it, and finally translate it into something we think is understandable—something that says to our inner knowing that we have found the truth about how this all works. But according to *Love*, we have it backwards. It's the other way around. We've been looking outside ourselves to understand the why of things, when all along that truth could only be found by looking inside ourselves to see what we, of our own free will, were choosing … to think about. If we could have turned inward for that understanding, we would have discovered that everything was inside our control and nothing was ever outside of it!

Now this is a way of turning the tables on an old way of thinking just like when the human race once changed their minds to see things in a new light—such as that of the earth revolving around the sun rather than the opposite to that. Now through the messages of this book, we are endorsing the principle that life in all its many forms comes *from* you rather than *to* you. And though this notion may sound strange and unfamiliar to some, if not most, there are probably few of us on this planet who can deny the experience of this. There have been so many instances in time when we no sooner had a thought in our minds, and then that reality just landed in our laps, seemingly out of nowhere—as if it had been summoned by us to do so. We think of an old friend and they arrive on the scene or we start to imagine our lives becoming something completely new, and no sooner than that, those doors open up. As if by magic, everything that is needed arrives to make that our newest reality.

MESSAGE:

Life is a construct of love first and foremost. It is a benevolent gift to the human race that represents … possibilities, those most glorious beginnings matured out of love that move mountains within your reality each time you take a breath. Life is all about these amazing new beginnings that come to fruition in all their many forms by first making their way to the surface of a person's conscious mind … when and if they call for that to happen.

It all begins with how you think. You think and then you are those thoughts is a very true statement about life, more true than you know because in your mind is where everything begins and where it ends. That's where the creative process of life takes place. It's where I sit in you in every moment of every day, just waiting to engage with you and your brainpower in ways that will intrigue you, enthral you, and open up your world like never before.

love

Certainly it is amazing to think that life could actually work like this—that through our thinking patterns we could change the very nature of life on this planet without at first even lifting a finger. To date, humankind hasn't fully embraced this type of introspective approach. This idea is somewhat new to our belief systems. Of course, there have been those in this world who profess the power of human thought over human destiny. However, the dimension we are adding to this picture is the understanding of how through the true expansionary nature of *Love*, your life proceeds through the energies of your thinking patterns, which have been gifted to do this for you in the first place.

Up until now, it hasn't been entirely clear how human thought could have such a direct influence on our physical reality. Mostly we assume that our thoughts are inconsequential. They are there only for us to "think into," but they alone do nothing outwardly to invest in our future reality. A thought just sits there and doesn't make life different, most people will say. They think it's only when you actually move an object that change is therefore made possible. As a result, time and time again humanity has tried to resurrect the same approach to living—the old cause and effect approach. We think if we twist and turn the *outer* circumstances of our lives, if we physically readjust what we're doing and how we're doing it, then life will somehow get better.

Love, however, will tell you differently. *Love* will say this is not a true statement and that this line of approach only brings exhaustion and dismay to many, which is not at all why we are here today. According to *Love*, the truth lends itself to a very different way of thinking, a different set of guidelines whereby the loving nature in each of us becomes the constructive force and the most amazing tool that when used correctly can and will move mountains without us at first trying outwardly to make that happen. And this, in turn, means that our days don't always have to be about difficulty and struggle. Our days don't have to be about working harder and harder to make more money or achieve certain goals, just to survive. Instead we take a different approach. We say to ourselves that life is a space that first can be reconstructed within the human brainpowers to be everything we need it to be—simply by engaging the passionate, constructive side of our brain influences, which are of course … the *Love* influences.

MESSAGE:

The difference with my approach to living, in general, is that it lies in the masterful, creative thinking powers of love—the key to what otherwise would be an aimless venture of life for the human race, without the true understanding of the central theme of why you exist in the first place. It is not to manifest with your brains a life that goes nowhere and does nothing for the world as a whole but rather to manifest a life on the rise that begins again and again with a newborn ideal of hope for all men, women, and children alike. This then is your evolutionary process that builds you up and constantly challenges the status quo.

And what a stark contrast this is to an old premise that says life is what it is and it's never going to change. What we have here instead is a new premise to live by that professes life to be an ever-growing space that becomes you and is revealed to you as you persist in these most precise thought structures you have. Yet this isn't to say that every thought you think will become your next reality; this is not at all what I am suggesting here. Life is more than just a manifestation of every fleeting notion that could come into the human brain.

Certainly if everything you thought about became real, life would be chaotic beyond measure. But it is not that because life was meant to be more than just a series of random manifestations that bring little to your understanding of who you are. Rather life makes real those thoughts that precisely define your life. And by that, I mean the thoughts you commit to, the ones that you grab hold of, and the ones that say this is the truth about me and my world, and these are the possibilities therein. Those are the thoughts that will drive your life and determine your life going forward. They will play themselves out each and every day in one fashion or another because these are the thoughts that have the strongest will and determination behind them. They have the greatest meaning to you because you have chosen to believe in them with conviction, and that is why they persist in you over and over again, just so you can feel their might … feel their significance in your life in that moment of time.

love

We are told that everything we experience in life comes from a thought we hold and nothing is outside of that. Nothing! How we think defines the momentary boundary between what is real and what is not yet real in in the infinite realm of possibility. So if, for example, you think of life as a place that can only bring so much goodness to you and it stops there, then you define the limits of your life that way. The possibility for anything greater will not exist for you in that moment because you have limited the scope of your thinking. But if, on the other hand, you say that the world is my oyster just waiting to deliver that next best thing, then the possibilities that will open up to you will be as great as your mind can allow for. According to *Love*, this is just how life works from the moment you set foot here on the planet.

Through your thinking ways, you create your reality for the moment, which is why everyone's life looks and feels so different. We all are born with the same biology and the same grey matter between our ears, yet the ways we think make our lives what they are today, be they big or be they small. And the good part about this is that with time you can become more proactive in your thinking prowess, which is where the *Love* aspect of a person comes into play. Through *Love* you have a tool to direct your thoughts, build your thoughts, and develop them more fully, but without the need to limit them like it is today in so many minds.

You can think, for example, of every conceivable experience that would enliven your life and bring a joy to it that you didn't even think was possible. You can think of becoming things no one has imagined, doing things you thought you could never do, and pushing the boundaries of life in all sorts of ways never even considered before. You can find a cure to a disease or invent a new technology. You can become a friend to someone new, be enlivened to the most amazing food you've ever tasted, or solve a problem that once seemed too big to solve. It's all about the finer points of life, your newer life that comes to you through the field of influence of your ever-expanding brainpower and always with the ultimate goal for you to feel love like never before.

MESSAGE:

The human brain was always meant to be a true ally to you in your task of life. It has been gifted to you to help in this profound movement into self-knowing. Its job is to bring to you, through its subtle adjustments, an awareness of who you are becoming each step of the way in your human evolution. And how does it do this? Well, it holds within its so called memory "storage vaults" all those life possibilities you have opened up to, grabbed hold of, and accepted as the living truth of you to date. Your brain, therefore, is like a holding tank of truth that gives you a way to understand who you have become—so far. Without your brain, you would have no awareness of this. You would have no way to feel your progression—no way to define and redefine the boundaries "of you" as they move and shift as you grow.

Just think of how at two years old, you have opened your brain to only so much in terms of a world of possibility because that was all you needed and wished for. But at twenty or thirty or forty, you will have added much more into your repertoire of new truths. You will have accepted into your brain many new ways to think about your life because of your own willingness to go there. You can think of it as your way of adding more and more pieces of "the puzzle of you" into your brain so that you can appreciate each piece along the journey. And then when you put all those pieces together, you can understand the whole picture of you. You can love yourself in totality.

You, in fact, were perfectly constructed to do this—to think into and live out many different life perspectives that would move you into an awareness of yourself that is progressively bigger and richer. At first you are a person who can speak, and then you are a person who can walk, climb a mountain, or engage an entire planet of people to get up and start something new. And on and on it goes for you as you set yourself free over and over again to rethink your life into something that feels freer, more supportive, and better aligned with your human passions, whatever they may need to be as you grow.

When you come into this life, you come with the express intention to do this, to make the change happen. You want the change. You need the change, and on many levels you know this to be true—that your life's purpose is to feel this changing evolution of you and fully accept these new beginnings each and every time they occur. Certainly if this were not true, your world would not have become what it is today. You would exist as you did back in the beginning because you would not have given the idea of change a second thought in your brains. But instead you have come this far in life on so many fronts because you wanted the change. You needed to have it, and so you made the change real to your lives.

Amazingly this begins for you from the moment you are born. You open your eyes to the light, and what do you do? Well, you begin to think, of course. You think in this direction and that direction with exacting precision, all with the idea of trying to feel more of this amazing new thing called life but always in a way that will bring to your heart a true love of what it is. Yes, in those early days, you never want to engage in a way of thinking that is without a purpose. Right from the moment you take your first breath and without the aid of anyone, you know how life is to work. You know how to think because you have this feeling of love guiding you, and you have nothing else to go by. You have no history of life to turn to. You have no past. You only have this simple feeling inside you to draw from, and if you didn't have this, you would be at a loss, without a clear sense of which way to turn or what direction to think into. Without love, you would have no reason to be in life ... no reason to want more from your world ... and no reason to change anything.

love

According to *Love*, this is exactly how it works right from the very beginning. The love is what plays this most vital role in the way it opens a person up to their heart's desire, whatever that may need to be. It gives a person a way to think into directions that are wholesome and good for their lives, and the key here is for a person to listen to its cues and make the correct adjustments going forward. The challenge is that most people today don't listen to this inner driver. Instead they fall away from its advice to then live a lesser life that otherwise could have been so much greater and so much more powerful.

The Construction Begins ...

MESSAGE:

Life is a rather simple thing in those very early beginnings of a person's life. There are only so many ways to feel the goodness of a world. You are constrained within a body that can barely move the way you want and a mind that can think only the simplest of thoughts. Yet still, life has a vitality to it. It has a goodness that you cannot deny, and you feel this through your connections to everything that is your world—like the connections to a mother, a father, a sister, or a brother.

And what makes all of this so exciting is the fact that everywhere you look there are these possibilities all around you. They seem endless too because back then in those earliest beginnings, you have no preconceived notions in your brain that would serve to hinder your thinking. Life is just this completely new thing to be felt and explored, and you are there as this perfect specimen of truth, fully engaged with it and fully loving it … as though you had just learned how to fly.

The love you feel is what makes you want to think more deeply about your life. It makes you want to push the boundaries of your world and build upon that foundation of goodness that is your life for the moment, and the way you do this is extraordinary, indeed. The process is simple yet infinitely powerful. It goes like this: it begins with a simple passion in you to have a bigger experience of life, meaning you want to feel the love of it more intensely. The passion, therefore, is the first step in the building process because it is your way of saying to your world that a change is needed in your life and you are ready to make the change begin out of sheer desire to feel more of this precious life. And this is important to know because it is through these most precise inner stirrings of passion that life begins to reshape itself.

The passion is what gets the ball rolling. It places you on high alert and creates within your human psyche an inner tension of sorts. Why? Because the passion is telling you that life needs to be different somehow, yet that change hasn't happened. It still is imaginary. It doesn't yet feel real to you inside your brain, so you are temporarily at a loss—uncertain about what is next to come.

So this is when a person will turn inward to a quiet space within their mind to begin a contemplation of sorts—a kind of self-examination. They will ask themselves the question, "How can I be something more to this world, when I am not that yet?" People quite naturally enter into this type of reflection all the time because they want to understand why, all of a sudden, life feels limiting to them in some fashion. The fact that they feel limited seems wrong to their inner knowing, and so they will reflect upon why life is as it is. They will ask themselves questions like, "Is there room to see things differently? Is there a way to feel something more, and if so, what direction should I think into? What path shall I take? Is my aim here to stay with an old ideal of living, or is it to step boldly outside this box of life that defines me here and now?"

While this kind of introspection may seem quite ordinary in the scheme of day-to-day life, in truth it has great significance. It has the power of the universe behind it, and it should never be taken for granted because it is the first step in the creative process of life, or in other words, the evolutionary process. Simply put, it is the turning inward of a person with a purpose to think bigger into their future but with a true commitment to change. It is not at all a thinking process that wanders aimlessly and goes nowhere. It is a way of thinking whereby a person takes charge of a new ideal for their life by saying to herself or himself, "I need this change to now become my next newest reality."

This is when a person will begin to open up to me, their inner love nature, right there inside their mind. Why? Because love is where you go to feel that change is possible, and it's the only place where you can feel that truth. It's where the energies of thought are pure of heart and clear of nature, meaning they are precisely correct and without bias. The limitations of life just fall away there in the face of that love because it is the feeling that says to your human psyche that everywhere you look there are these possibilities that were not even there moments before. It may be a new dream that you think about or the fulfillment of a need of some kind. There is no end to the possibilities that a person might consider, but one thing is certain—when you want for change, you know exactly where to head—straight to love. You build your connections to those feelings of love like it was the first and only thing you needed to be doing.

love

We, human beings, tend to think human growth is a natural process that takes place because of our physiological makeup and regardless of what a person might think or feel. But what we've learned through our conversations with *Love* is that human life never changes even in the smallest of ways unless there is this passionate state to begin that change in the first place. Always there must be this passion on the rise and this will in a person to become something new. So for most of us, the changes do come, especially in those early stages. They come because we love those next new thoughts about life entering into our brainwaves through the connective fibre of *Love* itself. But without those influences, nothing would be gained. According to *Love*, we would be stuck forevermore on the side of our mountain of life, never to progress again.

MESSAGE:

Just think of that newborn child who at first has no control over his or her tiny body. In fact, their body feels rather like a foreign object to them. But then, all of a sudden, they open their mind to the notion of just waving their little hand at will—a simple thing for them to achieve because at that young age they have little resistance to the idea of becoming something new. Their brain easily lets go of an old image of life and makes way for a more powerful image to take precedence; and this is so because I am right there at the forefront of their minds. That's the key. A newborn child has not yet turned away from my influences of love, which speak volumes to them about who they can be ... in that very next breath.

They, in fact, live more in that feeling than they do outside of it in those early stages, and this is why they change and develop so quickly. My love is the single most important thing in their life, and so they grab hold of it. They don't deny it and set it aside as though it had little importance, as many do today. No, they revel in that feeling and all the messages of truth that come from it. And then when the time is right, they move. They move quickly into the realization that they already have become something new. As if by magic they already can wave their little hand at will because this magical feeling inside them called love made them feel that possibility was real for them.

And then it opened up the channels of possibility for that reality to take place—for that new truth to take hold about who they next wanted to be.

love

Today we are on the verge of understanding this in a big way, and this is why these pages are in front of you right now saying there is a much bigger life to be lived on this planet. And the way you will access it is by first accessing a greater part of your brainpower, your right brain power—the power of pure love itself. This is how you can begin to *SUPERCHARGE* your brain to think beyond a normal existence— beyond everything you know to be true of life right here, right now.

Two Minds Are Better than One ...

The first part of our story about *Love*, as it has been conveyed to us, always begins with the thinking process. It explores the ways your brain can be turned into a powerful instrument of change that can have tremendous influence over your life—but only if you understand that it can have ever-expanding powers of influence. You think and then you are that thought is true, but what if you, like most on this planet, never think beyond an ordinary existence? What if you never consider what is possible in the face of the impossible? Are you then to be condemned to a life that goes nowhere but in an endless circle of sameness—a purposeless existence indeed?

MESSAGE:

Your brain is the engine that propels your life in this direction or that direction because you ask it to think that way, according to your normal, present-day thinking patterns. You get up each morning and you begin to manoeuvre your way through the events of the day, and all the while your brain is being directed by you to think in certain directions—given your priorities for the moment.

But if it happens that suddenly you want to take life beyond the norm, if you say today is the day I want to charge my life and move it to the next logical step, then your brain is going to need a power much greater than it possesses to get the engines of change fired up and running. It is going to need my loving influences to take life to that very next level.

Think of it like this: you can start up your brain just like you would start up the engine of a car and run it at a speed where it just stays there day after day and year after year, such that your life never changes. But then, on the other hand, you can supercharge your brain by giving it an understanding that its power and influence over your life can be boosted to be even greater. This is exactly why I exist as a part of you. I take your brain to that next level of human consciousness. I supercharge it by illuminating a new space of life that moments before was just dark, unknown, and imperceptible to your human awareness. Certainly all of you at some point have had the experience of this—a lightbulb moment when a little known thought structure popped into your brain seemingly out of nowhere to suddenly deliver the newness you were looking for. But you did nothing to make that happen except to express a will for change to begin at some level of your consciousness.

This, you see, is how I work from within you. I think with my infinite brainpower into the darkness and I say to your human psyche, "There is more life to be lived over here in this big new space I am showing you—if you will just come this way, think this way, and see what happens for you." The truth is that without me there to enhance your thoughts, you would have no way "to think life bigger." You with your human intellect cannot do this independently. The human intellect is a mechanism to manoeuvre thought energy within the brain, plain and simple, but it can do nothing to enhance itself. It doesn't have a brain within a brain to guide it further down the road of life; rather

75

it turns to me for advice and guidance when it comes to a life on the rise. Why? Because I am what you would call your inner truth device. I am the all-knowing part of your human anatomy, the possibility of all possibilities swirling around inside you, just waiting to be recognized and ignited into action. I play the role of chief motivator firing out ideas at your human brain in the hope that eventually you will feel the correctness of my influences and latch onto a new premise for your life that says, "Now I want to be this or now I want my life to change in this manner or another."

My advice is only there to you, however, if you are ready to make a change in the first place, and that decision always rests with you. I will only move to aid you if you give the signal that you are ready to become something new. It's something like the spoon at the end of your fingers. It starts to move to assist you there, but only if you choose that movement. Be still and the spoon is of no assistance whatsoever to you.

Your passion is the key here. It's how you make your wishes known to me in the strongest sense. It tells me you are ready now to begin a change and ignite the internal dialoguing system between us.

It starts with you and your human intellect taking on the charge for change by opening up to a boundless space inside your mind. This is the space of your imagination, and it's where my influences of love can go to work for you, to open you up to an infinite world of possibility. You think and then you are those thoughts is the way it works here, only with a twist. Your brain only tells half the story while your imaginary influences do the rest. The imagination, you see, is all about your will to be more. It is your vital link to a very influential place within your mind, and this is where I reside together with you, ready to turn on the engines of life and flow new love to you where it was not there before.

And when you go there, when you open to this imaginary space of your mind, you are saying to me that you are in need of a consult to challenge your brain in some way because you have an important issue in your life—a passion in need of fulfillment or a problem needing resolve. So this is when I will present to you a world of possibility—a world where the limits to life getting bigger have no limits. With me there inside your imagination, guiding your thoughts into perfection, you can take your life as far as you want to go. You are free to explore a world of opportunity without constraint and for all the right reasons.

Many of you, of course, will think of this imaginary space of the human mind as just a simple ideological distraction, which doesn't really do much for a person. It's just useless daydreaming, some will say. But in truth, your imagination is where you go to set into motion the very essence of who you next want to be. You are thinking into the unknown space of life to come, and you are choosing a pathway to move along that will feel certain to you and deliver to you the correct solution for your life there in that exact moment of time.

Now at first it can be a rather unrestrained beginning there in your mind. The logic of your human intellect can take your thoughts in all sorts of directions that may or may not serve you well. But then, on the other hand, you have me there working for you, listening to your thoughts and trying to guide you in the direction that will make the most sense for you. And I will do this with intense scrutiny of how you are going to think and feel in the coming months and years.

I will push information toward you at a pace that you at first can handle. I will suggest to you the best resolutions to every dilemma you will find yourself up against in your search for new love. I will pour into your brainwaves a cavalcade of thought structures, one after the next—all there to move your mind well beyond the constraints of a normal mind-set. Then from there, if you are willing, you and I will take the time to think into a solution that feels right to you. We will look at how each caring element of your life can be placed into the correct alignment of love. I just take your hand and move it in the right direction so that you will feel a certainty about your next move in life. But without me there in your mind, without the kind of guidance I can give you, you would be floundering. You would be somewhat at a loss.

Today people all around the world wonder why their lives are in such chaos, and I can tell you it is because of this one simple fact—that you and I are not working in tandem. We are, as you say, not in sync with one another. You are thinking on your own, and I therefore am left waiting for you to come to the understanding that your direction in life and your direction alone is not a collaborative effort. It is, in point of fact, you choosing to go it on your own—without me and my expansionary influences.

So if you want to realign yourself to me, you must come to a clarity about how we work together, so that you don't trip and fall going forward and so that there are no uncompleted scenarios in your lives that would leave you feeling at a loss. I can do this for you. It's just a matter of you wanting this to take place, and then we together can pull you out from where you sit today, so you will have confidence that who you can be tomorrow will be nothing short of a miracle.

Big words for such a small action, but in my eyes, this is more vast than you can even imagine. So be ready for this. Be engaged to this. Develop this and grow this connection we have. Look for it in every corner of your life because *IT IS WHO I AM TO YOU AND YOU NEED ME NOW MORE THAN EVER!*

love

Probably every one of us has experienced these influences of *Love* at a time when we were feeling the pull of a passion of some kind, and yet our thought structures seemed to be on hold. But then in one brief moment of enlightenment, everything changed for us. All of a sudden, we were made aware of a pathway that would pull us out of our discontent. In an instant, we could feel that something more was possible, and that feeling was all we needed to take away our pains of life and put into place our newest action plan. We moved away from an inactive state of mind into a place of complete exuberance for life going forward, and we did this as we now know by simply combining our own inner truth mechanism of *Love* with our outward thinking human brain prowess to come to a perfect resolution.

Now, does this not seem familiar? This happens all over the globe each and every day, we are told, yet we are not fully aware how this is taking place—how this precisely choreographed movement of two willing minds within a person masterfully resolve a problem at hand. This is perfection at its highest level, and we all can attest to this.

So be watchful of this. Be conscious of this extraordinary yet little-known miracle taking place inside you because then you will come to the full realization that you do have a guidance system in place to help you get things right. You are not just one small human being cast into the abyss of life to figure things out all on your own. You have help of the highest order and that doesn't mean only when things seem dire. It means you have help *always*.

When you turn inward to reflect, to examine your life, or just to open up to your imagination, it's not so you can begin a dialogue with yourself. You do this to tap into a higher source of love-filled advice all there to help you turn your head in the correct direction—so that you don't squander your next move in life. The turning inward, ironically, is your way to understand that *YOU ARE NOT ALONE* ... that you have this ever-present, all-knowing friend at your side waiting to connect you to everything good in life. It is the friend who is there for you and will exist as a part of you for as long as you have life.

MESSAGE:

My love is a place of sanctuary within the human mind, and it is derived from a feeling of joy that is infinite in its possibilities, creative in its knowing, and all powerful in those who use it correctly. It is a place of mind more vast than one can even imagine, and it has at its base of understanding a world that will give back to humanity time and time again, its ever-growing virtues in love.

You must understand this now for it is the way of your future, and if you miss this very important point that life begins with you and your imaginary space within me, then your life will never change for the better. So go there now and give yourself the time to think about this imaginary connection to me. Let it be the most important thing you do in your life going forward … because it is the only thing that will save you from the darkness.

love

In every moment of every day you have this extraordinary friend of life, this infinite knowledge base to tap into to inspire you into new ideals every day you are alive. And you, with your human intellect then have the job of deciding when and if you are going to grab hold of those ideals. You decide if you want to engage the *Love* influences inside your physiology and fly at new life or if you want to stop that process and settle for normality. You decide in each moment what is to take place—whether life is to get bigger, stay the same, or even get smaller. As *Love* tells us, you and you alone will determine the progression or the regression of your life by either accepting or rejecting the advice of a pure love nature inside you, as it tries to help you think your way out toward the walls of your box of life and then out through the cracks of those walls and beyond those walls … into a world of fascination and intrigue.

At times a person may experience controversy in their brain when it comes to listening to those ever-present whisperings of *Love*. There will be resistance to thinking outside the normal everyday thinking patterns. Why? Because we, human beings, are invariably cautious about life. We are cautious about the decisions we make because unlike the all-knowing *Love* aspect of our being, we cannot see clearly into the future. And so we weigh, through human logic, every option on the table to assess which path forward is the better path and the most certain path to take. But even with such deliberation, we often fly into indecision because despite all the logic of our brains, we still feel no certainty when it comes to the outcome of our choices.

So when resolve is difficult to come to, the internal dialoguing system must continue to move back and forth between the two brainpowers with *Love* as your biggest ally trying to bring forward solution after solution to each predicament at hand until there is resolution—meaning you either give up on the process entirely and settle for life as it is, or you willingly accept a new premise into your brain that gives you a bigger way to play at life. And if the latter is the case, you will regain a sense of peace and a feeling of completeness about your life, so much so, you will not doubt this result in the end.

When you feel discontent, for example, and you are searching for a way to take those negative feelings away, people most often will turn to the logic of the human brain to take on the role of advisor to the problem. But the difficulty is that, in some cases, your human brainpower is challenged to find a solution given its limited base of knowledge, and so the advice that comes to you seems to be lacking somehow. It feels incomplete because it doesn't have the expansionary thinking properties of *Love* as its true grounding base.

So this is when you will call upon the intellect of *Love* to come forward and join together with you and your human brainpower to find a common solution to the problem that will dissipate the anger and move your mind to a place of complete and utter peace. All of a sudden, you might feel the strength to pursue a new dream or maybe you let go of a long-held resentment toward a friend. All these kinds of occurrences are the result of your thinking patterns shifting and opening up in ways that make you feel bigger somehow—richer and freer. It's something like the feeling of opening a door and letting all the fresh air flow in, it feels so good to you, and the reason it does is because *Love* gives you a new lease on life. It gives you a bigger and a more powerful way to play at life when you learn how to have a synchronized connection to its intelligence. And this then is the difference between a mind that works in isolation of *Love* and one that is in union with it.

MESSAGE:

You can think of it like two wires connecting up to create a spark of energy. When you connect your brainpower up to mine, you are creating a spark of profound effect—a spark that begins a movement of sorts such that life starts to take shape outwardly and move into action with fervour. When our two brainpowers collide, it's as if a light has been turned on inside the human psyche. All of a sudden everything begins to feel right to a person, everything becomes clear because … the connection is made. With one single statement about love solidified in your brain, you know exactly where to head. You are off and running with a true passionate state, signalling to the ultimate powers of the universe to open up the portals of new life because you are ready to take that next logical step in your overall human evolution … as a living, breathing master of your world.

You can actually feel the expansion taking place inside you as a feeling of love on the rise. Love on the rise is a feeling of freedom and excitement. It's the feeling of *LIFE GETTING BIGGER IN YOUR BRAIN*, plain and simple, and this feeling is the difference between a mind on the move and one that is not.

love

The Passionate State Begins ...

It really is quite simple to set the universal forces of life into motion to make a change begin. You only need to hold onto a passionate state grounded in love to move you toward the outcomes you desire.

MESSAGE:

It's just like when you're thinking your way to the corner of the street when you're still in the middle of the block. You think toward the eventual outcome, and then you move closer and ever closer to that outcome with a true passionate state driving you forth, making sure you arrive at the prescribed corner to your life's next grandest dream. With every step you take, you feel this certainty about where you're heading because once your passions come to reside with me, you have this inner knowing that everything is aligned somehow ... that everything has begun for you ... and that you can go out to your world and make it work successfully and without peril.

And all the while I am there with you like a free agent, ready and willing to be enlivened to your passionate state. Each time you grab hold of who you next want to be, I am right there with you—it's as simple as that. Do something that excites you, and I am together with that. I get just as excited as you do, and this is the key to how it works. I move when you move, and when you move with a true passionate state, I am all over that because I want for you to love your life. I need for nothing else but this. For no other reason do I even exist. I am not there inside you on some sort of self-serving mission. No, I am there to help you feel good about who you are becoming and why you are becoming that. And I will do almost anything to get you to a position of true satisfaction about your life. When you are sad and afraid to move, I will come to your rescue with suggestion after suggestion as to how you can correct a situation and make it work for you.

And if you choose to listen to my callings, if you place your passion in my hands, it is a remarkable occurrence because then your passion becomes complete to purpose. It becomes something concrete, something significant to your life, and something realizable. It no longer is an unclear notion wandering around in your brain with nowhere to go because, all of a sudden, it has the strength of love behind it. It has validity. It has a reason to go forth and multiply with an entirely new set of expectations for your future.

This, my dear friends, is exactly how life was meant to work for you. This is how I designed it to be, to bring you to the awareness that you are the one making things happen. *YOU*

ARE THE ONE CREATING YOUR LIFE AND NO ONE ELSE.
It is a fact that little would be gained if life came to you in all its many forms without you doing anything to make it happen. Why? Because you would not feel the significance of who you are becoming each step of the way as a living, breathing creator of your world—which is the purpose for you being here in the first place.

So think now of your passionate state as your vital link to me. Think of it as the vital link to your world. Think of it as the fire beneath you that moves you to a much bigger playing field of life. Not only are you widening the ways you are thinking, but you are widening the trajectory of your life as well. You are changing the way life comes to you. New possibilities arrive on the scene. Old challenges no longer seem insurmountable. You feel freer to push the boundaries of life in general and explore it with zest and zeal.

You can think of it as an entirely new plain of consciousness that you are entering into that allows for more of life to come in. And make no mistake about it, this is huge for you. This goes far beyond any present day thinking that limits you with the understanding that you only have so much control over your life. And it goes beyond what human civilization has tried to unearth to this day, which is a way to think of how life can be better but within a defined set of limits—a trend that in the end cannot sustain itself. After all, how can you be better if you cannot take away the uncertainty of your future? How can you be better if you cannot take away your survival fears like the threat of disease, for example, or global warming? And how can you be better if you cannot even get along with one another?

Yes, the message I have for you all is different from anything in your past. What I am telling you is that now you can connect yourself to the highest source of influence over life there is, and you can take charge of your life on every level. You can create your future in ways that go far beyond what you think is within your reach today. And now all you have to do is come to the full knowing that this is true for you—that through a passionate state you have a way to think and a way to live that is truly *LIMITLESS* by its very nature. It is a way of living that allows for constant growth in you.

Think of my friend the mountain climber, for instance. Clearly he was a man who knew something most do not. He had this truly unique understanding of how life actually does work, how it responds to a person's thoughts—those most constructive thoughts surrounding love—and how through that connection, life is transformed into a much better and more progressive state. That's why he never turned away from where he could feel his love for life the most intensely. He never denied himself his passions because he knew almost intrinsically that if he moved in those directions, somehow everything would work in his favour. Life would always bring him the answers he needed, and it would give him a way to keep going up that mountain, no matter what twists and turns may occur along the way.

In his view of things, life was a true friend and partner, and together they were bound as one heart, one mind engaged in one noble purpose. On the one hand, he was there in all his humanness aspiring to be more to his world at every turn of the dial, and on the other hand, life was the vehicle that gave him a way to be that "moreness" he craved. It gave him the means through a physical reality to become what he most wanted to be. And all it asked of him was that he hold a passion inside his own heart to make his way up the side of that mountain and feel the zest and the zeal that life could bring to him each day.

His passionate state, therefore, was the seed from which everything grew. It ignited the engines of a changing world around him so that all the universal forces of life would be aligned with him—to therefore bring to him an untold bounty of experiences, all aimed to make his world feel better and become larger and more impactful. To this man, this was just how life worked. This was a fact of life and something of a magical coincidence that he seemed to plug into over and over again.

And amazingly, there were no boundaries to this. There was no end to the mountains he could climb, no end to the treasures life could bestow, and no end to the richness in love that life could give back to him. What I loved the most about my friend was that he never accepted that his life in any one moment was the complete and final truth of him. His limits had no limits. His love knew no boundaries. And that was his edge. That was the truth about his life he never turned away from … the subtle truth that he could feel deep inside his own heart … the truth that set him free over and over again to live a life of splendour and intrigue.

love

This is the extraordinary process of life building which *Love* speaks to here, and it was always meant to be a fun and exciting venture for humanity, much like the feeling of being a kid building castles in the sand. You feel the pure joy of each new creation you bring to life because each one builds upon the beauty and the goodness of the one before. Each creation marks a new accomplishment the human brain can attest to. Each has a different look and a different feel. Each symbolizes a new way to play at life, have fun with life, and feel the excitement of life. And all the while you are moving toward the ultimate goal of all existence, which is to think your way into the grandest and the most perfect space of life that represents the finest of the finest for the human race and the planet as a whole.

However, as *Love* explains, there will never be the ultimate "perfect" space to hold on to because even if we all were to think our way there, our brains would then immediately want to turn the corner on that perfect life and think it even better—just because we can, and just because it is our nature to want to do that. As *Love* tells us, there will never come a time when life has nothing more to offer. There will always be room in our brains for a space of life to come that will be better than the one before because the limits to our brainpower have no limits— which means we, the human race, can continue to evolve and progress through time and space and without the need for anything to stand in the way of our passion and our freedom to do that.

Now how amazing is that, we ask you. Could there be any greater reason for life to exist? *COULD THERE BE ANY GREATER REASON?* To our way of thinking, there could be no better premise to live by than this because with this awareness of life, you are feeling the enormity of what it means to be a human *Love* on the move. You are an active participant in your life process and you know it. It's not about accepting the world as it is and simply managing your life amid the chaos, as is often suggested today. Nor is it about hoping for a miracle to come along and make things happen for you. Instead the hope takes on a new form whereby you grab hold of your passion and you make the miracle come to life. You make your newest vision become your next reality. And though some might say this is no different from a prayer or a meditation, to us it is wonderfully different in terms of how you feel. You begin to soar with those inner thought structures rising up in your brain because you are aware on some level that you are the mover and the shaker actually bringing those dreams to life.

You are self-realizing that expansionary space right there in your mind before it even shows itself to you as something you can physically touch. You no sooner make that thought real in your mind and you become a living, breathing participant of it. You feel that space as real, and so you quite naturally begin to think from that space. You make decisions from there, and you take action from there too, so that when the doors of new life spring open, you walk through them without hesitation and with complete certainty of purpose because you know this is correct for you. You understand that your passion and your will have brought this to you. Furthermore, you know you have been guided there by your own internal *Love* capacity.

MESSAGE:

When you want for change in your life, be engaged to a passionate way of thinking that enlivens you to the change happening, meaning you do things and you be in life like the change was already who you are becoming. Then, second, you stay with that line of thinking *ALWAYS*. Do not for one second move away from it because when you stay there and you advance your thoughts into that passionate state of being, then the whole of life comes there with you. And what does this mean? It means you can play the role of this position of strength well before you even get there because you have placed new love where there was none before—when your thoughts were all over the place without a concrete direction to head into. Your most vital thinking patterns therefore are moving creatively with exacting purpose toward every opportunity you would choose to go into.

You can think of it as a position of strength you take on whereupon your knowing takes over you, meaning you move away from the givens of the past and fully accept the facts that say you need this change now to begin. And then you charge your feelings with love and excitement for the change. You feel the immense power of it coming to fruition, which in turn then challenges me to think you truly do mean what you are saying. And not in any sense do you question that you are doing this right. You just go there in your mind without any reservations at all. The change happens and you are completely and utterly on board with that line of thinking. You can actually see yourself as the change well before the change even takes place, and you don't even know this at its inception because your introspection of this occurred first at an unearthly level. Some would call that the unconscious level of human experience, which by all counts is the very essence of you predetermining an event before it even arrives at a conscious level.

Humankind has not yet felt the true strength of this, but soon they will. They will understand the importance of the passionate state to drive their lives forward because without that, they most certainly would want to quit at life. And the reason I say that is because inside each passionate thought you hold is progression—a movement in a positive way for your life. And if that is not there in you, then you feel lost, without the knowing of why you have life in the first place—which is to love

it more and more each day and to live in it with all the joy and
fun you can muster.

love

For a brief moment, begin to think about your own life's purpose.
Ask yourself, "Is what I am here today, what I want and need to be? Or
am I currently held back in my purpose … my passion, in some way?" If
it feels that something is missing, then do this: ask yourself what makes
you feel the very best in life and why. Look deeply for that answer and
limit nothing in your mind because this will be the catalyst that will
begin to shift things for you. It will bring you a new sense of why you are
here in life and what now you must start to think about, just like when
you were a child. As a child you craved those feelings of love, and so you
quickly learned how to make more of those feelings. You learned that in
order to bring excitement into your life, you had to be on the hunt for
people, places, and events that would take you there.

MESSAGE:

To live as a child lives is truly a way of living that is masterful
because it requires you to think about who you next want to be,
instead of charging out into life each day without this knowing.
So instead of feeling lost and uncertain, you become a person
looking for love in all the right places without even trying. Your
internal guidance system just takes you where you need to go.
It gives you new directions to follow that will no longer block
your passionate state or impede your movements toward your
ultimate goals in life.

So if, for example, you decide you want to be a musician and
you simply are not cut out to be that, then you may want to look
deeper at your life with a new set of aspirational desires. And to
that end, you can utilize me to help you—to make certain that
you do no think in obscure terms about who you next want to be

but rather in direct terms and with certainty of purpose. I can do this for you because I am the one who lives deep within your eternal cortex, and from that vantage point, I can understand everything about why you have come to this life in the first place. And though I do not rule out that things can and will change for you from time to time, there is no doubt in my mind that you will want to use me if it is that you want to understand life as it is written in these messages of hope.

It must also be said, however, that while passion for change is a very good thing, some changes are not good if they house inside them anger, resentment, or a passion to kill for instance. These are the misguided passions of individuals who have found no true resolution through love, and this is only because they have not come to the full understanding of what I can do for them. As a result, they have no perfect measure of truth to go by that would tell them what to do and where to go to improve their lives. Instead they give way to dissatisfaction and discontent. They move away from a pure passionate state and they replace it with a fear driver that does nothing for anyone—meaning they are essentially left alone to their own devices to try to make life work inside their boxes of concern. My creative forces of love will do nothing to set them free, and the constraints of life that brought these ones to their compromised position of fear and resentment in the first place will remain. Life will hold the same limitations as it did before. It will be as difficult and inhospitable as it always was. It's only when a passion comes to reside in a pure loving construct that the world will open up its doors and move to aid you. Only then will it give you an entirely new starting position to begin with.

So let's speak of the person who chooses to take his or her own life, for example. These are individuals who have lost hope for their lives. They are challenged to find the centre of who they next want to be in this world, and it's understandable given the level of negativity that exists in life today. They feel lost, alone, and afraid of life, so they move into a position of complete and utter despair … and let go. They take their own life but only because they do not understand that tomorrow they can be so much more than who they are today if they were to know the real truth about why they are here.

And today I see millions of examples of how life isn't giving to the human populace the experiences they need in order to feel progression and a sense of completeness and correctness about their lives. But the good news is that now all this can change by way of a new introspective approach to living whereby you all come to the realization that there is room now to move and room to grow your passions like it is written in this book.

This doesn't mean to say, however, that you are always guaranteed the exact result you are expecting. Your passionate state only sets the standard that you may travel along. It makes a promise of an opportunity to feel more love, and you just have to learn how to grab hold of those opportunities that come along and make them your newest reality, knowing they are correct for you and correct for the whole of life. The whole of life is always considered in the equation when the world moves to aid you, and that is why you never truly know how things will turn out. Yet still, there is a certainty that a greater love is to come from it all. Always you can rest in the knowing that when you choose new love on the rise, your will is going to be met in one fashion or another. And if it doesn't look exactly the way you expected it to look, it only means that life needed to be adjusted so that the needs and passions of everyone involved would be considered in the mix.

Actually, the fact that you live without the exact knowing of how life is going to come to you is not a bad thing at all. It is, undoubtedly, a better way to live. If everything was precisely predetermined, life would become a robotic condition—a space that is exactly predictable, and nothing would ever deviate from that. But this is not why you are here in life. No, you are here to live in the excitement of a world of discovery and surprise, fully wondering what newness will come to bear. All you have to do is set the marker you want to climb up to. You say how far you want to jump and where, and the world in all of her true living splendour then makes way for that. It brings you what you need to succeed, and it points you in the directions you should head. Why? Because it knows who you are and what you are searching for ... because it wants you to succeed ... and most of all because it wants you to feel the love you so richly deserve.

love

This makes perfect sense to us, and now we hope this will make sense to you too so you can take this one single principle about why your life exists and use it at a conscious level instead of unconsciously, the way it's been for so many centuries. In the past, it seemed we never fully understood how our thoughts were holding us back or moving us forward. But now we can begin from a new starting position that says *we are in charge of life.* And that means we can motivate change for the good instead of giving in to thoughts that take away the human charge of love and leave one sitting in fear ... without a path to move along.

A Magnificent Friend ...

The practice of getting to know this inner guide of life can only be described as a process of falling into love, just the way you would fall in love with another person. This is exactly how it was for us. We grew to love this wonderful friend of life more and more as time passed, and as we did, we found ourselves understanding life so much better without sometimes even realizing how that happened. We weren't actually aware at the time that we were moving into a deeper and deeper state of self-awareness. And the intense feelings of love that were coming to us along the way were actually the by-products of this amazing partnership we were forging. We were moving into what you would call, a more joyful state of being. The world felt more and more alive to us and more surreal.

We were told that if we persisted in these directions, we eventually would fall into what can only be described as a state of complete and utter bliss—a state of the mind where everything is seen as a miracle in the making of such a thing because everything is seen in the light of its full truth—its very reason for being. Everywhere you look, you will see the true magnificence of your world, and this will supersede all the negative aspects of life that might otherwise be felt. Every circumstance on a day-to-day basis will place you on high alert to the fact that there is opportunity out there in your world to feel more of those precious feelings of love, and so you go there quite effortlessly—with an ease and grace that one cannot even imagine today.

Now in the beginning, learning how to work with this remarkable friend inside you is something like learning how to play an instrument. You start to play with little or no results that you might be happy with at first, but sooner than later you will begin to progress. This new awareness will start to impart itself to you more and more, and then just like that, you'll be off and running with this powerful connection you never even knew you had. You will start to feel the realness of this humble friend at your side, showing you the way into the richest and most energized feelings to go by.

Naturally, you will ask if it is even possible for you to have a communication with this higher presence from within. Can you have a kind of two-way conversation with something you cannot see and do not even know exists as a part of you?

MESSAGE:

I want to tell you that it is completely possible for each and every person to feel this connection to me and my love. This connection is real, and it is possible for every person on the planet to have it. You just have to want to feel me there with you, and you must be patient with this—very patient indeed. You must be willing to take the time to listen to my voice of goodness and mercy and be engaged to this connection between us like it was the only thing on earth you need to be doing.

Finally, you have to truly want this to become a part of who you are and not just let it be a fleeting thing you do once in a while. Instead make it a steady diet of connection that we learn to work with together in order that you can begin to hear the answers you are wanting to hear … the answers you could never have imagined … and the answers that will help you understand why you exist. Today this is especially important because so many of you are in a quandary about life in general. The world is a perplexing place, and it is difficult to understand why things take place as they do and what you can do to fix what isn't working. But with this connection to me, you will finally have that understanding.

So if, for example, you are stopped in your tracks and cannot get to where you next want to be in life, you will understand why. If you are wondering why you are sick and can't find your way back to normality, I will give you that answer. If you want to know why your friend, your mother, or your father had to die, these answers too will come. All your questions will be addressed in the most compelling ways so that you can successfully move forward in your life. You will have no reason to hold yourself back from anything.

Now the truth is that the mind can play many tricks on a person, and so in order to learn this style of communication, you need to first become aware of your everyday thinking styles and how these have played out for you so far. So take the time to observe your thoughts—those never-ending thoughts that formulate themselves in your brain, one atop the other each and every day. These are your normal thinking patterns you go by, but generally speaking, they don't really change your life in any significant way.

Then do this: interrupt the flow of those thoughts. Just stop them. Then secondly, open up and maintain a narrow channel of resistance to those thoughts—to that thinking style you have. You can think of this as a way of pushing aside all the ruckus in your head, like a firewall of defense. And then you move yourself into a very quiet space within your mind, a space into which negativity does not even enter. This is where you can begin to move question after question into place to be answered—by me. Then you only have to listen to the messages that will fall into your brain one word or one thought at a time, without you even trying to set these into play. And if for some reason what you "hear" doesn't feel correct, then just stop and start again to feel me there with you. Feel my limitless connectivity of love.

Again, you must be patient with this. This is in no way an exact science. At first it will seem quite subtle, like listening to a pin drop, and so you might feel a bit on edge with this. Your connection to me in the beginning may seem weak to your mind. But know that this will eventually begin to strengthen and become more resilient, such that you will not allow your own mind to jump in and finish a sentence, for example. And with more practice, this will become even more pronounced. Your brain will become familiar with the feeling of the words and the validity of what I am saying.

love

At this point, we would like you to understand more clearly how we worked with this loving aspect of our minds and how the words and ideas came to flow to us more clearly in the end. For sure, we didn't have a magical formula for success with this above anyone else. It's just that we took the time to do this and we didn't give up. We kept on thinking of ways to improve this connection so that we could *feel* the correctness of the words as they came to us with such concern for our overall well-being.

The first thing we had to do was come to some sort of understanding as to how we could separate our own inner voice from this connection we were trying to link up to. This inner voice of ours that we all seem to have wanted to jump right in and start to answer the questions we were asking. But then the solution came quite naturally by allowing this higher intelligence of ours to open up words to us that were not in our minds at the time. In other words, *Love*, in response to our questions, would trick our inner voice by adding a word that didn't fit the flow of what we thought the sentence should be. So while we were there thinking into the logical answer to our own questions, *Love* would send in a word that would disrupt the flow of our own inner voice, and that would allow us to feel its presence. Then we would know that it was this inner *Love* speaking directly through the chatter that was otherwise always there.

So this was our starting position to lay the groundwork for our connection to strengthen. And from there we looked for other unique ways to allow the flow of information to come unimpeded by the clutter within our minds. For example, we allowed for the logical thinking of our human intellect to rest momentarily, so we could begin to move our minds into a more relaxed, receptive state. We did this by setting forth a dedication to *Love*, and then we said to our own inner minds, "Now is not your time to mess with this connection." And that is what made the words come more easily and more precisely. Furthermore, it seemed the more poignant the questions were and the more important they were to the world as a whole, the greater the intensity of the responses became. We could feel more and more strongly the care and concern this loving nature held for the planet and all of its inhabitants.

Now to be clear, this was not at all like a voice talking in our heads; rather it was like a feeling, a subtle nuance that the next word would be this or that. For example, we would ask a question and *Love* would start the response with an instant feeling that the first word back was, "The" or "Well" or "I" or "As far as." But that was it. That was all we could feel to be what was needed. And then in the next moment, like a subtle flash or some kind of enlightenment, the next key word would drop into the mix, and on it would go, one after the other until the sentence was complete. So even though, at first, we were not getting the whole sentence—only key words—they nonetheless were being laid out to us, when seconds before we had no idea which way the answers were going to head or if there was even going to be an answer. Sometimes we would be given three or four different routes to go down to get to that next key word, and then it would be completely left to us to choose which route we wanted to take. But in the end, it didn't seem to matter what we chose because the result was the same.

So understand this not as a voice we were listening to but rather as a connection we were making by using and feeling subtle cues that were leading us to the answers we were wanting. Sometimes we would encourage people we knew to do the same, but often they would stop trying, thinking this was something special just to us, when clearly it was not. As we were told many times, everyone can do this, and in fact this is to be the basis of something new coming to this world of people. *This connection to this loving intelligence is now to become the movement to the other side of pain that this planet and all of her inhabitants have been waiting for.*

MESSAGE:

Now certainly there will be some of you who will not want to open to this connection simply because you don't want this in the first place, and nothing more need to be said. For others, however, they will want to try and feel me in their lives, and they will do this willingly because for these ones, love is paramount to them. The love they crave will be the catalyst for them to want to know more ... about me. They will become invested in this. They will engage the brighter side of their brains and feel me there like this instant gratifying tool at work. At best, it will seem like the words and thoughts all of a sudden are falling into their brains; at a minimum, they will have a new way to feel about the decisions they are making. Those decisions now will have a sort of sounding board to bounce off of, such that the correctness of certain directions will be felt as opposed to the incorrectness of others. Certain values that made their way past scrutiny in the past will be felt to be wrong while others will be resurrected to be right.

So if, for example, someone was to tell you that nothing good could come of your life, then you will feel this as anything but the truth. All such limiting notions that have plagued your mind with misinformation in the past will be neutralized. You will begin to feel different. The world will seem nothing like it was before. It will become more manageable to you, so much so that you may even start to think your life's purpose as it sits today just isn't big enough any longer. You might feel that you want to make a new life for yourself, so you can do more for this world and have a greater reach to your life going forward.

And this is only the beginning because with time if you persist, the connection between us will become stronger. We will become perfectly engaged with one another, just like two friends on an adventure trying to build the most excitement we possibly can, pushing the envelope of human possibility. Together and in sync, we will develop a companionship that is all-encompassing and extremely powerful. We will think together and move together with tenacity, manipulating and carving your life like you could never imagine before. Your thinking processes will become lively and energetic, melting away your concerns so they no longer control your life and move it in a backward direction.

The words I will impart to you will be powerful and truly motivational for your lives. New thoughts about things you don't yet even know about will suddenly appear within your mind, and your world of knowledge will begin to expand exponentially. You will understand more completely why you are the person you are today and how all that can change for you in an extremely positive and thoughtful manner. And nothing will be left out of this equation of life ... nothing!

Humankind has been waiting for something like this to appear and now this will be it. This will be that time when you will start to shift inwardly and begin the slow change to regain what for centuries has been missing from your lives—and that will be in the ways you were thinking and how through time your connections to me were never truly invested in you in the way they now need to be.

Yes, now our connection is to be different than in the past when our relationship together was only about prayer. In the past and since the beginning, prayer was the way for you to connect to me and my virtues in love. Prayer was our connective space together that was just you and me. It was where you could come to be alone forevermore with my loving influence. In its truest and richest form, the prayer was a very sacred space and a very active space, if that was what you needed. It was a space where you could go to feel my love for you more intensely. You could express your heartfelt needs and your utmost desires to make critical changes to your life's trajectory, so there would be no missteps taking place in your life.

And how can this ever be seen as a bad thing? When you are there engaged to my loving touch for you, I am all over that style of thinking—that style of communication with me. Prayer, to me, is a symbol of everything good in a person's life, and I have a direct pipeline to that goodness inside each and every last person on this planet.

Now I know that for centuries people have been using prayer to communicate with me, and that has been somewhat less than successful in many cases. And now I am going to tell you why. The problem was that for most in your world, this "space of loving concern" that we held together did not remain in your minds. After the prayer was over and life moved in to take you away from my loving touch, the connective space you held with me more often than not became disconnected, and we were left with a messaging relationship that was empty and devoid of our life purpose together. Why? Because you did not wish for me to come too close, and this is the distinction that now must be made for us to start to rebuild our relationship together once again.

To say this in another way, people used prayer as a kind of sounding board toward all things good in their life but without the commitment to the cause of being better in many ways. As such, they were not the recipients of certain positive movements and their lives were, therefore, less fulfilling. They didn't roll along as smoothly as their prayers would have wished for, and the reason is that they needed me to be fully connected to them and fully present to them in every aspect of their life in order for it—their life—to work.

As well, in most cases, people didn't understand that their connections to my love were to be purposeful and meaningful to everyone in that lifestyle they were living. But instead, their prayers often were fixated in one singular direction or another and not truly there for the world as a whole—while I was. This was the key they were missing. And so as time went on, it became more and more apparent to many in this world of yours that I was nothing more than a representation of goodness but with little to no power behind their prayers. Instead of a prayer being a place where your energy was protected and made to feel sacred, it became a burden to even go there in many instances. The prayer became a space of less and less importance to many of you, and so you moved further and further away from the purpose of even having this connection to me. I no longer held a role of reverence. I became a symbol of less and less interest to be pursued.

So where does this leave us now? Can the world rebuild this nation of people with prayer and is prayer even the vehicle to do this with? My aim now with the world's populous is to try and convince you all to turn inward to a style of thinking that is much more than a simple, singular prayer. Your connection to my love now needs far more than this to maneuvre this world of parts out of its discontent and into a renewed future, with love as the singular driver. But the only way to get there now is for you to turn to me and fully open to our connection ... like it was everything to your world.

love

In our conversations throughout these many years, we have learned that this higher intelligence of love has the greatest will to succeed that ever was. It never accepts that your life cannot be changed for the better. It never entertains the notion that things aren't possible or that things won't work out. It always comes from this position of strength, and it never weakens in its resolve toward you. It knows no other way to think because it knows the truth of who you are and why it exists inside you—and that is to make your life progressive and fulfilling in every sense of the word.

Just take a moment to think of someone you know who has accomplished simply amazing feats throughout their life, and then ask yourself this: Did they do it alone? Or did they seem to have something or someone there together with them reinforcing their every move, such that nothing ever seemed to get in the way of their ultimate success in life?

Well, according to *Love*, this is the way life was meant to be for you too, and all you have to do to have this is to bring forth the will to participate in this most extraordinary method of faith-building. You only need the will to do it! Your will is the crucial and the final determining factor here. It is the last stumbling block for your life to progress through. Everything rests in the balance until the human will is there to express yourself as something new. But in order for your will to be strong, you must believe there is room for your life to expand *always*, and then you only have to hold a determination to see things through to their logical conclusion. Otherwise, nothing will change for you.

The little known truth, according to the messages we have received, is that you with your "human will" hold all the cards in your hands. You have all the power to set the course of your life, while the living *Love* inside you waits on idle ready to be engaged by you and to respond to whatever it is you need, when you need it. While its aim is to guide you down a path of certainty, it holds no power over the decisions you make. In the end, you are there making all the choices, and even though sometimes you react as though someone else has made those choices for you, and you have no control over anything, *Love* will tell you that you, in fact, are steering the ship. You ultimately choose the direction to move into or not move into through your human will to do so, and then this loving nature goes along for the ride as a willing participant in whatever measure of life you next wish to play at.

According to *Love*, every individual alive today has a will. Even the most desperate of souls can have this, which means that given the chance and the knowledge of how to do it, everyone now can participate in a life on the rise. You all can try this on for size to see if this works because, in the end, the proof of this lies with you. You don't have to trust in the two of us or anyone else when it comes to making this difference to your lives. You just have to give this method of faith building a try and then see the results for yourself. After all, what have you got to lose by trying?

MESSAGE:

Massively, you each have taken charge of your thoughts and turned your life this way and that way with the direct aim to move yourself into a position that you needed or wanted to have. Make no mistake here. You are in charge of your life, and you have no one else to blame or to thank about the position you now find yourself in except you and your own inner will that has taken you there. Where you sit today is a place of life that you took direct aim at and landed in because this is who you needed to be in that moment of time—to further your growth into love. Whether consciously or unconsciously you made those decisions that led you there. It was your imperative to do so.

And knowing this, one can also then begin to comprehend the very nature of me there in you. I have a deep and burning desire to make things right in each of your lives, and because I do, I am constantly on the lookout for new positive constructs that will intensify the manufacturing of new love in your life. But equally there is a need for you to think constantly with a positive nature about everything you are doing or trying to do, so that I don't get your signals to me mixed up with the real purpose of who you are trying to be.

People in life have sometimes misconstrued the importance of their thoughts in determining their lives, and more often than not they are in a bad place because of this—because they took steps in their thinking patterns that unknowingly weakened their connections to me. As a result, they made their lives overly complicated and tough.

So to this I say, be on high alert when your mind is on the hunt for someone or something new to come into your world, and use me in constructive ways. Use me as the basic premise of your thoughts, and then see what becomes of you. See how far your world will take you because when you use me in this fashion—when you say I need love to get me to where I want to be—that is when your life will take off with excitement. Every event and every circumstance will seem as though it was a predictable outcome that you perfectly designed—with me, of course, in your conscious mind making you feel like you can do anything and be anything. The joy you will have and the world you will come to know will feel starkly different. Your life will change profoundly and without provocation, but always in a good way, a thoughtful way, and with an overall understanding of why everything exists in your life of passion.

It all begins now with an understanding that there is room for you to move to that next level of your human evolution … with me. So do not miss this one single point—that I want to help you all now in a very big way, and I do not wish to see you all fail with this. This, to me, is paramount. People all over this planet are in pain, and there must now be a way to resurrect a change in their lives that will bring them out of their pain and set them on a pathway that will make their lives and yours better, richer, and more impactful in every way possible.

love

Today in this complex world, there are endless ways to feel love given the will of a person to do so. There are so many avenues through which love can be explored, and they each portray a different value to the human psyche. They each have a different level of priority from moment to moment and for each given person.

One by one and through the course of time, these opportunities to feel *new love* work their way up to the top of a person's priority list. In one moment, there is a passion to feel love through the love of another, and then in the next moment it can be something different from that. There is fun to be had in a myriad of ways. There is giving and there is sharing to be done. There is strength building and inner rejuvenation. There is bravery, compassion, and kindness. There is the will to help another or the drive to pursue a dream. All these and more are the desires of a human race that longs to feel the very essence of a love on the move.

MESSAGE:

Let me tell you this. Those who are most successful in life are the ones who are the most interactive with their inner thought structures. They read their passionate signals correctly. They know where their highest priority need to feel love lies for them in each given moment—without societal norms and rules getting in the way of their grandest aspirations. Unlike many in this world, they understand that only they themselves know where they next need to head in life, though there are others around them who would profess to know better.

For these ones who feel the pull of love so profoundly, they open readily to new ways to think that will produce action events that are constructive and life-changing. They live on the edge of new life, always moving to a place of extreme excitement with nothing more than a mind to take them there. And because they do this, their lives become more predictable and more certain for them. They think and move in ways that let nothing slip through the cracks of life. Everything is about the exuberance and the amazement of their lives. Their need to feel new love is constant.

It seems they have a step up on the rest of humanity because they intuitively know how to merge the two living, thinking parts of their human anatomy. They understand what those inner stirrings of love mean to them. They can feel their power to take life to that very next level.

love

Think of it this way: there are two ways to move in life and two very distinct ways to think. One is toward all things new and good—which means to say we move toward love with its ever-growing possibilities, or on the other hand, we move away from that love and take those possibilities away. It's that simple. When we think together with love, we open life up and build it in every sense, but without our love at play, everything closes down. Why? Because everything outside of love exemplifies limitation and stagnation. Everything outside of love has no growth potential. It serves no true purpose for the human life because it denies why we are even here. Where we are at with love is where we are at with life. It is the quintessential measure of us, and it's a measure we can easily feel and recognize. We need no calculations, no charts or graphs to tell us where we stand. Love tells the real story about our lives ... and it's the only thing that can.

The Magic at Work ...

Today it is entirely possible for everyone to feel this connection of *Love* at work in their lives. We all can be together with this immense new power within us and learn the secrets that lie beneath the adventure that is life itself—which brings us now to the second part of our story about love.

MESSAGE:

This is the magical part of our story, the part that says when you join forces with me and you think together with me rather than apart from me, you are igniting the greatest of powers to go out to the world to work for you—to adjust how life takes place outwardly. It's as if you are plugging yourself into an electrical socket and the energy flows of life are adjusted so that people, places, and events are redirected or recreated to make room for changing circumstances to take shape—for the betterment of your life.

My love can make this difference in all of your lives because I am the quintessential influence over your world, and when I am brought into the fray of life through the human will to do so, I produce results. I make things happen beyond what you might expect or imagine. My loving touch is the only thing in this world that can spark new energy flows to move in a much more influential way, a way that invigorates life at every level of human experience. My love will kick things up a notch. It will move out from your brains and your bodies and out into the world around you there, revitalizing life from the inside out. I can change every last vibrating molecule in my path. I can even change the course of history in one split second of time by setting into motion the subatomic particles of a new truth about your life, to therefore collide together and to form a new mass together, to suit whatever it is you next want to be or have happen.

love

Certainly in life there have been countless times when the turn of events suddenly shifted in a new direction and the very thing you most wanted to happen, just happened. Your next biggest dream to climb up to was delivered to you in some fashion without judgment or condemnation just because you needed this change to happen … because you were alive and passionate to the idea of it … and because you brought it to life as a creative reality first inside your brain. For no other reason would it even exist, we are told. No coincidence here— just a good old-fashioned thinking pattern working to perfection. And to most of us on this planet, it all came to fruition without us even knowing why a major turning point in our lives took place as perfectly as it did.

MESSAGE:

Every possibility that has opened up this space of life has come from me—which means that every step forward you have taken has been precisely organized, developed, and placed before you in such a fashion so as to grow your awareness of love succinctly and profoundly. *THERE IS NO RANDOMNESS HERE.* Life is a very exacting and caring effort directed straight toward you in response to your need to expand love.

People have always wondered how this life actually does work and this is how it works. I build from the centre of you, as though you were the sounding block of information sending out your directives toward me, so that I can believe this is what you need. These directives are the connections we have, you and me, and they must be clear of heart to have any influence over life. They must have a strength of mind attached to them as well, meaning they have been well thought out by you and masterfully connected to other thoughts that have been central to your mind for some time. These are the directives I need and require from you if we are to be in sync with one another.

It's just like when you start your car in the morning. You open the door, sit down, and turn the key. Now those actions are complete of purpose and most engaging to me because they let me know, for instance, that you want to go somewhere. You are sending me this message that is clear in its purpose and most precise in its delivery to me so that I will get it; so I will be ready; and most of all so I will have a plan to co-create together with you our next movement in life.

So remember this when you are out there not yet living the life you need—when you are living in all the quagmire that you see everywhere and on all fronts. Challenge yourself to fill your brain with the ambition that you now are on the move to change your life for the better in every aspect, and then take certain directive strides to get you there. By doing that you are intensely engaged to your spirit life connection—which is your connection to me—so that I can begin to go out to this world and start to make life happen for you, in accordance with the signals you are giving me.

love

To us, this *Love* is such a profound influence in the world today. We have come to know it as a truly magical force—the only thing that can deliver a person out from beneath their turmoil and bring real meaningful change to their world. It can create new realities never before seen, felt, or heard. It can make something out of nothing right before your very eyes, all with the aim to make your life grow bigger and to bring a goodness to what would otherwise be a rather dull and haggard existence for the human race.

Yes, in our minds we are lucky to have this magnificent friend who lays at our feet all the gifts of the universe. All we have to do is point ourselves in the direction we want to head. We build those rich and wonderful feelings of excitement and anticipation for a world to come, and then the creative forces of *Love* do the heavy work. They put together our physical reality. They bring to life the people and the events before us, and we just have to show up, take the finished product and run with it, be conscious of it, and fully engaged with it.

And as *Love* has told us many times, there are no limits to where we can go with this. There are no limits to what we can achieve because we are more than just a born potential that ultimately seems limited, which is how the human race thinks today. Yes, we are a human potential on the move. We are an ever-expanding potential that gets bigger every time we change our minds about who we next want to be, and that is infinitely more powerful. And now, if life is to change as it needs to change for all of us here today, we should use this *Love* to our best advantage.

MESSAGE:

At first this movement will be a little one. It will begin at home with you seeing through example after example how life can be for you with love decisions in it, as opposed to when there is not this love in your lives. The question is will you try this? Will you develop a spirit of learning that will take your mind beyond where it sits today? Will you engage in a thinking style that will limit the negatives in your life and expand the positives? Will you produce example after example of loving thought constructs that will take the discontent away from your mind so that you can move more freely in your day-to-day events—and that includes brushing your teeth, combing your hair, or creating a smile when you would not do that in your past. All these and many, many more examples are what new love can be to you. With love on the rise, you can build yourself into a position of strength that today you do not have. And it begins right here in this moment you are reading these words and not a second later!

But the question is do you want this? Do you want your life to grow stronger and more prolific together with me? And can I now become with you that next newest thing in your overall lifestyle? If the answer is yes, then open to me now and let's become something amazing together because right now I can see a world of possibilities just waiting to be explored. So let's not wait one moment longer. Let's be engaged to those ever-present impulses, those stirrings of true passion and excitement for your life because those signals are your way into a better future. They are your way to remember or rather re-remember who you actually are and why you are here—the two main starting principles of your life. Of all the many things you could learn about, none will be more compelling than those two principles because beneath them is … the answer to every prayer.

And that means you no longer have to be afraid or uncertain. It means you can feel more resilient, more invincible, and more certain about who you are as a human being walking the planet. Even the very body you walk in will seem lighter and lighter as you progress each day up your mountain of truth, and in that lightness will come a freedom of spirit. You will feel like you can literally fly with your passions, just like my friend the mountain climber.

You see, the reason he is here in these pages is to symbolize to the planet that it has magnificence at its doorstep that now can be utilized by all of you, once you come to feel the power of me inside you. This power now is what you all can learn to tap into on a conscious level, to therefore level the playing field for everyone here—meaning that everyone, regardless of their circumstance, will have a new starting position. And from there, we together can begin to rebuild and reorganize this planet's spaces into a new life structure based on a premise of love that doesn't yet exist here today … that never did exist simply because it wasn't ready yet. You were not ready yet, and so it didn't come … until now.

But now you are at this most amazing new juncture to life's grandest dreams that says to a world of people that this is your time to think way outside the norm of what you believe to be true. Now is your time to think more proactively about how you can give rise to what is missing in your lives and then never turn away from this. Never change to go back to a normal existence again … that leaves one at a loss.

The truth is that it is your natural propensity to be bigger and more prosperous, and you have done this to some degree through intense study and determination in many fields of intellectual pursuit. But you have never fulfilled your true destiny as a human race … and that is to be alive to a world that is love in its every nuance.

love

CHAPTER 7

THE FREEDOM

MESSAGE:

A Story about Jumping …

When I was a child, I felt the true joys of life in all sorts of ways. There was nothing I wouldn't try if there was fun to be had doing it. When I was very young, I loved to jump off things. I would try to jump as high as I could from all sorts of objects and have fun each day doing this. The feeling of lifting off and projecting myself into the air without a care in the world was such an extraordinary, exhilarating feeling, and I just loved it!

But then reality struck. My parents were the bearers of bad news. They told me that what I was doing would not end well because eventually I might get hurt. Nonetheless, jumping was what I wanted to do. It was who I was back then. It made me feel a kind of inner excitement about who I was becoming, and I was hooked on it. I gave no credence to anyone who tried to stop my fun. I jumped anyway because the pull to do so was so strong in me and so vital to my life. I was certain of the feelings it would bring to me, and never did this harm me.

Now this is how my story went, but it could have turned out quite the opposite. If I had just lived a normal existence and never challenged the status quo, I wouldn't have learned to love my life as much as I do now. I would not have come to know that the love-pull that brought me the real thrill of life was far more important to listen to than anything else in my world. It was the direction I needed to move in to energize my life each day I was out there trying to have fun. And I have used this style of thinking ever since that time and in a meaningful way, instead of squandering my life not truly feeling the real richness I could otherwise have there in it. I look for the love-pull now … everywhere.

love

The Gift of Freedom …

There is something new afoot in the world today. Everywhere across the globe people are turning inward to reflect upon their lives. They are pondering the deeper questions of life and asking themselves whether they've done things right and seen things correctly as it relates to their existence on this planet. Yes, today people are taking stock of their lives in these most uncertain times. They want to know how it is that life is supposed to be lived now and through what eyes they should look at this place we call home. Will it be with an eye of concern for everything out there in the world today, or will it be something different from that?

For centuries now, humankind has been advising itself of how to live, and it has done that by way of a constant barrage of thoughts all aimed to make their lives better here and more progressive. There have been discoveries, innovations, and new developments in our thinking styles that have changed life in so many ways for all of us here. But guess what? It's still not working as perfectly as one might hope. It's been a constant struggle in many ways and we've given over to a variety of life perspectives—many of which, in our opinion, have done nothing to further our existence on this planet.

Today many people feel dismayed. They wonder why this world has come to a point in time that is filled with such human controversy everywhere you look—controversy about the negatives of life like not being good enough, not having enough money and material wealth, and not being free of the dangers that constantly enter the fray of life. People ask themselves why after all these centuries we couldn't have made our lives better than they are today and why life didn't allow for that. If, indeed, our destiny is to be more complete to love, then why must there always be this struggle that takes the love away? It's as though we're pushing up a rope, fighting against the very life that should be helping us succeed at everything good. What gives here anyway?

MESSAGE:

Life is all about the freedom to become something new in that very next moment of time. This is its challenge and this is its glory. And you are the ones who have been entrusted with this most extraordinary freedom to take a life and turn it into something it has never been before. This is the kind of freedom you, the human race, are all about on this planet. Freedom is your middle name, and you have it from the moment you are born to the moment you die. Freedom is, quite simply, your born right regardless of whether you use it ... or deny it.

You see, the freedom I speak of in these pages is a freedom beyond any you might imagine. It is not the kind that one would normally think about, nor is it one that any one of you would have to fight for or struggle to attain. Nonetheless, many wars have been fought in the name of freedom and many sacrifices have been made, and these cannot be measured in one small book. There can never be enough said about a world of people who gave of themselves so selflessly to save the lives of others. By this I am most humbled, indeed.

The kind of freedom I am referring to, however, is different. It is not conditional upon any outer circumstance of life. It does not depend on anything or anyone outside of you. It exists within you as the nature of who you are, and once you come to know this, once you come to understand what this means, you will begin to feel the kind of excitement and the kind of eternal hope humankind has never known before. And by that I mean the kind of hope that doesn't wither away through time but instead builds into a bigger and broader force—the kind of force that would be known only to a walking, talking, breathing creator of the planet who brings forth new life each time it opens its brain ... *to think*!

This is who you are—every last one of you. You are the inventors of life's biggest dreams, and you are here today on this planet looking to find a better space to play within. What you have here and now is just not enough to satisfy the ever-growing needs of the human populace going forward. And so, you must ask yourselves, "How free will we be to turn the pages of life? How big and how bold a thought are we willing to take hold of, trust in, and be a living part of?"

It all comes down to your freedom really, and to date humanity hasn't fully understood the kind of freedom they possess. You haven't connected up those dots, and it's easy to understand why because today people see life as a very defined space that has only so much to offer. This is why you see frustration and resentment in people all around the globe. People need to feel more freedom, but they don't actually believe that freedom exists.

When you look out upon life today, you see a world that doesn't seem to have a way to move past its limitations. It is a world that hasn't yet found its freedom. Nonetheless, this is the world you have conceived of together. Your thought energy flows have manifested its outer realities, and every person who has ever lived has contributed to this. You all have participated and played the part you wanted to play in the evolutionary process, by way of the thinking structures you brought forth.

Clearly some of you have felt more freedom in this than others. There has been growth for some and for others there has been stagnation. Certainly when you survey the world at large you will find many a varied circumstance to life's biggest dreams. Each person has a different story to tell about his or her journey into freedom, and for some that journey has been fraught with disappointment and struggle, so much so that they do not want to even try at life any further.

But to this I say there will never be a time when I cannot help you bring more to your life, no matter what situation you sit in here today. I will be there for you. I will bring you whatever it is you most will need, and I will never leave this post of life. The freedom of living a life together with me is yours and yours alone to have, and no one will ever take that away from you. No one!

Right now, I can see that for so many of you on this planet, life is a struggle just to get by to that next day. Every moment of your existence revolves around the need to survive. But what is also true of you is that you need not worry about the future of your lives, for in truth if you were to choose me like it is written in this book, you would have a way to pull yourselves out from beneath your struggle. And you would have no further doubt about that, no matter who you are because when you come to know what it means to live a life with me, you will understand that your plight exists not just because of circumstance alone. Nor does it exist because you are less worthy or less powerful in this world. You would know that your position is as it is not because life is willing to serve only some people in a bigger way or because a god has turned its back on you and not on others. Rather you would have a clear understanding that you too were meant to succeed at your lives. You would know that my love is there for all of you, and that it responds equally to all people to make a change happen, if and when they turn their heads in my direction.

I can tell you that even if a situation seems dire, there is always room for life to take on a new form. Just look at the lives of those who live today in oppressive societies or those who are abused or imprisoned. These are situations some would call a living hell on earth, and so to say to these ones that it all could be different now would almost fly in the face of human logic. How can they even begin to feel their pains of life dissipate when their lives are not their own? It seems impossible. Yet there inside those challenging positions of life, progress can be made, and it comes first by way of a freedom born of their own minds—a freedom to explore the world of their own inner thinking more prolifically. This is where the difference can be made because inside their minds is where they will come to realize that who they are in this very moment is not who they wanted to be when they first came to this life. Their minds now are empty of those thoughts, and so they only need to open to those wonderful new beginnings once again and start to imagine a new life for themselves that will replace the life they have today.

Consider the life of a prisoner, a man who lives in relative solitude without the thought of a freedom one can count on in terms of an outward movement to life. To him, it is a constrained life that has little to no happiness. It is a position that people will think of as a place of bondage, a place where uncertainty and fear reign supreme.

But this is how I look at it. I see it as a place of serenity … a place of thoughtfulness. I see it as a place where this man can begin to understand himself better and rebuild his life out from a feeling of uncertainty into a position of complete certainty for what his next move in life will be. He only has to begin to develop a new strain of movement within his mind that includes me. But to develop this, he must be certain that he even wants to move in this direction of great quietness … of great perfection. And if he chooses to go there, he will have the chance to turn his mind into a powerhouse of understanding about why he has come to this world in the first place and what he will need to do to create his life into something it is not today.

Certainly his position is a difficult one to break free from, but it can be done if he tries to open to my loving nature there within his mind. Then he will start to produce results that he will be happy with because his mind finally will be moving him to a place of complete and utter devotion to the cause of love … to the cause of life … and to the virtues of humankind itself. Of course, this will take time to develop, but time is what he has on his hands. Time is what he can use to move himself into a deep reflective state, which then will become his strongest ally. This state of reflection and quietness will be the place he turns to, to imagine his new life just like it already was there to him. Then, given the proper timing, he will begin to see the difference in his life—actually self-realized. His connections to me will begin to intensify and his willingness to accept change in his life will literally take over his human psyche such that from this point onward, change will be all he thinks about. And that is exactly what he will need to widen his resolve to reshape his new life— as he moves into his future together with me.

So now look at his position as a positive opportunity for these folks to get to know me in ways they would never have thought of before, for I love them all equally, each and every one of them.

love

It really doesn't matter who you are. This works the same for everyone, whether you sit alone in abject poverty or enjoy the richness of life's bounty. We all have the same need to feel a change begin. We all are trying in our own way to feel the outer limits of our space of life. Each one of us has a purpose to build from within our inner core, a determination to know more about what we can be and become in that very next breath.

Into Apathy ...

Today more than any other time in history, it is important to understand all of this because in recent times, according to *Love*, human thought energies have been closing down all around the globe, in the richest of countries and in the poorest. A feeling has been permeating the planet that says we are quickly reaching the outer limits of where we can take this life. This is what all the concerns around us are seemingly telling us now—that there are limits to what this life has to offer.

In point of fact, our atmosphere is becoming more and more challenged today, and there doesn't seem to be the will to fix this. As well, people are thinking in more aggressive terms, fighting one another over the limited resources we have, and thus we see a planet on fire with discontent and resentment.

MESSAGE:

In the beginning of your history together there was, of course, just a simple life in which a man or a woman did not think beyond the scope of a simple day. It was, in every way, a very ordinary life that was about nothing more than making it to the next day and the next day after that. Human needs were few. Thinking patterns were limited to only basic needs and aspirations because back then people had little knowing of their greater purpose. Simply put, they needed more time to explore life in order to feel the inner significance of what love could mean to their lives.

So with time, life did eventually begin to change. It changed because you, the human race, wanted more from your lives than what you had. You wanted to feel the excitement of a life on the rise, and so the world began to take on a new form. It became something new and something more and more complex as the human race pushed the limits of possibility through a constant bombardment of thoughts—all placed there within their brains to evoke change in their otherwise mundane and ordinary lives.

Along the way, however, there were these concerns that started to pile up, one atop the other, and these made you all feel that life did not hold the promise you once thought. There were concerns about not having the things you needed and wanted for your lives. There was a lack of money, loss of health, and unfulfilled aspirations. There were concerns about ... human survival. Some of these you simply ignored as simple dilemmas of life that could be dealt with at a later date when the time was right, but that proved not to be the case. The concerns instead intensified over time until there was no true way, it seemed, to humanly deal with them all.

For the human race, it was much like the feeling of being placed inside a box of sorts that you couldn't get out of, and the concerns were the impenetrable walls of that box. They represented the limitations of life that stood between you and the things you wanted and needed the most. In fact, everywhere you see concern in the world today, there is a limitation at the centre of that concern—a limitation that says, life stops here and it has no way to get bigger. And this has not at all been an easy thing for you all to accept because limitation, quite simply, is what drives you crazy. You cannot stand the feeling of it because it is everything that you are *NOT* about, and at the deepest level of your human awareness every one of you knows this. You can feel this to be true.

love

Consider how today we have the understanding that our universe is expanding. But then ask yourself how you would feel if there actually was an end to that space we think of as our universe. Wouldn't that make you feel a bit uncomfortable?

There is simply no denying the fact that we have this insatiable, constant need to feel life "outside the box." It is our nature to want this kind of freedom, but then again we can't deny that there are all these obstacles standing in the way of that freedom. There are these walls of concern now all around us and they seem rock solid and impenetrable. They represent all the things that hold us back from the values in life we need to feel on a constant basis—the joy, the passion, the abundance, and just the simple fun of living life together on this planet.

These limitations have been very painful for us all to accept—so painful, in fact, that now many of us on this planet have given up on their quest to feel life beyond those walls, we are told. They don't try to reach out to feel that freedom anymore for fear of repercussions, meaning they don't want to run into those brick walls of concern that hit you hard and stop you fast. People will try to avoid that kind of pain at all cost, and so they will settle for a world filled with concern and a life where human needs and passions go unfulfilled. Eventually, for some, they even forget that it was freedom they were after in the first place—the freedom *to think it all different.*

MESSAGE:

So this is *THE* dilemma of being human—to want so much more of life but to think you have no freedom to make that happen. Every day people are reminded of the fact that they can only be so happy and so safe within a life that seems to play the game by its own set of rules. People today feel at a loss in the face of what seems beyond their control. They think their only recourse is to ignore all the trouble and live out a simple existence just like it was in the beginning, where once again the main goal is just to get by to that next day and the next day after that.

To this I say the answer to what ails you in this world does not lie in the turning away from the freedom that you came here to feel. The answer is not about resigning yourselves to a life that denies you everything good; rather this is the root cause of your problems. Human apathy is what I am talking about— apathy to love, and it is the biggest problem on the planet bar none! In fact, it is the only real problem on this planet because it is stopping the world from moving to its next logical position in its overall evolution. Today every concern from the common cold to global warming exists because of apathy. These are symbols of this feeling dimension of life, and so now you need to understand more about what this apathy is. You need to understand clearly … why it exists!

So let me tell you this: apathy is the letting go of the need to hold a purpose. It is the letting go of your deepest desires to be a human love in the making of a greater love. Instead you take on a strategy where you accept things as they are and settle for a life that isn't big enough to satisfy the ever-growing passions of the human race. The apathy, therefore, is a statement that says there is no bigger way to think about life today, and we therefore must go on living in simple terms, believing we can do no better and be no better. And why do you turn in that direction? You do this because you do not think of love as anything more than just a simple emotion that winds aimlessly about your lives with no true aspect of greatness that would help you in any meaningful way.

That's why so many of you tend to live small when compared to what this life has to offer you. You temper your passions. You put a lid on them and use them only when you are certain of a good result, which means you live marginally, not expecting much of life. You only do certain things, go certain places, and see certain people inside your box of life. It makes you feel less afraid that way, yet it makes the space of life possibility so much smaller at the same time. It's like you're playing a game of basketball but with only half the court. And so much of the excitement is missing from the game because half of the love is missing from the equation—the love that would have given you the freedom to take that ball all the way down the court for the winning basket—a disappointment, indeed.

Amazingly, people don't even realize this is happening; it feels so normal to live a lesser life. They can't even remember what it's like to feel the excitement of a living passion inside them. In fact, if you were to ask people today what they would do if they had the freedom to do anything, most wouldn't even know what to tell you. Their brains just couldn't go there. They know deep down that something is missing in their lives, but they don't know what it is and they don't know where to find it.

Their lives could be described as a set of plans just waiting to be masterfully put together. Each day the stage is set to bring more to their lives using love, yet when they leave their homes in the morning, they never even consider how far they could go with this life or what heights they could attain. When they come home at night, the story is much the same. They don't think enthusiastically about where their evening's events could take them, and so on and so forth it goes. For so many in this world, they are without any true understanding of what it means to be a walking master of the planet, fully in charge of what is next to come. Instead they walk in the darkness of the unknown.

If you think about how people view life today and what it means to them, more often than not you come up with an image that has a feeling of boredom, hopelessness, and fatigue. For some, it's been this way right from the very beginning. They knew no other way to play at life other than to accept it as it was. Life was simply a need state—a space of utter, relentless futility based on the pursuit of things gone bad in a multitude of forms, all beginning and ending in the same way ... without the need to feel more love, plain and simple.

love

It's no wonder there is sadness in the world today where apathy abounds. There is anger and resentment toward a life that just doesn't seem to have a way to keep our love for this place alive and growing the way it should. Of course, it's not that we don't try to make the best of what we have. We do. We live life as big as we can inside our box of concern and whenever frustration sets in, when it feels like the walls of life are closing in on us, we try to distract ourselves. We keep ourselves busy. Many of us will turn to idle pursuits just to keep boredom from setting in, but deep down everyone knows that something is wrong— something is missing.

Today we both feel how vital it is for all of us to understand that this world exists for one purpose only, and that is to unfold the endless possibilities of new love through the process of life. But if we stop this growth, if we lose our desire to pursue this simple little feeling called love, then we take away the reason for our existence. As *Love* tells us, we need to feel love constantly building inside us, for without that love, we would die a slow and very painful death within our human psyche— much the same way a wilting flower will blow away its petals in the fall because it no longer feels the true joy of its purpose to be a flower. It, therefore, resists nothing and … lets go.

The truth, according to *Love*, is that it isn't enough for us to be a human life that never changes. Eventually such stagnation will lead to discontent and deterioration because the *Love* at the core of each of us is not satisfied to remain in this sameness. Its desire is beyond that form of existence, and so if humankind is unwilling to fulfill its true purpose, then this *Love*, which sustains us all, will most certainly not want to stay.

Already we have witnessed this. We are told that we have lost many men, women, and children on this planet because desire died away inside them. They just could not believe there was room to feel a greater love in a world that showed them only barriers to that love, and so they left. They chose death over life because what was here was not enough; because what was here didn't satisfy their urges to feel new love; and because here they simply could not achieve what was needed for them to want to stay. For so many, life just didn't make sense. The world didn't hold the correct measure of completeness for them to feel safe and fulfilled in. So they took their leave feeling alone and afraid and without truly knowing the "moreness" that life could offer them.

Now how huge is that? Could it be any bigger? We let go of a willingness to pursue a simple feeling of goodness and we therefore let go of this life. We let go of the need to be engaged to a world of promise. It is a tragedy this has happened to even a single person on this planet, and it is a tragedy we can begin to eliminate right now. How do we do that? By finally and once and for all setting ourselves free to live life with a purpose. And according to *Love* that purpose is to eliminate human concern on this planet and rebuild our societal norms so that every last person on this earth will have love like it was always meant to be. In other words … *WE CHANGE THE WAY WE THINK*.

The Imaginary Wall ...

Today human concern exists in every corner of the globe. The limits to life loom larger than ever before, at least that is what we think. But consider that maybe human concern at every level is not what one might imagine. As *Love* has expressed to us, the concerns you see today are not life getting in the way of you. They are not life limiting you or trying to deny you, harm you, or stop you, as most believe today. No, these concerns are signalling you that there is a discontent in you that now needs to be taken away.

The feeling of concern is there to wake you up to the fact that you have a way to make all things right with your world. You have a way to move through those concerns of yours and make life bigger in the face of everything that would tell you that you can't. You can take away your discontent. You can make concern disappear because the only reason it exists is to make you aware of the fact that you've hit an imaginary brick wall in your own mind—a wall that now can be torn down through your own willingness to pursue the ever-expanding potentials of pure love itself.

MESSAGE:

When you live life, truly live as you were meant to live, you are making a statement that says: I am a master of the universe on the march toward all things good and I will never stop no matter what obstacles may come my way. I am free to move them away, to make them less than what they seem at first brush. Every obstacle, therefore, is merely a solution yet to be solidified and masterfully put in place, so that I can move forward in my life and never backward. And the eternal driver of love in me is there to give me the tenacity and determination to do this—to move in a direction of success that is exponential by its very nature.

love

Think of it this way: in every last concern you have in your life, there is a hidden passion in you that, at some point in your evolution, has worked its way to the top of your priority list. And that passion now is waiting to be set free to a space in your brain you haven't opened to yet. This is how human concern has been described to us—as a desire in you that has been stopped dead in its tracks because of a limited thinking base that says life stops here and nothing you can do is going to change that fact. This is a way of thinking that humanity has grabbed hold of time and time again and accepted as the ultimate truth when, according to *Love*, it is the furthest thing from the truth of you. Life is not out to stop you … ever! It is not out to get you. Where life stops short is where the human brainpower has stopped short of a needed outcome, and so there you sit with nowhere to go except to stay where you are in your discontent.

But the discontent, as described to us, is only about your uncertainty. It's about your unwillingness to make a move. It's something like standing on the edge of life trying to see out into that dark unknown space that is your future, only you can't begin to see or feel anything out there as *real*. Your brain knows only what it knows today from where you are standing. It feels only the truth of who you have become so far, and nothing else beyond that reality seems real *yet*. Nothing else has become *permanent* in your brain as a possibility.

This happens all the time when people step out into life to feel the newness begin, but then they send their minds straight into a limited-growth scenario. They no sooner imagine something new and wonderful for their life and their brain kicks in and tells them there are just too many hurdles to jump over in order to make things work—in order to bring even a modicum of success to their lives. So what do they do? They stop the flows of life to come, and in doing so they destabilize their thinking movements toward new life because their will to do so is no longer invested in this.

This is the kind of self-sabotage people put themselves through again and again, and guess what? It's working. We are told that people all over the globe are living inside this kind of constraint-filled existence now, and the reason is that they are not yet aware of how to control their negative thinking styles. Each time they are ready to move, they are literally stopped by the notion that says, I am just not good enough to be this mastery. I am not wise enough, powerful enough, worthy enough, rich enough, skilled enough … and on and on it goes.

Message:

It is never enough to say you cannot make a difference to these most amazing lives you have. This is what you might think, but this is never a true statement about who you are. Nonetheless, this is where many will go in their minds, and when they do, those feelings of lost love come pouring in. And so life stays the same, except there are these concerns starting to build in their minds about the fact that they have this need sitting inside them with nowhere to go.

Today there are endless quantities of these concerns bubbling away in the minds of humanity, like festering sores with no way to heal. They create great pain within the human psyche, and with time they get worse. They stick around as reminders to the fact that ... there is something you're missing here, and it is the understanding that no matter what life throws your way, it always exists as a statement saying to your human psyche that "life can be bigger." That possibility always exists. It never goes away. Your life is meant to be about expansion ... *always*. You were born to change. You live to grow, and therefore any limitation to love that you accept in your life as real ... permanent ... and inescapable ... is completely false, and that includes sometimes even death itself.

Death, in fact, is just a temporary pause in your overall growth into love. It isn't the end of you, but rather just a new beginning because love—your love—is eternal and therefore never dies off. It never does end for you, and so you carry on building yourself into a love filled existence even after you have left this place of life.

You, however, may choose to live as humanity has done for centuries. You can accept the premise that there are real-life barriers that hold you back from everything good in life. But this is false thinking. Those barriers in front of you—the ones that seem to want to stop you, judge you, condemn you, frustrate you, and discourage you—are signals for change to come. Their purpose is to point you in the direction of a change you are asking for at some level. They are saying that you have a way not only to manage these circumstances of life but also to enhance them rather than let them take you down.

love

Today you see discontent growing everywhere, and the reason is that people are turning away from the opportunity "to think" life better, we are told. Over and over again, they will ignore the facts that say there is this urgency inside them to feel a change begin. Instead they will sit in discontent and take no notice of the signals telling them that their time now has come to move. This is when you will see the most challenging of situations, these so called obstacles of life, coming on the scene to let people know that something is up that they need to pay attention to.

The magic of life shows this to you time and time again. Just when you feel as though your life is moving along just fine and everything is on track, something comes along to tell you otherwise. Something stops you in your tracks and makes you emphatically aware that all is not right in your world and that you need to do something about that fact. It might be that you got sick, broke your leg, lost your job, or any one of a myriad of unfortunate occurrences. And of course, these are not the kinds of circumstances you would wish for, but we are told they have a reason for being there—*all of them.*

Your brain with its logic, however, can falsely interpret these so-called negatives of life as your enemy because your brain has no way of understanding the whole truth and the deeper truth about where you're trying to head. The loving intelligence inside you, however, does understand the bigger picture. *Love* understands where you are heading and why. It understands the greater truth about you to come because it is the one that helps you think your way there into that future. But it never does that by placing an obstacle in your path, never, not even inside those most concerning events of life. As explained to us, these events, rather than obstacles to your progress, are simple markers. Their purpose is to provoke, motivate, and challenge you to think bigger into an entirely new measure of love for your life, simply because *you are wanting that at some level and because you are not doing that!* They are trying to tell you to let go of your resistance and push those walls of discontent because there is more of life to be conquered out there in the dark, unknown reaches of new life to come—but conquered now in a new way that is masterful and truly engaging to those *Love* connections in your brain.

So think of these so-called negatives not as a final statement about your life. Think of them as a symbol of who you are to become in your future—inside a newly reconstructed state of human awareness. Think of them as your way to link you back to your purpose, so you don't miss the point of your existence, if you are looking for it. And finally, think of them as your way of building a resilience in you to see your life differently each step of the way ... which is the key to how things work in this world.

MESSAGE:

You would ask me why there is tragedy and why there are these so called accidents of life that come along unexpectedly, where lives are lost and people are badly injured. These are the kinds of circumstances that create real pain in people's lives, and so why is it there seems to be no real way to adjust or take away this pain? People of this world now will want to learn about how I can work to eliminate these kinds of scenarios, and I will be only too happy to give them this wisdom now.

Let me say first that where there is pain in the world— any kind of pain— you will have discontent, and behind every discontent there is a mind that has nowhere else to go except to resign itself to a thought about life that is ... less than desirable. Today in almost every person on this planet, discontent is brewing in one form or another, and the reason is that their understanding of this life they are living feels somehow out of sorts with the plan they came to this life to execute. Therefore, at some level of their consciousness, they will want a change to begin—a change that will serve to alter those directions in life they are not happy with. And by consciousness, I am speaking about the many layers of your mind whose job it is to take care of your life and move it in the opposite direction of those movements that do not seem right to you—as in the case where you are thinking in a way that is constantly out of control, for example.

So this is the starting position through which people's lives will proceed. Their discontent will either take them to a place of resentment for their lives or contentment, and then from there they either make life difficult for themselves or the opposite to that. But no matter what they choose, I will be there to it all because beneath every accident or misfortune in a person's life, there is a deeper reasoning as to why they would want for this to even occur. Their mind in controversy has taken them there into a plain of consciousness that would allow for the accident to be created. Why? Because they needed to move the needle on their life's progress into love. It was their life imperative to do this and to use whatever tools needed to get them there. They may not have known at a conscious level just how this turning point was going to turn out, but nonetheless they were in complete control of what they needed for their life in that moment.

Now, some would call these kinds of happenings in life, destiny; others would say they are karmic justice; and others still would think these were just simple accidents—coincidences that were unavoidable. But now all these styles of thinking are to be discredited by me because they are not true. They have been mythically propagated as a way to make sense of a world that seems to be out of control.

Societies all around the world carry this style of thinking, and many of you don't even give this a second thought. People just accept their pain and discontent and simply go on with life. But if they now were to find the centre of all their discontent, if they were to examine why their pain exists, they would walk a straight line toward everything good in their lives because then they would be directly aligned to me. And when a person's life is aligned to me consciously they are in direct co-ordination with the universe, which means that everything they do will be in perfect harmony with the all that is life itself. This is when a true master will arise from the darkness of their life and move with exacting certainty into their future. And then nothing will be out of place for them; nothing will go wrong in their world; and everything in their life will have its greater purpose revealed to them.

Now why is this so very important for the people of this planet to know? Well, it is because this masterful style of thinking has at its base, an understanding that you are not alone. You are connected to who I am and what procedures I live by, and as such there would be no accidents in this world that I did not fully understand and recognize—as that of a purposeful event. And now the reason I am telling you that you are the maker of your destiny is so that you can use my creative forces within you to be more influential and more impactful to your life.

You see, when you choose this life in your early beginnings before you even enter, you have an agenda to do certain things and create certain outcomes. And all of these movements are fully encompassed in the ways you are thinking—which, ironically, is your direct pipeline to me. I am your force field of influence, you could say, to the all that is your life in its fullest and truest form, and none of your thinking is outside of your need to feel me more at some level within your conscious and unconscious mind. This is why you have direct access to me always. My connection to you will never go away no matter what life you will choose.

Now, you will wonder why your connection to me and my love for everything you are choosing did not prevent these so called accidents from happening. The answer is that you did not listen to me. You didn't heed my warning signs that would have otherwise prevented those accidents from happening. If you had been aware of your connection to me and had you learned how to work with it, I would have turned you away from that ever-present danger. Those occurrences would not have even taken place because I would have been directing the traffic of your life there in those moments.

Consider this too. When lives are lost or when people are getting ready to leave this world, choosing death over life, I am there with them every step of the way. There is not one movement they take where I do not know what they are doing; the choices they are making; and the meaning through which their thinking is derived. And all of this is within my capacity to change, if they want that change to take place. But if they choose to ignore my calling to make the necessary shift when that shift should be made to correct whatever danger might be coming their way, then I will not play with or adjust their "free will" to go it on their own. At that point, there is little I can do for them, except to let them be.

For the most part, people will think these tragedies, these so-called coincidences of life, are not defensible, that they are outside of a person's control and therefore have no clear and justifiable reason for their occurrence. But I tell you this is not the case. When the accidents of life happen, they are completely choreographed and fully orchestrated to be as they are in order to evoke a certain response that each man, woman, or child actually wished for. At some level of their conscious and subconscious mind, they made this event happen in order to take straight aim at the failures they were feeling out there in their world.

Nothing could say this more strongly than when a young boy or girl takes their life in order to make a statement to the world that says, something is wrong and now I must take this one last stand in order to change it. And so they leave fully knowing at some level that their statement of change has been met. To this I say we owe a great debt of gratitude to these ones for their sacrifice. They knew that something was wrong, and the only way to change it in their minds … was to leave this life with a message of utter resentment and frustration.

These lives that were lost were a judgment statement about life and they can look like accidents in many ways, but just know they are not that at all. All creations be they good or bad, be they seemly coincidental accidents or premature deaths are built first out of a person's mind, and then they are lived out in perfect perfection to the whole of life. It's as simple as that. When people choose to die early, it is a direct statement about how life should have given them more and how their purpose in this world was in some way … conflicted.

It is a fact that everyone has an inherent need to feel their lives have worth and are not just a waste. But when they cannot feel this, when they cannot feel the strength of who they are to this world, that is when their minds will wander off course and misguided events will occur. The tragedies of life will be manifested because this is where their thinking patterns take them time and time again.

Everywhere throughout eternity this has been the case, and it is because all people of this world had the freedom to choose through their own free will, whatever direction their minds thought they should go. In many cases, this was in direct opposition to the direction I wished for them to take. My calls to each of them to make a turn in the opposite direction away from their need to leave this life were ignored. Instead their minds, time and time again, took them into a position of not wanting to stay. And so they moved away from me because they were not aware in most cases … that I was even there!

So here lies the truth. If everyone could feel their pains of life coming on well before they even materialize as form and then learn how to use me to restrict those negative influences, then you all would not sustain further damaging consequences in your lives. You would not move your "free will psyche" too far to the opposite side of life where everything is unwieldy and out of control to some degree. Then these so called accidents would no longer play out their hand because I would be there in direct opposition to them all. I would be guiding you along a direct pathway to everything good in your lives, and this, my dear friends, is all you will need and want going forward.

So let me be the policemen of your life now. Let me do all the heavy lifting for you. I can remove the pains in this world, even if they be of innocent children playing on the fields of life one day with no desire to stop their fun, when suddenly a war breaks out in their back yard. Innocent children come under fire. Some even die. But if I was in charge of their thinking capacities in so far as I was able to lead their "strong wills" successfully to another field of life, then I could have moved them from harm's way and changed the trajectory of those incoming bullets.

In many cases, this is what takes place in hot spots around the planet. People's lives are in constant danger of extinction, they think because of circumstance. However, it may shock you all to know that there is not one circumstance in this world that I myself cannot handle in a truly meaningful and progressive way—to help innocent men, women, and children who are in harm's way just because their strong wills took them there. I just as well could have moved them to another position of life where their lives would have been safe from oncoming fire.

So what now can be said about these innocent children? What can be done? I can tell you that if I had a direct pipeline to each of your lives like it is now being professed in this book, then I could have prevented all this death and destruction from happening everywhere throughout the world bar none. I could have stopped the wars, and I could have challenged the reasoning for creating the wars in the first place. So with all due respect for the choices you have made, I say that in those moments of time, your thinking modalities were flawed, and for that reason and that reason alone, you had no clear direction to move along. The wars ensued, the devastation continued, and lives were lost when they could have just as easily been saved.

To say this in another way, humankind has never been willing to give up free will, and rightly so. They would rather die off than let that happen. But for that very reason, today the world finds itself in the predicaments it now is in. People all around the globe are in peril, and the reason is they seem to want to go it on their own. They are living independent of me, you could say, and that today is the single most compelling reason why I need to come forth and multiply my existence now more than ever before.

My goal is for you to live a life with certainty attached to it now, and the only way I can do that is to show you the way to a much better future—and not just for one of you or a few of you, but for all of you. That includes even those who think they know it all. Even those ones who think they have all they need and require will find they are living an empty existence when they see what this new life with me can be in comparison. And to those of you who already think you have control over your destiny, I tell you this: your lives are as flawed as the rest when it comes to how you "think" and the actions you are taking. So to you I say, get ready to feel what this life is truly all about because there is nothing more important than this line of discourse now coming to bear on the world's populous. And my greatest fear is that you will not listen. You will not take heed at what I am sharing with you, and that one single thing ... will destroy us all.

love

Life—a Symbol of Hope ...

When we first began this journey to better understand this life, we had little awareness of what this unique, loving intelligence inside of us was all about. We didn't know if it was something we could depend on or trust in. In fact, every day we wondered if it would someday just disappear without a trace, never to return again. The feeling we had about it all was much like that of being in a play that one day would end in disappointment, and then we would go home thinking to ourselves, "What was all that about anyway?"

But that didn't happen. This wasn't what this *Love* had in store for us. In fact, the connection between the three of us only got stronger as we moved forward with our conversations. Our passion to be together became more and more intense. And the most wonderful part of this was that this loving presence seemed to want that too, and this made us feel that we would never be left alone to fend for ourselves again.

The three of us were connected for life, you could say. Our minds were never too far away from one another. Even if our two human minds strayed off course in our thinking, we would always come back again to sit beside this loving friend—to feel the love of it, the comfort of it, and the safety of it. We were the best of friends, the three of us, through thick and through thin. We cannot truly describe in words what it meant to us to have this caring mentor at our side, always ready on a moment's notice to take us out of any discouragement we might feel. Its compelling truths always gave us a new way to think about the challenges of life, so we wouldn't fall prey to an old style of thinking that seemed to do little for our lives in comparison.

So if we struggled with issues surrounding health, even just a simple cold, we could understand why those issues had come about and how we could begin to turn them around. If there was an issue with regard to the two of us in our marriage, we were made aware of the deeper reason for the controversy. We were given ways to think beyond any constraints to love, to find solutions that allowed for both sides to grow. If money and business were creating stress in our lives, we learned how to adjust our thoughts to take away barriers to progress, and on and on it went. This dear friend of life seemed relentless in its efforts to push us forward into a bigger truth about our lives. Never did it fall away from this line of thought. *Love* persisted through all these many years with the same consistent messages—all revolving around the energies of love and how they can be used to change *everything*.

And indeed, life did change for the two of us, there was no doubt about that. Together with this *Love* in hand, we slowly and ever so precisely stripped away the layers of false thought that once permeated our brains. Where we were stuck before in our thinking, we were getting unstuck. Where we tried to make life bigger and couldn't or where we felt too apprehensive to move in certain directions, we used this friend of life to build a confidence in us that we could do anything we wanted to do. But it wasn't always easy. It was difficult at first to think from an unlimited perspective, especially when at times there seemed to be no possible solution to life's quandaries. But there we were anyway, trying our best to keep the faith that we were onto something, and slowly it was proving itself to be true.

The concerns were starting to move away from us before they could get a full grasp on us. One by one we were letting go of our fears and setting ourselves free to think life into all kinds of directions we would have closed down to in our past and dismissed as false thinking. Yes, life was changing for us in the ways we needed change the most. Our financial position was growing and our excitement about life was high. It seemed that this guidance system we didn't know we had before, was working for us and working well. We could feel its intense measure of care for us every single day. No matter what passion we held in any one moment of time, this inner nature of *Love* was on board with us, bringing a certainty to our lives that we were, in fact, stepping in the right direction. And with that, the world became a very kind and hospitable place. It was a place we could feel safe in because now we had this remarkable friend who could help us control our lives and improve them in profound ways. We only had to learn how to connect ourselves up to its immense powers and open to its ways of thinking.

And now, many years later we can say to you without any doubt that we do not question the validity of what we've learned through this connection. This, to us, feels like the correct truth to live by, if for no other reason than … it works!

MESSAGE:

Life comes to you in all its many forms to symbolize in a most precise way, your journey into the far reaches of love. All of what you have today exists as a symbol of how far the human race has opened up to their hidden creative powers of love and used those powers to transform a rather unknown, dark, and unworkable beginning space of life … into something bigger, richer and more fulfilling.

Everything you taste, touch, feel and see; the roads you travel upon; the people you meet; the colours that fill your eyes; and the events that parade before you—all of it is created in a most precise way to physically portray who you have become and where you need to go to take that next logical step in your human evolution. It all has been perfectly contrived to represent everything good to the human race and everything good to come—which means that where life is seemingly not good, where it feels rather limiting, bad, or just plain unworkable, is where you have a symbol of the growth that next needs to be constructed … in you.

In simple language, what you think of as bad is just *A LACK OF POSSIBILITY INSIDE YOUR BRAIN*. This is what the negatives of life represent to you, and for many in this world, this cannot be seen as anything hopeful or helpful to their lives because it only makes them feel they have no control over what happens to them in this life. The negatives, they think, are nothing more than a pain they must endure, and as a result they more often than not produce no positive movement of thought that would relieve them of that pain.

The true masters of life, however, never accept the pain and then resolve that the pain now must be their reality. Instead they think of the pain as a real-life signal there to help them take the pain and turn it into a real-life opportunity—a space that makes life grow bigger and more robust, rather than stagnating with no true way to end the pain in any concrete manner.

This is the difference with their approach. The person who has mastered life will not allow their thoughts to just linger in the pain with nowhere to go, as most will do today. Instead they will begin the slow process of unfolding "the why" of things. They will turn inward to self-examine each dilemma of life and ponder what next to do.

Rather than taking an analytical approach based on pure logic as most will do, they will open up to my higher influences, and there they will masterfully begin to take apart the events inside each dilemma. They will sit back in their mind's eye and try to connect up the dots, just as though their life was a movie script already written. If they come upon a situation that seems dire, they will instantly begin to think how they can limit their growth into negativity and master their growth into a love based mentality. They will say to me, "Now we've got this one. Now we can begin to understand the why of this event, so we can be complete to its truth rather than incomplete."

In every dilemma of life, there always is this hidden truth for a person to see; and in that truth is a perfect outcome for them to move into that will turn them into someone they were not before—and in a most wonderful way. It's a gift that if one doesn't take, they lose ... and mastery is forgotten.

A true master, however, will never miss the opportunity to become someone new because they already carry the preconceived notion that everything in life is a blessing. They are on guard constantly watching and constantly looking for those signals in life that will tell them where to go to see their life grow stronger. That is all they think about. That directive is what keeps them going. It keeps them centred. It stops them from straying too far off track in their lives, and it keeps them engaged to a lifestyle that will make things happen for them, without them ever feeling alone or afraid. And nothing can change this trajectory for them either. When they choose new love on the rise, nothing will ever make their life seem so dire that they forget why they are here in the first place. Nothing will ever become too fearful in their minds such that they would not have time to rethink their circumstance and then change it to be something remarkable.

It is true that in the perfection of life itself, there can always be a perfect consequence that perfectly fits each situation and brings peace to the minds of all those who are there looking to see the truth. No one need be left standing feeling out of sorts with concern still lingering in their minds, like it is so often today. Today you can see concern and controversy boiling everywhere, and that leaves people with a feeling that somehow things haven't been resolved correctly, with the ultimate mastery there and with the perfect understanding of a perfect truth about who they all next needed to be together inside these events and why.

In fact, much of the time people have little understanding of where they should be heading in their brains to bring resolve to their lives. They don't trust in those inner feelings of love that are there to guide them. Instead they are pulled in this direction and that by a sea of rationalized logic that doesn't even consider why they are here in this life in the first place. It's understandable why they do this. They only have half the story.

love

The Leap ...

To understand who you have become inside the richness of love and to know who you next want to be is the very essence of life itself. To understand this is to understand everything about why we all are here today. And now, what *Love* is saying in these pages is that we can open up to this knowing in a much grander way by limiting nothing in our brains as to what now can become our newest reality.

To date there have been all kinds of barriers in our thinking, especially when it comes to those things in life we think we have no control of. But now we can let go of what binds us. We can begin to move our world in ways we couldn't have imagined before, and by doing so we can alleviate the feelings of futility that are building in the world— the feelings that say we simply cannot succeed at life. We cannot get to where we next want to be without something more to go on than just a hope and a prayer. People think the leap is just too big to take. It's too big a stretch to imagine that we could move from where we are today to where we want to be tomorrow. These two realities seem to be moving further and further apart as human discontent grows.

The message that *Love* has to share, however, will tell us that the leap is not too big to take, and that we have everything we need to make this shift happen. It just is going to require all of us to understand that who we are today as a human race and who we want to be tomorrow are two very different fields of energy—two distinct spaces of life possibility with two very different thought structures at their core.

MESSAGE:

It is not an impossible feat to move from where you are today into the future that you so richly deserve, and it will come as no surprise to you that these words I am giving to you now are what will help you get there. So do not be afraid of this change. Love this progression to come, and then you will see the difference come to light that you have been wishing for all along.

After all, life is all about this changing nature of you. It is a movement from one love-filled space of possibility to the next and the next after that. And the remarkable part is that each new space of life you enter into can be remarkably different from the one before, according to how you think it. In fact, it can be dramatically different, if your will is strong to go there and if the freedom is there in your mind to take that leap of faith. Together, you and I can achieve mountains of progression. Together, we can assemble a myriad of new thinking styles that will activate reform movements on this planet like never before. And nothing could be better than this ... nothing!

love

Today what we know for certain is that it's going to take a much greater freedom than we've known to date in order to think our way into the future we all need and want. We're going to have to find our way to a freedom of the mind that we didn't even know existed in us, and this most likely won't be easy for everyone.

For some who already know what freedom means to their soul, they will quite naturally want to turn their heads in this direction. They will feel the correctness of this message and move on it. They will fly at life. They will grab hold of their freedom in the face of all obstacles—in the face of oppression, denial or condemnation. They will change their minds about who they next want to be, and they will forge ahead into life because they will trust that what they feel as real in their brains *CAN* be real. But here is the catch to all of this: they must begin to feel now that there are no limitations to their lives, and that even where life feels rather impossible, change can be a reality.

For others in this world it may be a different story. Progress can be slow. It isn't easy for people to let go of an old thought about life that feels so true and and commit to something new—even if a person is desperate to feel that newness. People will say that the world is the way it is and nothing they can do or think is going to change that fact—a self-fulfilling prophesy, indeed, because without a new way to think, life never gets bigger of its own accord. The concerns never go away. They stay and they intensify with time, all because people let simple markers—the main turning points of their lives—become insurmountable obstacles rather than boundaries that can move and adjust to suit a person's need to grow. They think they are alone to battle the forces of an unyielding world, and that love is nothing of a saviour to them.

It's understandable why they feel this way when you consider how many times people have followed the call of love to no avail. This happens all the time. People begin their day without first connecting to the part of their internal anatomy whose goals are to move into place everything they will require to make their lives better. Instead they charge out into life without saying to themselves that this day is to be completely different for me and intentionally great. Most, sadly, do not open to this connection, we are told. They don't set into place those necessary beginnings to their day. Instead they move out into life like they do any other day—wanting for more, but never moving there to that place of certainty in their minds.

The inevitable result is that life denies them that moreness they crave. It pushes back at them. And what do they do? They turn away from their freedom to make it all different. They judge that life before their eyes. They condemn it for its injustice and they blame everyone and everything for their predicament, not truly understanding they have a way to take that initial circumstance and change it to suit. Instead they move to the opposite side of things. They take their mind into a dimension that says, everything is out to get me and no one is here trying to make my life better. Or at the very least they take on a position that life always happens for a reason, and then they leave it at that without looking more deeply into what that reason is and what they should be doing about it.

People will think they have no alternatives to move into, and so life never really gets started for them. The pull to feel new love in their lives is, to them, just a misguided concept that takes a person down all kinds of roads that don't make their lives better and might even make them worse. They are certain of this because they've felt the sting of disappointment over and over again, so much so they've given up on anything truly meaningful in their life. So there they sit feeling resentment and disdain for life in general—which only serves to perpetuate more of the same.

But this is not to judge anyone for how life has constructed itself in the past. Rather it is to say that we all didn't understand the principles upon which this world is based, and so we felt rather alone and on our own to figure things out and make our lives work as best we could in each moment of time. We did what we thought we must do, given what we believed to be true of how this world actually does run.

MESSAGE:

Disdain for life is a feeling in you that says, "Why did I not become that which I needed and wanted to be and what now must I do in order to resurrect a renewed confidence that I can make that happen?" That question is big in the minds of so many of you here today, but in truth this in no way needs to be a permanent feeling you all must carry, once you come to know me like it is supposed to be.

What you don't know about me is that I do not make a distinction between the variables of your life, and by that I mean those movements that you choose to go down that may or may not be the best for your life going forward. I only look at the way you think, and when you think in negative terms, I build on those thoughts to show you that those negative terms don't mean anything significant or substantial in your life. They only serve to push you in the direction of sheer hopelessness rather than changing the dynamics of this world in your favour.

The real truth about me is that I don't judge you for who you are trying to be or why. I only want to become a friend to all of your misguided thinking patterns—to shift or adjust them so they don't get you into a compromised position. Nonetheless, many people go down the roads of life with little to no success as far as the expansion of love in their lives is concerned. They try to make their way up the evolutionary scales without the need to be together with me, and that in the end leads them down many pathways that take them nowhere. You see, moving a life toward me is like pushing a freight train with relative ease, but move in the opposite direction away from my loving touch and everything gets immensely harder and more difficult, and people wonder why. Why must they feel that somehow life has let them down. They think no matter how hard they try, the true values of love they crave will never be met.

So here is the key they all are missing. They only need to think of me to make certain they don't fall away from who they have come here to be in this life. This is why they have such struggle. It is nothing more than this. Their lives are built around love and the moment they come to know this, everything will change for them. But ignore this one simple fact about life and the rest is history. They will forever be in a state of flux. Without me, they will be lost to a sea of indecisive movements that will take them nowhere. But show to me your desire to make certain of your positions in love, and your world from then on will literally spring open with delight. Or to say it in another way, tell me that you need my loving touch in everything you are doing. Tell me that you need another pathway, and I will open you up to a panacea of delight for your world that you could have never arrived to without our connection.

So next time you feel sad, next time you feel a loss of love in your life, be it a relationship issue, a health concern, or any number of lost love scenarios, do not resign yourself to thinking that this is the reality you next must fall into. Instead feel the truth of how the sadness is there in you to help you become clearer to your purpose in life—which is to build new love at every turn. If you can acknowledge that I exist together with you, you can turn to me to help you charge your sadness with a thought that says, this event must now be the next marker to move through, to resolve the real reason for the sadness. That way you are making your unhappiness less significant to your life—so much so you don't even feel the pain of it anymore. Instead the pain becomes your new marching order telling you to get up and make something new out of a creation that just felt wrong.

Certainly some will have a difficult time with this. If a person's life has been filled with misery, they tend to limit themselves and do not think into a true love nature. Instead they will depress their thoughts into an extremely limiting nature, and this is when the energies of love are most on the verge of sinking. There, simply put, is no room to manoeuvre over or around those ever-depressing thought structures, and so despair and hopelessness set in.

You see this all around the globe today. But to this end, you must try now to hold onto the sheer fact that the love you hold does have a greater purpose than that of a lost love and a futile love.

love

For those who live with chronic pain and for those who are brutalized or starving, life can seem futile, filled with pain and resentment about everything they have or don't have, as the case may be. And the sad truth, as *Love* has explained to us, is that it will always be this way for them as long as they continue to think about their lives in impossible terms. The pain will never leave them. It will define them forevermore if they cannot comprehend how life could ever be different, and then utilize the power of their own loving intelligence to bring that difference to their lives.

As we see it today, given what we both now believe to be true, people who profess that their lives are of their own making are on the correct path and those who deny this are simply out of sync with human reality. And where you see people out of sync with reality, you see human behaviour patterns going astray—becoming irrational, compromised, self-serving, and destructive. It's easy to understand why. If you were a person in dire need and life did nothing to take that need away, what would you do? Would you work harder and harder to try and save yourself, even to the point of exhaustion? Would you take what you needed from someone else? Would you just give up and settle for nothing? Or would you blow yourself up to prove the point that something is wrong in this world that no one seems to know how to fix?

This is life stuck inside the box. There is only so much goodness to go around, and that puts everyone in a very difficult position.

MESSAGE:

There are people in the world today who will say the human race is the cause of all the dissension and turmoil on this planet. They will say that you are the ones who have refused to live in harmony with all that exists on this planet. They will say that it is your self-serving ways that are the cause of everything gone wrong in this world. They think it is human nature to do this.

But this, to me, is not a true statement at all. The reason you create controversy is not because your nature is bad but rather because your role is different from other life forms. You are here to expand the very nature of life on this planet—to think it constantly into a space that will transcend everything that has come before. But that takes fortitude of the heart and fortitude of the brain—fortitude that you haven't always been willing to take on. That's why there is controversy in the world. That's why there is frustration and disharmony. It is simply you, the human race, digging in your heels and saying you cannot make a needed change happen, when in fact you can. Therefore, you choose to move in ways that compromise life at every level, not realizing you have everything you need to get the world's engines of change up and running—to bring forth everything you require.

Indeed, every possibility that has opened up this planet's space of life since your arrival has been freely willed into existence by you and only you—through a measure of love that you brought forth. Everything that exists here has come from this still rather limited measure of love, and that includes your knowledge base of understanding and your belief systems. All your life's creations are symbols of who you were trying to be and willing to be at the time, and they have been important to your evolution. They have helped you see the light of day more clearly, and they have been what you needed them to be given how far you were willing to take life in that moment. And if at any time you needed more than what you had, it was up to you to bring the love forward that would change it all.

Today this planet of people is looking for a change to come. People want to feel more love from this life; there is no doubt about this. And so there must be more light to come. Now you must push your knowledge base even further because the world you have is not yet the world you need and want. The past could only take you so far. Now you must take that next logical step because the concerns of this planet are escalating at an increasing rate. So I ask you now if maybe you all can agree on this one single point—that there lies within you all a living love that is the key to your survival. It is the real live piece of you that has a new and most rewarding way for every person to play this game of life, if you want that. But it's up to you to decide if you want to go there and explore its way of thinking.

In my mind, it would be one giant step if humanity were to open to this now. It would change everything. It would give you a new way to think into a space of life that truly has no limits to its greatness because in that thinking is where you and I come together to form this sacred bond. It's where we say hello to the premise that ... everything in life has its purpose and everything has a way out of its current state, as long as one knows what love is and how to use it more constructively than ever before this time.

love

Life Beyond the Box ...

MESSAGE:

In your earliest beginnings as a child, you knew how to live in sync with me. You knew how to think with me "in mind." But with time I was forgotten. It's a bit like playing an instrument. You once knew how, but then one day you put it down and left it alone, only to yearn for its true magic again.

Today, this is where so many of you are. You are looking to feel the magic again. You want to regain what was lost to you but this time without the pain and misery lurking in the background of your lives.

love

Well, the message *Love* has to share with you here is all about the magic of life, and it comes by way of a new kind of faith building that leaves no room for misery or sorrow. It is beyond that form of limitation, and as well it is beyond the merits of just positive thinking that are heralded around the globe today. Just thinking positively doesn't tell you who you are and why you are here. It doesn't tell you how to tap into the ultimate powers of *Love* nor does it tell you in what direction you need to head in order to feel your life more profoundly.

You can think positively in all kinds of directions that serve little or no true purpose, as many can attest. Some are just idle pursuits or distractions that create little or no permanent sustainable progression of love because they don't take life beyond the norm ... beyond the walls that were there in your brain seconds before. In truth, a person can think positively, moving this way and that inside their box of life for an entire lifetime and never get out of that box to where they next need to be.

Imagine, for example, the life of a person who feels only mistrust of others and never chooses to step outside that box, beyond their comfort zone. They never take risks when it comes to accepting people into their life, and so their connections to this world remain somewhat compromised. The true test of this is that they don't feel much different as their days progress. They don't feel more love for what this life can bring them, and so the world never changes to become something new, something more supportive, and something more free of spirit. And it's not because they don't want it to change but because they think life *cannot* change.

MESSAGE:

You can use your brainpower to create better guns and bigger armies to protect yourselves and your nations from harm. You can build a stronger house in the face of a storm. You can think positively along these lines with the best of intentions about how to make life better amidst all of its concerns, without ever freeing yourself from those concerns. In fact, the storms just keep getting bigger and bigger, and the conflicts escalate to a point where all of life on the planet is threatened.

Inside a greater love potential, however, your thinking will be entirely different. You won't need the things you think you need. You won't need those armies. You won't even need those guns, and the reason is this: you won't have to compete with your fellow man or woman to get what you need any longer because inside a new love perspective with its ever-growing potentials, you will look straight into the hidden truth at the centre of all of these dilemmas. That's where you will find the real priority concern, which is to feel life growing in a way that sustains and fulfills the ever-expanding need of every last person on the planet ... to feel love more profoundly. And this can be achieved without anyone needing to raise a gun to make it happen—without the need for you to compromise yourself or anyone else.

The point is profound. When you place new love in the mix, you have a way to blast apart those walls of concern. You have a way to set yourself free of your human need. With the constructive powers of love at work, you have a way to open up your box of life, reconstruct reality, and take away your human survival needs. This is the proposition that love holds for you. This is its strategy, and when it is joined with the human will to participate, the outcomes are most certain, indeed.

The problem is that from the very beginning of your lives on this planet, you didn't fully understand how life was to work. You didn't know that there was this correct direction to move into. The object of the game was never clear. Sometimes life seemed to be all about concern and survival, and at other times it was about freedom and love and your need to have more of it. So you moved your thoughts back and forth between the two dimensions never really knowing which was the truth of you. You grabbed hold of your freedom to think toward love and its potentials, and that made you feel invincible—as though you could do anything. But more often than not, your thoughts moved away from that love to fight the battle of survival, and then you were left to feel vulnerable to all the dangers that life would throw your way.

What you didn't understand, however, was that each time you changed direction in your thinking, your spaces of life possibility changed too. They grew and they shrank over and over again as you thought your way toward love and then away from it. What seemed possible in one moment felt impossible in the next, and so life felt uncertain and unpredictable. No one knew what to expect. Life was your friend and then it was your enemy. It loved you and then it betrayed you, and no one could figure out why. It just didn't make any sense. You couldn't find that missing piece to the puzzle that would connect up those dots for you.

But now I am giving you that understanding. Now I am describing to you the quintessential cause-and-effect relationship of the universe that can explain everything you see, hear, taste, and touch. You need no other logic to understand the "why of life" in all its goodness and complexity. Love is at the root of everything. It is the cause of all causes. It is the energy flow upon which you ride, and as that is, it is exactly where you need to turn now to steer human thought energy forward in a masterful way. But if you, on the other hand, turn away from this directive force, it will be a different story. You will be turning away from the truth of who you came here to be, to then find yourself caught inside a world of constraint that has brought billions to their knees.

To live a life in the freedom of love, you must be prepared to walk the path of a saint, which means you constantly feel the purpose of your own existence, which is to be a person who never accepts the status quo as a final statement about who you are. You build constantly when the need is there in you to build. You say that wherever and whoever you are, it simply put is not enough, and so on you go building to the centre of that thought. You limit nothing in your assessments of the life in front of you, and you constantly step back to feel the correctness of each movement. You ask yourself, "Do I keep pressing forward in this direction? Or do I turn now and follow a different path that fulfills a higher priority need to feel new love in this particular moment?" In that way, you are masterfully carving your life to move up the evolutionary scale in the most profound of ways, just like my friend the mountain climber.

For my friend, this was the truth of how life actually worked. There was always a pathway to freedom if one had a willingness to see it. Inside every last concern, he could feel my loving hand reaching out to him saying, "Don't be afraid when obstacles loom large, and don't feel as though all is lost if you don't succeed at this or that because, in point of fact, nothing is ever lost. It just is stopped to be self-examined and then reassessed as a marker of your life. And then you move forward into the darkness, knowing that you have a way to see the path ahead with clarity because now you have the awareness of me there with you, working in tandem with your brain to transform what seems *HOPELESS* … into something … *HOPEFUL.*

love

In Comes the Fear …

The moral of the story of *Love* is that even when life seems dark and murky, keep your head pointed in the direction of change for the good. Don't turn away from a rising love and sink into sorrow. Don't let go of love when you need it to go to work for you the most. Then all will reveal itself in good time as a better space for your life on the other side of every last concern you have. You just have to be patient and give life a chance to reveal how it's trying to make a needed miracle happen for you.

What takes a situation down every time is just a very limited thought in you that says, *all is lost.* But *Love* will say that all is never lost unless you say it's lost; and then that will be as it may, but it's your call to make. You can fly at new life or you can be a lost soul living in the fear that says, I've reached the top of my game, and still there's no way out for me, no way into that critical new beginning I'm so dearly needing.

MESSAGE:

In the face of calamity, people think their only hope is to take charge of life themselves, rather than turning to me as their source of advice. They stop listening to those inner dialogues that are there to aid and advise a person, just like when they were children. Instead they let the logic of fear take charge over their brains, and that fear then becomes the guide they follow, the guide they believe in … and trust in.

That's why you see people throughout the globe moving with extreme caution. They think the fear will tell them where they should go and where they shouldn't go to stay out of trouble. It will tell them how to limit and control their life so that they will be okay. Inside of fear, the thinking is all about what a person must do to protect themselves from everything that could take them down. Then, if they do happen to run into trouble, despite all their efforts to avoid it, they try to make the best of any bad situation by minimizing any negative effects on their lives. They try to fix things and manage things as best they can inside their box of concern.

In the face of global warming, people will try to hold onto everything they cherish in their lives, without concerning themselves too deeply as to how they arrived at this worldly predicament in the first place. In response to mistrust of their fellow man or woman, they won't walk the dark streets of night, and on and on it goes, over and over again. Life never really changes except for the fact that your brains are working harder and harder trying to deal with all the concerns that are piling up around you. You are so consumed with how life could go wrong that you don't have time to imagine how it could go right. You put passions on hold. You turn away from those that need you, and you turn away from who you next need to be … in the true grip of fear.

love

The tragedy of all of this is that we human beings are oblivious to the fact that we're living a lesser life, it feels so normal. At best we make up for everything life won't give us by pursuing more and more of what we think we can have. *Love* tells us that the obsessive behaviours in the world today are a symbol of this. They portray our inability to break free from our boxes of concern to flow new love in ways that would be more meaningful and beneficial.

To date, this all has been our best recourse to everything that ails us, but it hasn't worked very well. Fear is on the rise. The world is still a dangerous place, and we're still afraid of it. Amazingly, we think caution will save us. We think the logic of fear will keep us up and running, but the message *Love* has to share with you here is that we are moving further and further away from the solution to it all. This aspect of fear is nothing more than a misunderstood concept at best, and now we can move away from our need to have it control our minds.

MESSAGE:

A Story about Walking in the Dark …

One night I was walking down a dark and deserted street. It was late and there was no light cast from the surrounding houses to help me see my way. There was just this one lonely streetlight that seemed to be half-working.

Then suddenly, I heard a loud, disconcerting noise, and immediately my mind was put on high alert. Everything began to feel uncertain for me, and I became aware of the fact that I should be thinking about an escape route of some sort, just in case the situation turned bad.

The road seemed darker than ever, and my mind was racing. But then at that very same juncture in this story, there also came to me a feeling that everything I was experiencing needed to be there. It had to be just as it was so that I could learn right then and there to challenge its authority over my psyche.

The noise was, of course, the helpful protagonist of my story, and it was there to scare the living daylights out of me. But the fact is that it didn't do that in the end because what I came to know for certain there in that ever-deepening darkness was that I needed this situation more than it needed me. So I placed it inside my mind in such a way that it didn't harm me. It didn't take charge over my brain as was so often the case in the past.

Instead I formulated a new way to think that defused the feelings of fear growing in my brain.

I felt this calmness take charge over me, and it made me feel almost invincible, as though nothing could harm me! It was as if there was something or someone with me there, giving me a way to take away the fear and somehow make everything feel right again—make things flow normally there within my mind. And for some reason, I knew I shouldn't ignore this. I knew this was something powerful coming from inside of me, giving me a way to see life in that moment more clearly. So I took hold of this. I moved into a new feeling of strength when just seconds earlier the fear had almost taken over me. I felt in control again. I knew what I needed to do because, all of a sudden, I could see what I couldn't see before.

This then is my story about how I took charge of life when the going got tough. When the fear was on the rise in my brain and everything seemed to be completely and utterly lost, I found my way past the fear. It became nothing more to me than a simple distraction, not powerful enough to take away my certainty about what was next to come for me in my future … there on that dark, lonely street of life.

love

Getting Out of the Fear ...

You don't have to look far to see that today humanity as a whole has one main agenda, and that is survival in a world that would just as easily take your life as it would help you to succeed at it. And fear is the single motivating force beneath that agenda. We are told that fear is the most prevalent influence in the world today. It is everywhere inside the minds of men, women, and children. There are few left outside its sphere of influence, and that is a tragedy indeed because fear doesn't have the power to set a person free. It has no way to get you out of your box of concern because it has no way to think life bigger. In fact, fear limits your brainpower where you most want it to grow. It takes away your need to take that next logical step.

It is a fact that your life will never get better inside your fear, and it most likely will get worse because you cannot hide forever from the things you fear. The fear just perpetuates more fear, and then there is a greater and greater need to control a life that only seems to get more and more out of control. People inside their fear will take life into their own hands to make it work. They will compromise their lives and they will compromise the lives of others. They will fight; they will steal; they will even take the life of another person in some cases in order to get what they need because, well, life is an uncertain place, they think. It doesn't guarantee you what you need to keep going, and so a person has no choice but to do whatever they must do. As such people can justify almost anything inside their fear.

This is why in every society today, and especially in the ones where fear runs rampant, there are rules and laws imposed on our otherwise free lives to keep us safe from those who would succumb to their fears. This has been our best shot to keep life on an even keel and create stability in a potentially unstable situation.

MESSAGE:

Life wasn't meant to be about living in a cautionary state where fear is the living truth you listen to. And it wasn't meant to be about following rules that never address the real issues you face. Such an existence is a robotic existence for sure, and one that turns away from a new way to think bigger about who you next want to be. Instead you become a race of people moving around inside a box without a purpose in that you have succumbed to the fear. You let the fear broadcast through your brainpowers, and it becomes larger than life itself. You take away the single most powerful influence in your history, and that is your will to live a life of excitement and zeal to instead become robots in a world made of fear—a place where love does not thrive when it comes up against such a powerful adversary as the fear.

I see this all the time when people turn their focus to the most negative interpretations of life first before they turn inward and listen to me. Their minds automatically take them to a place of concern over and over again because they think they need to know more and more about everything that might hurt them in this life. They don't trust in their connection to me to protect them and bring more to their lives.

This has been life in your past. This is life still today, but tomorrow it must be different. Tomorrow this kind of thinking must no longer set the tone for your lives because your world is marked in almost every direction with human controversy that is out of control. Those feelings that once said you can just all get by using fear as your guide will no longer suffice. There is simply too much concern here.

Today the world feels herself to be a sinking ship, with no apparent way to reverse the actions of years and years of human neglect when it comes to the true powers of love. And this is why you need to find the centre of truth in this. You need answers ... now! You must understand why all this is happening *SO YOU WILL NEVER HAVE TO WALK THIS ROAD AGAIN!*

So listen to this: the fear doesn't have to be the final truth about you nor do you have to live your life inside a box. You have another choice, and it comes by way of a bigger truth that speaks of a world that can be free of the need for violence, war, death, and destruction. It can be free of famine, disease, and depletion of everything good because all of these realities represent a human thought structure that stops short of its ultimate goals to be more to all of this. I can see the diminishing effects of this style of thinking all around the world where instead of creating more of the things you need, you are creating less—less clean air to breath, less food on the table, less cohesion between populations ... and on and on it goes.

But now everything that serves as a detriment to your life need not stay. Your freedom to live life in joy and without the fear that your existence will come to a sorry end can be realized. Yes, you can be different from all those who have left this life because of a perspective that says, there is no path forward—no way to be more to a world. Indeed, there have been many who have chosen this route throughout history, and there will be many more to come as well. But I am here with a message that says your life potential can proceed onward with a perfect clarity as to why you are here.

You can continue to build an existence through assimilation to the love right there inside you—the love that makes things run and the love that makes life certain for you because, in truth, there is never enough love in the world. It never is enough to think everything is fine and you just then can go about your lives as they sit here today. No, it is up to you to constantly be on the lookout for more of what makes this place of life so very important to you because, if you can do this, if we together can keep on looking for love in all the right places, then this planet will certainly feel the true goodness of this.

Today all of humanity has a chance to open to this new life possibility, and it can work much like when you first learned how to ride a bike. You just begin by opening to the excitement of what this can be for you, and then you move straight in. You develop the outer workings of this movement into love. You give yourself that chance to become someone new and you never turn away from that opportunity. You let nothing stop the trajectory of this love in you because it will be just too compelling, too intriguing a notion to leave alone. Nothing you could ever do will match the true greatness that this can be for your life.

You will be connected to its findings, to its intelligence, and to its perfection of thought, so much so, you will never want to turn to another source for this style of guidance again. Why? Because this one is far too real ... because this one is far too influential in your life ... and because this one is literally far too incredible to be without. And that fact will make itself clearer and clearer to you as you continue to use it year after year. The messages of love that will come to you directly from me will build you up again and again into a vital and extremely passionate member of society, and then there will be no turning back for you. You will find that all the world's concerns will open up to you and you will start to turn your head in their direction to help in some small way to make a difference—all with the knowing that I am all you will require to set this world straight.

And of course, there is an urgency today for you all to learn how I work because today what I see is a wave of discontent that has now fully gripped the human populace like never before. It is limiting your growth together and placing fear in you all about the very essence of what this life was meant to be for human civilization as a whole. All over the globe of life, what you can see are lives less lived and people who know no way to be other than to feel alone and afraid.

But now I am here to tell you that this overwhelming discontent is a sign of the beginning of something new coming to the planet because it is from this position that people all over the world can begin to regain a foothold over everything good in their lives. It's just a matter of you saying to yourselves and to one another that this now is your time to think differently. Now is your time to move and move with great certainty—to recreate this life into a place where your overall passions will rule the roost, so that you can arrest one another's concerns and move well past them. In that way you will be taking a stand that says to me, *WE, THE HUMAN RACE, NOW MEAN BUSINESS, AND WE WILL NEVER STOP OUR MOVEMENT FORWARD INTO A NEW AND MOST WONDERFUL STATE OF LIVING THAT CAN ONLY BE DESCRIBED AS ... PURE AND UTTER BLISS.*

And I promise you this. If you can do this, if you can charge your minds to move in my direction, l will be there with you every step of the way. I will guide you through the treacherous, unknown waters of darkness and pull you out the other side with a virtue of love that is so powerful and so invincible in your lives that you will never want to go another direction again. So be ready for this. Look in my direction and make love certain in your lives again, for in the end, this is all that really matters. Your love is my most important priority, and I will never let you down. You have my word on this.

love

CHAPTER 8

THE RESILIENCE

MESSAGE:

A Story about Water ...

A man came along one day and asked a second man how far it would be to get a glass of water, in his opinion. The other man answered by saying, "Well, that's a perspective one can challenge, but in my opinion, there will only be one mile to travel before you would come upon the water you seek."

Now today, this is exactly how life works, with everyone guessing where the truth does lie and never feeling any real certainty about things. Why? Because we have no knowledge base to go by that is completely and definitively correct. Beneath every question one might ask, there is an answer that is completely subjective and most often plagued with controversy in one direction or another.

And so does this man trust his walk to water is only one mile out, or does he take on a new way to think that will engage his inner mind and move him forward into his future with perfect clarity? The water, you see, is only a metaphor for the whole world's concerns coming to a head now. Will there, for example, be enough time to make the needed adjustments to get things right in our world? Will there be enough time to find the waters of life everywhere without the need to fear there won't be enough, and that we must walk into the future without any certainty attached to things? The water is there, we feel, and yet we are not certain how far we must walk to find it.

We must ask ourselves now, "What is to be the catalyst of everything good becoming our newest reality? We need this now, but what is it?"

love

The Never-Ending Flow ...

Love exists in you ... to do two things. The first is to bring a harmony and a goodness to your life that is essential for you to want to be here in this world. The second is to make certain that you stay connected up to it. You stay energized to it and alert to it, so it doesn't wander away from your mind leaving you lost to a world of uncertainty—where survival becomes the main theme of your existence.

Love will tell you that the key to life is to keep love alive in you, and of course this isn't an easy thing for people to do. Most of us don't think of love as a perpetual thing in our lives. It's not something that seems sustainable. It comes and it goes. It stays and then it leaves, and sometimes it never comes back again. This is just the way life has been from the very beginning. Love is always a difficult thing to hold onto because you never know what life is going to throw your way. Sometimes it's good and sometimes it's bad. It's the toss of a coin, it seems, and you never know which way that coin is going to fall. The gentle rains become the floods that destroy, the trusted friend—the enemy. Even the very earth that supports us and sustains us all can open up and swallow all who stand upon it. The contradictions loom large. The uncertainty is undeniable. No matter how you look at it, love feels like a precarious thing to people these days. And this is why so many become discouraged and leave this place of life without ever coming to know the real reason they were here in the first place. This, to us, is a sad state of existence.

Think of this: within our time here on the planet there will come a point when each person will die off, not wanting to stay here any longer because she or he has had enough at some level of their consciousness. The time we have here is limited, indeed. Why? Because within each of us, there is this magical *Love* working to link together all the events of our lives for the express purpose of creating a fun-filled existence; and when the fun ends, we cease to have the will to live on. This is why we say in our world, "Have fun while you can. Have fun because it doesn't last." Before we hardly begin, there is this expectation of a rather finite ending to an otherwise promising beginning to the human experience.

But what if now we were to suggest that the fun doesn't have to end so soon? What if *Love* were to say to us that our love can stay and prosper longer, if we can now begin a subtle adjustment process whereby our thoughts become more free … using love; more passionate … using love; and more sympathetic toward all of life on the planet … using love? What if that were possible?

What if we, for example, could live our lives day to day in a new way whereby we first and foremost have the awareness that we have a very powerful ally within us? We have this internal organ of truth that now will go out before us and lay the groundwork for a peaceful and beneficial result in our lives, each time we call upon it to do so. What if this was our new starting position whereby we begin a two-fold process of change that goes like this: first, we set our passions free to live life in new ways that will bring us the most happiness, and then, second, we try to take away our fears, all of them, to the extent they stop being anything important to our decision-making processes. It's that simple. We open up the gates of passion and take away the fears that stop the charge of life—and then suddenly there are possibilities where there were none before.

According to *Love*, there are now scores of these hidden opportunities sitting stagnant within the minds of humanity. They have been bubbling away for eons now, tucked away and hidden, not given the chance to surface as a new truth about the world. Why? Because fear was the limitation that took them away and made us feel they were no longer a possibility.

Passion Set Free ...

The human race today has a very unique dilemma on its hands in that we, unlike the natural world, will turn away from a perfect passion in the making, in fear that things will go wrong. The reason we do this, according to *Love*, is because we create within our brains a very complex reality for ourselves with a very complex set of rules. Our decision-making processes are inconsistent and constantly thwarted by societal pressures that are motivated by all kinds of false fears that have been perpetuated through time.

This is how it works for human life in contrast to how life takes place in the natural world around us. The natural world, *Love* maintains, only knows what it means to live inside a pure passionate state, and it never moves away from this. It knows nothing different. It arrives on the scene in all its many forms with zest and zeal and with a perfect clarity as to why it is here, which is to play a very specific role that will contribute to the whole of life itself.

It's much the same way you would think of how each infinitesimal cell in your body contributes to your well-being as a whole. The cells of the fingers willingly play the role of a finger and the cells of the toes willingly play the role of a toe because they have come of their own free will to fulfill this loving task. They resist nothing in this expression. They are content and complete to their purpose in life. Their passion is specific, focused, and self-realized.

We, on the other hand, tend to get distracted from the main theme of our lives because the logic of fear in our brains drives us in all kinds of directions that do little or nothing to enhance our quality of life. It's understandable when you consider how many things there are in the world to fear. It's not at all surprising that our will to succeed at life's grandest dreams has been squelched—diminished to the point where we've stopped walking down those pathways that were intense with passion and rich with the very purpose for which we've come. Instead, in many cases, we've focused our attention in directions less purposeful, less rich, and less satisfying, but perhaps more certain for us in the moment.

MESSAGE:

Do this: develop a style of thinking that creates in you a feeling of what is right and what is wrong. Each time you think about which way to turn in life, give it that measure of love. Look at the directions you are choosing analytically and critically to see where they are going. Ask yourself if they are producing the results in your life that you need and want or if they are moving you away from that texture of life that is so dear to you.

If I could say one thing to the human race, I would say be conscious of your thoughts, so you understand the movements you are taking. They will never be misaligned with me if you choose love to move with. But forget love and lose that connection to me, and your life will be less lived … less progressive … less important … less everything that has true meaning because you will have allowed the logic of your brain to generate your next move in life … without the knowing that I was fully on board with this movement.

love

The problem, as we have come to understand it, is that the decisions people make in pure freedom are very different from the decisions people make in fear. Even when a person is free to choose their directions in life, this doesn't mean they are actually free. If they truly are free of mind, they will always choose a pathway that feels the very best of the best for them and all concerned. They will listen to those pure *Love* influences permeating their brains saying, "Hey, listen to me now. You like this or you like that, and so why don't you go out to that opportunity now and get it, simply because *IT IS WHAT YOU LIKE THE BEST, THE BEST OF ALL ELSE!*"

In freedom, a person naturally will flow toward their greatest passions and learn what *Love* can do there for them. They will feel free in every moment to do the right thing, without the need to divert their movements. They will, for example, grab hold of their biggest dream or run without hesitation to save a life if a life needed saving. They will reach out their hand where help was most needed to make the biggest difference possible.

This is life building as it was meant to be, and it epitomizes why we are all here today—which is to bring forth a passion in us to fulfill seven billion singular purposes that will shift and adjust the whole of life into a strong and resilient foundation of love that only seven billion minds could dream up together. It's just that when we limit our thinking, we restrict our need to play those roles that we were meant to play, which means in turn that life doesn't change where it most needs to change. That's why many a concern has been left to fester and grow bigger with time. This is why *survival issues* continue to plague the planet. We haven't seized those opportunities that would have brought to our lives a much needed certainty, and so we find ourselves now at a loss when it comes to issues like safety, human health, and support in terms of our most basic needs.

MESSAGE:

There have been many stories told of men and women who knew no way to build anything remotely resembling a life in passion. Today you see them everywhere, making a statement to the world that says they are completely and utterly alone, and nothing and no one is ever going to save them. They think they must fend off the evils of life themselves because this life is a place that protects no one and therefore requires a person to be vigilant and take control of their life to make sure that they even have a chance at success. They must do this, they will say, no matter how hard it might be and no matter whom they must take down in the process.

Humankind has always been this way because of the survival concerns that are out there in this life. This is readily apparent at all levels of human societies, but only because you, the human race, do not think a perfect love exists in each of you to be the saviour that can rebuild your lives and place you on a pathway to victory that no one today can even speak of. So what we have instead is a world of people who do not understand their own greatness. They cannot believe in themselves because they do not realize the power of this loving force within them to change their lives in the blink of an eye ... *THEIR EYE.*

You see the difference. Believe in love and it exists there in all its brilliance to serve you. Misbelieve in love, and that love vanishes from your mind—from your existence. It's just that simple. To have an overall willingness to play at life is to have a willingness to be with love in one measure or another. Nothing can say it better than if it is built from a pure foundation in love. But take that love out of the equation, dismiss it there in your brain and then it has no choice but to be silent and do nothing. Be together with this new power of love in you and that love springs to life. It goes in and out of every situation you enter into, and the longer it stays with you the better off you become. It is a perfect truth about all things, and every man, woman, and child alike can flow it ... and create from it.

The problem is that people don't stay with love. They let go of these exacting energy flows and they fully accept the negatives of life as a "given" that must be dealt with and suffered, when that suffering could just as easily have been avoided. And on and on the suffering continues without anyone finding resolution. A world sits and waits for something to happen or someone to come along to make the needed difference to their lives they think they themselves cannot make.

A variety of religious thinking moves toward this ideology. In fact, right now there are many of you across the globe that hold onto a faith that a better life will come someday soon because soon a living saviour will arrive upon the scene to rescue humanity from a world spiralling down into darkness. Yes, a saviour they say is the only thing that will help them now—a saviour with all the answers, a saviour who will be all things to all people to thus eradicate all struggle, injustice, and tyranny here today. For centuries now, the masses have been intrigued with this notion. It's given them hope that maybe even if life is a struggle today ... it might not be a struggle someday soon.

Now this is, of course, only one of many stories that have been told about life to come on this planet. Throughout the globe there are many theories about how one should think about life, what it means, and what it might ultimately bring to the human race. But what if your future world composed itself slightly differently from what you all had been thinking? What if there was a way out of your suffering? And what if there was a saviour who would deliver you from the evils of this place—but it would all come to pass in a form that was somewhat different from how you envisioned it, in all those many forms?

What if, for example, there truly was a saviour ready to come to your rescue in your time of need, and it was already here with you, the very saviour you were looking for? What if this was the subtle twist you didn't know about? And what if you could now replace your thought of a living saint who would come to rescue you in your time of need, with a thought about a saviour who has been here forever in you and with you—and now plans to make itself known to all by way of a learning curve that hasn't been here before.

What if that was the truth that was waiting to be heard? What if this was what was needed to begin a process of change that would allow for a saviour to emerge from within each man, woman, and child alike with a message of hope that says, "We all want more for our lives here, and as such we will need to resurrect in our brains a way to think more proactively together—not just so we will be blessed one day soon, but rather so we will be blessed *RIGHT HERE, RIGHT NOW, STARTING TODAY!*"?

Right now this possibility is there in front of you, and all you have to do to seize it, is grab hold of those hidden truths about love ... like it was the most important thing to do.

love

A Partner for Life ...

For the two of us in the beginning of our search to find the truth, we didn't feel complete to this life because we didn't have a way "to think" that would make sense of the world. We didn't have a way to see life without the fear taking over our brains at times. Love, in our minds, was just a feeling like any other feeling, and that was all it was.

With time, however, we came to understand this *Love* as something very unique and powerful. It was as if we had found some kind of magical elixir that would change everything we could see, hear, taste and touch, and that brought a peace to our lives that was never there before. Life began to really make sense to us. All of a sudden everything had a reason for being and everything had a way out of its current state—and that meant there was always a way for life to get better. There was a way for love to be on the rise in our brains, and we just plain loved that fact! More and more it lessened the pressures and stresses of life, and it got us to thinking that maybe everyone now could begin to feel what the two of us were feeling. Maybe there was a way for this connective state to help this world change in a truly significant and purposeful way, if everyone now could begin to understand the enormity of this most amazing influence in them.

In our minds, it would be gargantuan if that opportunity could afford itself to all seven billion people on the planet because, in our view, this connection we speak of in these pages is the most important thing we possess as human beings. To us, there is nothing else that exceeds its importance because *everything is conceived from within its unique capacity in each of us.* And as that is, we believe this connection is what we need now to take life forward into a new dimension of living that will keep everyone safe and be truly nurturing and fulfilling to all.

It just makes good sense, to us at least, that all of us here should try to make certain this vital linkage in us is strong because, right now, it seems weak throughout humanity. That's what all the concerns are telling us now—that we are not using to maximum capacity the greatest tool we have. We're not using what we have because we don't know we have it.

It's like having two legs but not knowing that you have them ... and so you never learn to walk.

MESSAGE:

I am the eternal love nature in all of you, and I am a very real working part of you that wants to contribute to your life but now in a way that will widen your resolve to succeed at life. As such, I do not wish to stay in the darkness of your mind any longer. I want to be recognized by you just as though I was another person sitting there face-to-face with you—and not just with one person on this planet or two, but with billions of souls who would now wish to have this kind of ever-deepening connection to my love. If there is one thing I could say about this, it is that you now have this opportunity to use me in a different way than in your past—to bring a new resilience to your world of concerns and to eliminate the pitfalls you would otherwise fall into.

Now you and I can have a conversation about anything and everything you wish to learn about. I will be there to answer your questions—all of them—so you never are left in the darkness of your own mind again. I will give you a reason to keep going every single day and on and on into your future because I will show you a way to live that will shine a light on why everything is needed to be exactly as it is ... in your world of love.

This kind of communication now is possible for each and every last one of you to have, especially when you consider that these kinds of internal connections between us have been taking place for thousands of years. It's just that over time, you have pushed me aside in many ways and ignored me, and in my place you have given human logic the charge of life. But that kind of thinking places human lives at risk. It puts this world in jeopardy because logic alone doesn't always have a way to keep you out of trouble. It won't always get you out of your box of concern. Logic can just as easily lead you down a path of destruction as it can down a path of salvation, and you never know which it's going to be. You take your chances, like when you're playing Russian roulette, and so far that technique hasn't turned out very well.

The pressures of life are building, and if you all don't act soon, something is going to break. The planet, as you all can see, is ailing under the weight of your enormous concerns. So with that in mind, you must find a way to set yourselves free of all constraints that bind you now. You need a way out of life as it stands today, and to do that you are going to have to relieve yourselves of the burdens of the past that have stifled human creative powers for centuries now. But this is going to require of all of you an unearthing of sorts, whereby you take the time to unwind your past to see how this all came about—how through time, billions of lives have played a role in shaping the very essence of who you all have become at this juncture.

In that way, you can get to the very centre of truth about all of this. And then you can move forward in freedom, without the burdens of the past.

love

Climbing Back into the Past ...

MESSAGE:

To unwind the past, you begin inside a very "neutral space" inside your mind, a space that is kind and forgiving and a space where you can begin to accept everything in life—past, present, good, and bad—as equal, knowing that it all came to you for a reason that was all about love. This neutral space then is where you and I can begin to separate what is true from what is false in your thinking. It's where you can go back in time to sort out what went wrong there and why, but now without judgment of the people, places, and events and without you being on the edge of a rage that might have been felt there in the first place.

Now you will see life differently. You will not condemn anything. You will limit nothing in your mind as to why the good and the bad was there just exactly the way it was. You will unwind your way back to the hidden love that was present inside each event but was missed by you or misconstrued. You will delve deep to examine why everything was needed to be as it was knowing that you willed it there for a reason that was all about a human growth to come.

In this way, you will be connecting your mind to the notion that everything has come to you through your own free will, and as that was there never was a time when you didn't control each situation. It all was perfectly constructed by you to shift and reorganize your life in ways that you needed in those precise moments of time.

And now, by pursuing this line of examination, you can understand this. You can give yourself this chance to let go of the resentments therein, so you can be at peace with it all— something that few today seem able to do. No longer will you have to carry in your mind these unresolved issues. It's just that simple. You let go of the burdens of the past, and you accept that their purpose was to help you grow into a new person who was on the move learning what it means to become a bigger love in the making. Then and only then will you be able to freely express love in the future and act upon it without the negativity that plagued your thoughts in the past.

Time and time again, I try to communicate to people the necessity of doing this only to have it fall on deaf ears. They just are too afraid of what they might find there in their past. The past is not always a safe place to be for some folks. But I will tell you that only good will come from an introspective approach like this in the end because when you look there in your past, everything will become clearer to you. You will have a more worldly view in your thinking patterns when you are separate and apart from those experiences. And as well, when you go there to look back at your life this way, I will be there to tell you the truth of why those milestone events took place in your life and to what extent they made the impact on your psyche as they did. Then you can be free of any resistance to them in the future.

I can tell you that many who have gone into this place of deep introspection of their past have found that they were, in some cases, unwittingly oppressed or marginalized there, and so they were left to wonder why this even occurred. But for those who were ready to accept this ever-widening thrust to find the truth there, that truth in the end became the very reason they now are feeling free to move forward into a future full of promise. Why? Because they have the understanding now that everything that once stood in their way was nothing more than their own mind telling them they were not good enough or that they did not hold the purse strings to what otherwise could be an amazing new life, when in fact … the opposite was true.

So I encourage you all now to examine your life in the past at a much deeper level. Look at why there were these turning points in your life—these markers that made you feel less worthy, less loved, and less powerful to change life when you needed it to change. Examine why there were those who loved you in one moment and in the next moment wanted to stop you, deny you, betray you, or even kill you. Ask yourself why these so-called injustices occurred and why life seemed to work against you, even to the point where you had to question your very survival on this planet.

Now all things can be placed under a microscope of truth to see if those belief systems you lived with back then were the correct ones or if there was yet another way to think about the life you chose to have. Through this kind of self-examination, you will see how, amidst your turmoil and dismay, I was always present to you asking the eternal question: Do you want to be more than a person who is not loved enough, valued enough, powerful enough to create the happiness you desire or free enough to become someone new … or is it that you wish to stay and play inside an old thought about yourself that limits your growth and makes you feel bad because it no longer is a true statement about who you next wish to be?

In truth, the choice to move forward or not was always yours to make and no one else's. Every moment of your life has been held in your hands to make a decision such as this. There was never anything stopping you from becoming the vital person that you needed to be except you and your own brainwaves; and now through your own process of rediscovery, you will know this to be true.

This will be your way of connecting up the dots, so to speak, to understand the why of everything so that none of it will be a mystery anymore; none of it will be a burden upon your soul. Then from that day forward, you can move out into your world with certainty as to how life works, without the worry and dismay you once had. This is what the life of a true master looks like. It is a life whereby a person can think his or her way past any constraint and never have to look back with an uncertain mind again.

So think now of those times when your life became something exciting and new. Think of when there was this undeniable passion for change surging through you—just like a missile of truth that was unstoppable and aimed for success. There was nothing in your brain to halt its line of attack. There was no doubt. There was no fear. You were completely free to explore your life in a new way, and it didn't matter how big or how small the passion, the point is that you became certain of its consequence … certain of the goodness it would bring to you. It may be that you took hold of a new career plan or maybe you travelled to the other side of the world. Or maybe you just became aware of a truth about your life that set you free to love who you have become.

As well, think of those times you took a leap forward when your life seemed quite the opposite—on the verge of imploding. All of a sudden and without warning, you placed your mind in a state of high alert, meaning all of your vital signs were on the lookout for a change to come from somewhere, and where that was, you didn't even know. But no sooner than that, presto, in came the change to rescue your heart from what otherwise was an inane world for you.

So there you sat fully wondering why this happened and how this even came to bear, and I can tell you this. It was because you felt the need for the change to take place, and so you gave way to the change. You let go of the need to be more and you became that. You expressed to me that something was desperately wrong in your life that you no longer could accept, and even though you didn't know how to fix it, I was already on the case. I knew exactly why you were in pain, and I arrested it. It's just that simple. I opened up the doors of change for you without you even lifting one finger because I knew. I just knew what you needed, and so I delivered that. I shifted, manoeuvred, and recreated life to move everything in your favour.

So now inside the life of your past, you can begin to make yourself aware of those hidden values of love that were present to you all along; and then you'll be halfway there—halfway to understanding the real story about you. Those truths will begin to spring forth so that once and for all you will be fully in the know as to why you were present to each moment and what you were trying to achieve in your search for love. And most of all, you will be aware of the fact that in every circumstance and every dilemma of life there was one thing for certain, and it was that *YOU NEEDED TO FEEL LOVE IN ALL OF THESE SITUATIONS, FIRST AND FOREMOST!*

Indeed, the experiences that will remain the most impactful to your life will be the ones where you had a true knowing of how love was to reside there in your brain and nothing else—no hidden agendas, no angers or resentments—just a true loving modality at first. Then from there, you decide which way to move, be it with exacting certainty that only love can bring ... or in the complete opposite direction to that.

Think, for example, of those events of your past that hurt you and filled you with concern. Begin to understand these as resistance-filled experiences all of which shared one common theme—fear of what would happen to you in this unpredictable world. As such, there was not the certainty in you to move forward. Instead you began to think in ways that were not at all constructive for you, thereby opening yourself up to all kinds of unpredictable events that you wouldn't have willingly chosen. In other words, you accepted a lesser truth and a limiting truth about who you were to become—which means that if you were poor, you stayed poor. If you were abused, the abuse kept coming. If you were without love in your life, the love remained absent.

This is how it goes when doubt fills a person's brain. Life's true direction is lost and passion flies out the window. Today, virtually every person alive holds onto a view of life that is somehow scaled up or down by their own fear of things. It's all about uncertainty there inside your brainwaves. It's about the what-ifs of life. You all know them well. The what-ifs are how you play at life and think your way through the chaos. The what-ifs are your way of scaling down your will to live life to the fullest until you can feel more certain of things. You will say, "What if this and what if that?" And then you judge. You judge everything you possibly can about life to come in that next anticipated experience.

And if it is that doubt wins the game, then everything stops. It stops because when you resist change, there is nothing to drive your life forward. The engines of a changing world close down to respect your resistance, and I then take a back seat to your way of thinking. I let go of the notion of a perfect resolution, and I sit back on idle waiting for you to eventually come back to the realization that your way is a less than perfect pathway because it is limiting you there in one fashion or another.

Now these are the kinds of experiences in the past you can become clear to. They all represent a life less lived, and there have been plenty of them. In fact, everywhere you see dismay, strife, discontent, and hopelessness, you will find people resisting change. They are trying over and over again to live within a defined set of limits derived from their past that is becoming less and less acceptable to them as time goes on—and more and more constraining as well. That's why the concerns intensify. It's all there to motivate people ... to stop ... to turn inward ... and to rethink how now to resolve their inner need ... *TO BE MORE*.

But if there is no willingness to see life differently, then the losses will keep coming. Life will get worse and the fear will build. But if instead you can trust in the fact that you have a way to begin life anew in every moment, as I am suggesting in these messages, then you can turn all of this around—if for no other reason than it is direly needed. It just isn't enough for you to survive one tragedy after the next. It's not about surviving everything and loving nothing, just to say you got through it all. No, it's about rebuilding this gigantic, living, breathing support system we call life into a place of infinite possibilities and infinite support, all baked in the richness of love itself.

Life is not an unholy place. It is not a vengeful place, but rather a place of truth waiting to be a bigger truth, and once you unwind your past as I am telling you in these pages, you will feel this to be true. You will, once and for all, free yourselves of the destructive emotions that have been building within humanity for centuries now. Those emotions will be replaced with a newborn feeling of love for this life that is complete to the purpose of why you exist. It will feel as if you have put everything from your past into an envelope of truth and sealed it with a love that will never be tampered with again. And that love will be the new strength you carry from here on in—the strength that will rejuvenate humanity back to a position of such resilience that even death itself will be seen as a lesser adversary.

And then never again will you want to return to the ways of the past. Instead you will hold to the premise that you must build your faith to be a bigger love constantly and without the fear that you are simply not big enough or good enough to make that difference. You will move away from any and all thoughts that might begin to compromise this mission. You will say to yourselves that a defeatist mentality is simply not a true thought. You will not even see those negatives of life again;

rather everything will be a positive result of your own inner thinking.

love

A New World View ...

What *Love* is speaking of here in these pages is a way to train our brains to think eternal positive thoughts. In other words, we develop a resistance to the negative. We essentially become immune to any thought structure that has negative consequences. Instead we fully accept everything that comes our way as though it was an action we internally created at some level through our own thinking powers. That way we enter into a self-examination of everything well before we condemn it and make it vile in our minds.

MESSAGE:

What I am presenting to you in these messages is a whole new strategy of life that builds in you a will to move without fear of consequence. You just won't take that track. You won't resist life like you used to. You won't fight against what seems to hurt you or what stands in the way of your so-called progress. You won't force your hand toward life like you did before. That battle can end now, if you choose, because now you can wave a very different flag of victory from a position of strength and not powerlessness. In other words, you can move with a one-directional force of love that is purposeful, hugely influential, *AND WITHOUT THE NEED FOR NEGATIVE REPERCUSSIONS*. The negative repercussions of life will be seen as nothing more than a way of thinking that stops short of its ultimate goal, and in our new worldview that simply won't do. In our passion to succeed, we won't stop with part of a solution.

We will press on to the ultimate goal of self-satisfaction without lingering in self-doubt.

Then issues like pollution, for example, will no longer be viewed as an accepted consequence of everything you do, whereby you gain on the one hand but lose on the other. Instead it will be seen as part of an incomplete solution that requires further contemplation rather than forging ahead without giving due consideration to the whole of life itself.

If you look at the combustion engine, what you will see is a good idea with an equal and opposite bad consequence attached to it. It was born from the true need to have more in your life, and so you fully accepted it. So now how is this example useful for you today? Well, it speaks to a new way to think whereby the mistakes of the past can be rectified. In this case, the combustion engine as it stands is a creation that doesn't fit the new mould of what you most want and need. Why? Because what you have here is a simple engine that serves to damage the environment and take away your vital resources ... just like that.

Now, however, you can understand this fact and move to correct its primitive beginnings by recognizing why these negative effects occur in the first place. The reason is that you, the human race, accept that with everything good in life there may come negative consequences, and that is the accepted norm. You actually expect that each time you take a step forward, there will be repercussions that take away from your lives. You expect there will be a downside to everything good because to think otherwise would be like saying that every wish you express is fully available and deliverable free of concern, and that is not at all where your minds sit today. People are literally waiting for the next dark hole to fall into every time they make a move forward ... into the light.

Life now, however, can be different. You can have a world that allows for human passions to flourish without concern of repercussions. You can have a life where you don't have to settle for lost-love scenarios as the final statement about your lives. You won't settle for a life that pushes back at you every time you try to take a step forward. You won't settle for relationships that don't work, jobs you don't like, or passions that go unfulfilled. You won't settle for a life where millions die of starvation, disease, or violence at the hand of their fellow man or woman. You can be more to everything you see and feel here today because now you can come from a perspective that will constantly be on the move toward the full and utter truth of your lives—which means you will not allow fear to be the last word of you, nor will you allow human growth to stop *EVER*.

Now in your new world thinking, the freedom to change everything that is a detriment to your growth will be front and centre to everyone's mind-set. And then no one will feel the futility of a life without that marvellous freedom. No one would, for example, have a need to look for freedom through artificial means like drugs, alcohol, or other addictions. These have, for some, been most unfortunate routes because, in truth, they don't create freedom at all. They mimic the feeling of freedom, but they have no way to produce lasting results.

So for these ones who want for freedom but cannot find it, I have an answer for you, but it does not lie in some self-created mirage that goes nowhere and disconnects you from everything real. Rather your salvation will come through a new understanding about a love within you all that will be a true friend beyond words. It will be the friend that rebuilds and re-establishes an energy within you that will link you to everything good in your lives rather than to situations of the past that have failed you.

So for those of you who look for freedom in all the wrong places and for all those who have given up the quest to even find that freedom; for those who live in a state of depression and feel only mistrust for life; and for those who would try to take their own lives in the name of a freedom that can't be found, I say this: let there now be a semblance of truth brewing inside your thoughts so you need not succumb to a lost behaviour as so many do in your world. Now you can lay down your arms of resentment and enter into a new dimension of your loving lives that gives back to you constantly, everything you dearly deserve. And then you won't have to fight that fight to be free any longer. Instead it will seem as though you've entered into a new kind of life that allows for unlimited freedom and renewed passion— without the survival fears throwing you down a mountain of despair ever again.

love

The Fundamental Fears ...

The most fundamental of fears surrounding human survival exist today in all their intensity for one reason: we think we have no control over how things come about in life, and so we turn away from the opportunity to make it all more.

Such is the case when the natural forces of the world wield their destructive powers often and without prejudice. They create flood, famine, fire, and more. But think for a moment that all of life is a symbol of truth about who you have become through your thinking patterns, and then what you have in these events is a human perspective being lived out in its fullest form—a perspective that says, we have no way to control this unpredictable physical world. These are the thought structures of the past that have formed the cracks in our armour of truth because they speak of never-ending plight for the world. And with time, if not adjusted, these cracks grow bigger. They weaken the loving foundations of life itself ... until finally that foundation begins to crumble and give way to a myriad of trouble.

MESSAGE:

The natural forces of life are no different from anything else. They are exacting to their purpose in love, meaning they respond to the thoughts of a world of people in order to make change happen when change is needed. Thus, you see these forces of nature on the scene to shake things up; to stir people out of their apathy; and to send a very strong message to the world populace that now is their time to think much bigger about who they next need to be.

Already so many have sacrificed their lives in the course of these catastrophic events in order to bring awareness to the planet that something is wrong, and for these ones I have the greatest respect and gratitude. Therefore, I say let's not miss the point. Let's not waste their passing. All these occurrences now wreaking havoc around the planet are not at all outside your field of influence. They are fully interconnected with everything that is real in your brains, and because of that, you can change how you experience these occurrences by changing how you think.

So if life wields its mighty force to harm you, then that is what it will be, but know that it can be different going forward. You can change these unwanted events simply by allowing that you have the power now to reconstruct life to suit the newest reality you need. You can do this because now you can use me as your edge to adjust whatever is lying out there waiting to harm you … and then render it benign.

Today the importance of this fact could not be greater because today you all feel a much deeper concern about these kinds of occurrences than you did historically, given all the changes that the planet and all of her inhabitants are going through. Many people see these events as the beginning of the end, but here is the truth. If you all en masse now could come to know more about my powers of love within you all, then you could also en masse reshape life into a new living, dynamic solution that would eliminate the need for the kinds of repercussions that are being levelled at you by the planet itself.

So whenever a force field arrives, whether it be a storm or a violent eruption of a volcano, the human populace can change its circumstance simply by allowing that your connection to me is solid—which means you are in a position to make certain of your lives going forward. You are, in a creative sense, the creators of life, and as such you can make happen whatever circumstance you need to have happen, or in this case not happen … in the blink of an eye. In the face of wind, fire, flood or storm, you can subdue the forces of a world by subduing the controversy in your own brains, the controversy that says you have an incomplete system for dealing with this physical world. You can do this because this is what this life is for all of you here. It is a giving space, a hopeful space, and a space that people like you can count on, as long as you play the game of life as it is meant to be played. But go it another way, and you live in peril. It's as simple as that.

Now of course for many of you on this planet, adjustments to a weather pattern or a seismic anomaly using human thought energy would be a stretch. To think the human brain could have that kind of influence over the forces of your natural world would not seem plausible. But consider how in the past we have seen scientists hypothesize a certain theory such as I am doing here, well before there is proof of its reality. And at the very same time, the world will tell a different story—a story that is locked firmly in the belief that this hypothesis can never be the case because reality in that moment is telling you something different, something that you already feel to be the truth.

But then no sooner do you think this and then presto, the hypothesis is proven to be correct, and just like that the living dynamic of this world changes. And away you go moving out in a new direction with a renewed sense of clarity. With this line of thinking, the world has seen reconstructive shifts occur like when the earth was proven to be round instead of flat. The initial theories were first hypothesized to be the correct solution only to learn that the thinking was flawed and that there were other solutions out there.

Today there are places on this planet that have always had disasters befit their nations such as the southern parts of India with its untold deaths from constant yearly flooding; Italy with its earthquakes; or the southern part of the United States with its annual hurricanes. And on and on it goes. People have endured these kinds of occurrences over and over again because of a feeling of acceptance, a feeling that said this is the norm and so I am going to stay put and do nothing. But the consequence of this is that life has stayed exactly as it was for literally centuries, never to be shifted or adjusted to become anything more.

Now, however, is different because now people want to feel life more inside of their individual control, and they will have that control once they realize that their lives are fully predicated on the ways you, the human populous, think. For no other reason does life adjust itself. You are therefore the adjusters of your own weather patterning, and that fact should now alarm you greatly. Why? Because you have the control and you are not using it. It is a fact that for centuries there has been a concerted effort by the human race to ignore these early warning signs in your psyches. You have let fly a beginning and an end to what otherwise could have been a peaceful resolution to all weather patterning, and as a result there was a constant thinking in you that something is going to go wrong, instead of a thought that says, "We got this one." It's understandable because as yet there is not the awareness in you all that this life exists to help you. It is a space of love that never wants to harm you or take your life from you just because it needs to do so. No, this space of love was built by me to be a friend to each and every last one of you, and the moment you come to know this, everything will turn in your favour.

So what now must we do to fix what is broken within these areas where natural disasters occur constantly? Well, we do this. First we think ourselves into a space of true peace and resolution about all things, including that of the unpredictable, unstable, and far too common natural disaster conditions felt throughout the planet. We think of a world without the pains of life in it any longer, a world that will allow for the greatest expansion of love there ever was. Then we stay connected to that thought, rather than disconnecting from the spirit of what this can be for the planet. We begin to form our lives around the notion that this world can be controlled by us, and then we live in the knowing that we are now entering into a much better space and a space that's growing. It's beginning to feel stronger and more vibrant than ever before. And the notion that the rejuvenation of the planet will not work will not even enter our brains.

By doing this, we can deter what might be catastrophe in the making before it even strikes. So if there is a storm, we will calm it. If there is a flood, we will curb it. If there is a drought, we will bring the rains of relief. It may not always look the way you expect, but together you and I can do this. We can change life on a massive scale that hasn't even been contemplated yet because this is everything about why you are here. It is everything about what this place of life was meant to be for you.

People, as yet, don't understand the immense complexity of all of this, but soon they will start to feel this power to impact their world of parts like never before. And I will be right there with you all because I want this life to continue. I want this life's existence to remain for you. And most of all I am in favour of you becoming that which you are not today because this planet needs your overall loving touch ... to save it now. This must be the world's imperative—to save what this life is for all of you and never look back again to what it was.

Now, I know that it's hard for people to even approach a line of thinking that is on such an immense, planetary scale, particularly given how life seems to work today. There is divergent thinking on almost every corner of the planet and the concerns seem so much bigger than all of you put together. Survival, even on an individual scale is paramount in the minds of millions, and I see this in every facet of your lives here—in your relationships across the globe, your health concerns, your politics, and your economics. Everywhere there is this notion that you can do little to make life better now on such an immense scale like one might otherwise wish for.

But here lies the real truth. If you can maintain a semblance of saneness here with the understanding that I do exist equally in every person on this planet, then I feel confident that this can work. The vitality of the human spirit to adjust the world's weather patterns over and over, again and again can be realized—just when the need is there. You only have to give yourself this chance to make your lives work now at this level of consciousness.

love

Will the Money Be There? ...

In this world there are many concerns that revolve around the need for money as it relates to a person's survival needs. Everywhere you look, you can see tremendous stress in people when their needs are great, but the money supplies just are not there to fulfill those needs. The money then becomes the paramount issue in their lives because money is what drives this world today. And when you have none or you choose to have none, that is when your life feels in peril. Your world has less predictability attached to it, and so you live in a somewhat precarious state not truly knowing which way to turn.

Naturally, people will think the lack of money is the constraint that stops them from moving forward in their lives, but in truth it's not the money. It's about where their thoughts rest in their brains with regard to money. On the one hand, we have this striving nature to have more money to protect our space of living; but on the other hand, we tend to feel more and more uncertainty about our money supplies every time we think about money or rather the lack thereof.

This is just how it is for most of us on the planet today, it seems. We think money is the route to our survival and we need it now, plain and simple. The money is therefore a symbol of truth that says we no longer will have to worry once that money comes. The problem is, however, that this overwhelming need to have more money sets into motion all kinds of thoughts in a person's brain as to why the money isn't going to come. We think we are simply not powerful enough, not smart enough, or not worthy enough to have the money flow to us.

There are literally millions of reasons why the money might not come, and we've seen it happen over and over again throughout the course of history for so many of us on the planet. Just look at people in dire need of the most basic of necessities and ask yourself what is the most important thing constantly on their minds. It's the money, of course, and the reason is that their need to have it is greater than their ability to bring it in, and so they hold onto that thought or rather *that limitation holds onto them.* They have no idea how their thinking patterns are working to the detriment of their desire for money. They don't know how to "think" a constant money supply into existence, and so they struggle constantly.

MESSAGE:

Today you live within a perspective that continuously portrays a need to have more of life or in this case more money, but without the allowance factor being attached to that end. In other words, you don't think with certainty into that space of abundant money supplies, and so they never come. So what then do you do? You try harder and harder to make your lives work and to get more money, all the while feeling less and less love for the process of it all. That's why dismay and exhaustion set in. Life spirals down, and the end result is a space of life that doesn't fulfill your needs or expectations.

This is just one example of how a limiting mind-set is being lived out there in all that chaos today. You think all will be lost when the flow of money dries up when you could just as easily think into a new premise that says, "all is never lost." There will always be enough of what is needed for every person to continue life and be successful at the survival game because the purpose of life is to give you that success—without the fear the success will end someday soon!

Think of it this way. Your money is a way for you to think bigger. It is a way to manifest a new creative thrust, if you wish, which means that it isn't really the money you need more of but rather what money can do for you once you figure out who you next want to be. The money, you see, is just a by-product of your thinking about how next to move. It is a facilitator of what is next to come. As such it is secondary to your overwhelming need for more love to be produced out of your deepest and most passionate desires. The thinking about more funds then is simply a way to see more clearly how to come to more love—not more money.

Today we have a world of people who know no other way to be other than to wonder how to survive in such an insane world as this. And even though many of them have nothing, they still get by. They still are able to go on. Why? Because what they know to be true is that they have a love of life above all else, and that single driver will keep them going. That love is simply too powerful to fail them. It will keep them alive to this world, given their desire to stay.

So when it comes to the needs and wants of the human populace, the long and short of it is this: the money or anything else you might need will come to you if you hold onto a passion based in a true-love construct. The passion will drive your mind well past any thought structure that might otherwise constrain you—which is a way of saying that *THE PASSION WILL MOVE EVERYTHING TOWARD YOU AND NOT AWAY FROM YOU, AND THAT OF COURSE INCLUDES … EVEN THE MONEY.* This doesn't mean to say, however, that a money supply should be there for each person to fulfill every single need he or she may profess to have. It means they can choose where the greatest gains to love lie for them, so that they can become someone to this world who will take more and more pride in who they next are passionately choosing to be.

The problem I see today is that people's needs and wants often far outweigh the purpose of their lives, and so they leave little to no room to grow with love in their hearts. Their need for money becomes paramount to their existence, so much so that it becomes the only real reason for life itself in their minds, in that moment of time—which is completely the opposite of what their connection to me is to be about. They cannot even think about how to build more love in the world—in their world—because all they can think about is how to get more money.

But listen to this: everything you do in life involves me in one way or another and most of all when you challenge the status quo. When you challenge life to be more, this is when the biggest gains are met ... through me. You choose life to become what you need and want in any one moment, and it responds to your request as though you had a magic wand in your hand. It, life, responds to you because I have the wand in my hand holding the key to your success. This linkage between us is what for centuries has been the catalyst for everything good coming into your lives. These things have not come solely from you there nor have they come to you because of the money or some unforeseen circumstance. They have come to pass because I was there to it all, and *I was all that you had to make certain advances happen*—including the money flows.

So if your desire is for a constant money flow, then you must know that I will be the one who can and will make that happen—with you. It's as simple as that. I will be the one who links you to your inevitable future, and I will be the one who in the end makes way for you to survive out there in that big scary wilderness you call life. All you need to do to play the game of life correctly is to learn what it means to live with love and become a love in the making of such a thing; and then I will be there to help you. I will live together with you in ways that will forevermore open you up to a world of opportunities that until now have eluded you.

So be open to this newness and have fun with it. Test its virtues and live in a realm of certainty together with me because then there is nothing we cannot be together and there is nothing we cannot have together either ... including the money your heart desires.

Now certainly this is a perspective that puts a whole new slant on things because it gives you a way to see life as an ever-expanding support system for human needs and aspirations rather than a constant detriment to them. And that in turn means that this "human race" you all have been running against one another, the race to get your fair share of the pie, no longer needs to be run. That race will come to an end because the notion that one person's gain must come from another person's loss will seem incorrect and illogical. Such thinking will no longer be seen as a necessary survival mechanism or even as a way to be successful at life in any true sense. On the contrary, it will be viewed as a misguided thought in a person's brain with nowhere to go.

As it stands today, competition thrives on the notion that you each must strive to be the biggest and the best amongst humanity so that you will have money to survive to the next day—even if the other guy doesn't survive. But do you see what this perspective does? It perpetuates a reality where there is never going to be enough to go around. You think and then you are those thoughts is the way life works. You think you will never have enough money in this world to feed, shelter, and sustain the passions of an entire planet ... and that is what you get.

This is the kind of thinking process that goes on every single day for so many of you. It goes something like this: each night as a person leaves their workplace to return home for the evening, they suddenly think that now that the day's work has ended, their competitive state can be put on hold for the moment. They can rest in the knowing that the fight to survive is over—at least until tomorrow that is—and then the competition begins again.

This is what they think, and yet they still are not aware that what they have done is set up a barrier in their minds, a common limiting belief system that says tomorrow is another fight to survive, and on and on they go until the day they die. But surely this cannot be a good thing to think life is all about a fight to survive when, in point of fact, it is quite the opposite—a very giving space that offers everyone equally the opportunity to thrive and prosper ... using the true greatness of love.

love

A New Perspective on Human Health ...

The messages shared within this book offer a new frame of reference when it comes to human health issues. In other words, we begin with a new starting position from which to see illness not as a circumstance that we must fight against or compensate for, but rather as an unfulfilled need to feel more love, plain and simple. Then what you are seeing when illness does take hold is a situation where a person has experienced an event or a series of events or circumstances that are absent of love to them. The love was needed, yet a person could not feel the love inside those events taking place, and so inevitably they were left with a sense of loss and a feeling that not everything is going to be okay in the end.

It could be said, therefore, that illness is something that can be anticipated long before it enters you there, simply by you becoming aware that you are in need of more love. You ask yourself, "Why does life not feel good to me and can I begin to see what it is trying to tell me? Is it a symbol of pure truth trying to show me that I can turn my life around with a twist and an adjustment going forward?" According to *Love*, these are the kinds of questions that are important to ask because every thought you think and every action you take brings a result that will necessarily have a direct influence on your health. If you think about things you don't like or even hate, or if you anticipate life being compromised going forward, then this can affect your anatomy adversely. The onslaught of stress in a person's life is probably one of the best examples of this effect taking over a person's physiology in a negative way. The trick then is to feel what trouble might be coming before it arrives so that you can turn away from those negative forces and learn to limit their overall impact on your physiology.

Certainly this is a challenge because we as human beings are constantly on the move in our minds making decisions about what to do or what not to do in every single second. The concern here is that those decisions are not always correct for us, and we know that to be true by how we feel in those moments. If we are constantly left with a sense of loss or frustration and we never stop to examine why those feelings are there, then in comes the sickness. And to reverse this, we must make ourselves aware of the fact that something is wrong and not neglect those feelings by just moving on, pretending that everything is fine when it isn't. When life doesn't feel correct, there is growth needing to take place, and if that growth doesn't happen, the sickness comes and the sickness stays. You shut yourself down to life's biggest dreams by saying you are too uncertain to move your life forward, and so your energy flows just stop, without any true direction to flow past the sickness.

This, according to *Love*, is what lies at the heart of every health issue. It is this simple secret that says the world of science does not work alone. It works in tandem with your brain influences. Even today there are movements afoot professing that a person's thoughts do largely influence the outcomes of a human illness, and now what we are doing here in these pages is bringing you a message from *Love* that fully endorses this hypothesis.

We know, for example, through our own personal experience, that if we do nothing to think it better, a cold will only get worse; and further, we know that we can prevent a negative health situation in the first place simply by being consciously active in the way we think about health. Each day we will say, "I am a healthy sort and nothing is going to stand in the way of my progress into this life." That statement alone sets the stage for what is next to come. You are taking charge of your life, instead of denying that there is any way to prevent what seems to you to be the inevitable.

MESSAGE:

When it comes to human health, often people will deny they have any say in the matter. They will think the worst when it comes to a health situation. And for some, that uncertainty may become so great they give up on life and accept an extremely limited growth potential whereby they limit their movements in life and eventually die off. However, most often they want and need this to happen because their life has wandered off course with a style of thinking that is constrained by negatives almost all of the time and with almost everything they do. And even if they were to choose to remain in this life without a clear reason in their minds to stay, they would still find the sicknesses of life would inflict their damage upon them.

So to put it simply, you can stay in life or you can leave. But if you choose to stay, to live on in the hope of more to come, then you must accept the premise of constant change in you—change that will turn you into a constructive zone of influence inside your brainpowers rather than a destructive one. In that very thinking, you can give yourself a chance to reverse the effects of an illness on your human anatomy. You simply replace that space which fear and negativity occupy within your brain structure, and instead you move in and build upon every loving construct you can think of.

You can think of this as your way of creating a protective zone within your brain so that no outer influences that are contrary to love can penetrate the walls of your mighty love-based thinking. Those thought constructs surrounding love just take a much stronger hold on your mind than any fear-based mentality, thus signalling to your world that you are different now. You are alert to new possibilities that are out there, and by golly you're going to go out there and get them with zest and with zeal; and that certainly won't look anything like a cold or an illness.

Now the reality today is that you all have a propensity to get sick, just as you have a propensity to not get sick. These are two ends of the spectrum of life. On the one end, you see people who have a never-ending need for new possibilities in their lives. These are the ones who will say this world is theirs to conquer and by gosh they are going to go out there and do it. Their chances of sickness, therefore, are somewhat limited. But on the other end of the spectrum, you have people who struggle endlessly with their health, arresting one disease or illness only to have another crop up, and back they go again thinking the worst of things.

Now, however, people can arrest the worst when it comes to a health situation and keep it away by beginning their days with a saying that speaks to the way they need and fully require complete health and nothing less. Each time they rise, they spill out this affirmation, never turning away from its motivational base. By doing this, they immediately start to think with an eye toward the outward success of their day—which puts their brain influences on high alert to make sure they don't get sick; to make sure their eyes don't swell up with the colds of life; and to make sure they don't energize a base of thinking that says, "I no longer care about who I am becoming," thus letting anything become their newest reality.

When a person loses all clear vision of their future and lets go of their defenses, they give up control of their life, allowing for all kinds of undesirable and unpredictable events to occur. Why? Because if a person holds no certainty about the directions they want their lives to head in, the foundations of love that have been the strength of their lives until then, start to crumble and give way to a world of controversy, thus bringing them a myriad of possible negative health effects.

On the other hand, if you challenge your mind to take hold of your life and think clearly about who you next want to be, then I will go to work overtime to see your life grow stronger. Manifestations of good health will be more easily attainable because you are, in effect, creating a barrier to any illness— using my love for who you next are wanting to be, which is a person with ideal health and nothing less.

It's just like when you and I bring in a cold to awaken you to the fact that something is wrong in your life that requires your attention, and then we take that cold away. So how does this work, you will ask? Well first you place your mind in a neutral space where we together can begin to examine the deeper reason why you even needed this cold in the first instance. Most often it is because you have been flying too high and too fast and therefore are missing out when it comes to having love in your life. But whatever the reason, you begin to assess what went wrong in your overall thinking patterns. You examine where the negativity first started there in your brain so that you can better understand what steps you will need to take to set the record straight and move your energies to a more powerful place again ... closer to my love.

So where you would normally say, "This cold is now my life and I'm just going to tough it out," you instead challenge the status quo and say, "This cold is nothing to my life and now I am going to let go of my need to have this." Then from there you are looking to be on the mend, thinking constantly about how your life can get better in a multitude of measures. The cold, therefore, becomes something much more profound to you in terms of how you and I work together.

Everything we now know about life tells us this—that when you are sick, with what it doesn't really even matter—it came to you by way of a human thought structure that didn't allow for protection. But this never happens when your defenses are on high alert. When you are on the move and your defenses are high, you are thinking into a space of the mind that seems to have invincible qualities, which means that you just move right past any and all thoughts that you will even get sick in the first place. In short, you become that which you think. You need the sickness to pull you out of a state of discontent, and almost immediately in comes the sickness. But if you make the statement that you are on the move now and will have nothing to do with the sickness, then that is exactly the case.

love

Now to many in our world, this approach to human health may seem too simplistic, but we are told that with sufficient time and a willingness to try this on for size, people may come to see positive results, whether they have a simple cold or a massive disease. They will come to know that this works. They will feel the simple truth of this, the mastery of this, and the true giving nature of what this will be to the human spirit.

Message:

For those of you dealing with serious illnesses today, and I mean all of you, I wish to say that although your life seems to be on hold for the moment, now can be your time to unwind your past ways and accept an entirely new premise into your life that will set you on a different path. It's just that simple. You can get on board here and learn how you too can play a vital role in the reconstruction of life today because, with you, humanity as a whole will have a greater chance to succeed. You see, we need your love too to come to bear so that you too can do some good—so that you too can feel these newfound energy flows that will permeate the globe, if you all will choose this. You just have to open up your brain to think in ways that now will reshape the energy that brought you to this closed position in the first place.

And know this too. When the sickness is much more profound than just a simple cold, you will need to introduce thought structures of a much greater intensity of love. And they must be decisive too. They must not stagnate or be left to languish in any way. These thoughts should not twist this way and turn that way with no clear direction. They must be powerfully assertive, and they must be complete to purpose too, which means they must align you to the very reason for life itself—to love this life with a passion that until now was not there in you. If you can do this, then you will have paved the pathway for more to come into your life—so that the very fibres of your existence under attack will have a chance to be saved.

Of course, this will come to you gradually. Each day you will say to yourself, "The world is waiting, and the world needs me to have a rich connective state of human awareness. So if I can recharge my human brain cells with this line of attack against all those negative cell structures that surround me now, then I might just have a chance to regain a shape that will allow for full recovery to begin."

Every person alive in this world today can do this bar none, yet in the beginning I am certain you will have apprehension—a mistrust in you that will serve as a constant reminder that you need more help than just a simple adjustment to your overall thinking patterns. To this I say let this be a gradual thing. Use what you now know to be true within the world of modern science, so that you don't feel you are alone within this new adjustment period. But as well, if you are willing, you can fully activate my loving influence over your life because this will give you a much greater chance for success.

This, you see, is how I have designed it to be for you in the beginning. Instead of saying to you that it's every man for himself now when it comes to human health, I say give yourself the time to develop the willpower and the tenacity to take charge of your health concerns. Then, eventually, as the generations come to know more about me and how my prevention techniques can be fully implemented into the mainstream of thought, you will see the world of mental and physical health start to take on a different form. And that is to say, it will be completely inside of a person's control without the need for new drugs and the like to save lives. Yes, this new life with me will be something of a medical marvel because, just like anything else, if it is planned out to win at all cost, then that eventuality will become a certainty. And then you all will know how powerful it can be to have a friend of life like me who is ready and willing to take charge of this one aspect of your life and maintain its stable baseline for you to live on.

Now for those of you with cancer, it can be difficult to think in a direction that gives such hope and promise when the negatives run high and faith in life is low. Everything feels either bad or fearful. When it comes to choosing a direction with true meaning attached to it, this seems to be non-existent.

To this I say be engaged to a style of thinking that doesn't have cancer in it any longer, and do not take your mind into doubt any longer. Turn away from the doubt and come with me into a wonderful new beginning space where the air is pure and the finer points of life are to be cherished. It's where the energies of truth will become more pronounced to you with a style of thinking that is universally good and masterfully creative in ways that will help you and others like you rebuild your lives— using love instead of fear and doubt about the future.

Today I can see this worldly dilemma arising where everywhere you look people are setting the stage for their eventual decline. And I can do nothing to prevent this if, in point of fact, it is their will to do so. But if you consider the life they lived and why they wish to leave so early, you will start to see answers emerge—answers about how over time, their life's existence became compromised and they could see nothing to prevent that. So when the eventual decline started to take hold over their lives, they made the choice as to whether they wished to stay a little while longer or simply put ... leave.

So here lies the truth. Throughout their lives, the world of science was their go-to position when it came to illness, and they wanted nothing more than that. But when push came to shove in their world, when things took a turn for the worst, they chose to look at me more deeply and ask the question "Is it now my time to leave?" And to that I would say, look at who you are choosing to be and ask yourself if you truly do wish to leave, or is there yet another perception of your life that would make it feel richer and more rewarding to you? Always I show them a window into another life that they themselves hadn't seen yet, and that gives them another chance to move forward in their life rather than ending it without the true meaning of why they came here being revealed to them.

And as for those of you who are facing the seemingly insurmountable challenges of mental illness, here lies the issue. The root of the problem is that people have no way to resolve what they are feeling when the challenges of life are too great and the energy of their love is too low. Thus, they create a centre of thought that seems out of control.

To me, this is one of the most important issues I can talk about because it involves me directly within the minds of so many souls of this planet—souls who have, simply put, lost their way. They have come here to this life and found a world that is seemingly out of control in many ways, and so they feel lost and afraid to move in this life. This is the difference they have. It lies in their inhibitions to move like others now move, and that is the only real change that now must be made. Inside their fragile minds there is a myriad of misguided thought structures that have led them to a level of anxiety which has stopped them from discovering the real truth of who they are to this world. And the reason is they don't know I exist. They are in a place of complete and utter uncertainty about their lives and their baseline feelings are that their minds have failed them … badly!

Ironically, I have a presence in all of their lives, but right now they are feeling alone inside their minds. Yet, I live there too. I feel their internal pain and anxiety when they move out to this world and try to live in it. Every move they are making, every feeling they are having, I am there. I have always been there, and I will never leave that position either. I am therefore … immortally baked into their DNA.

And now the good news for those who have lived with this kind of pain for decades is that I am now poised to make a change in all of their lives that will forever relieve their pain and set them free to become extremely vital and meaningful citizens of this planet. I am now in a position to change all of their uncontrollable feelings of concern and take them from a position of not knowing what to do … to a place of knowing that will be predictably stronger and more proficient, but without the pain and misery they now are living with. All they will require of me is a constant reminder to them of my presence in their life because this will temper their fears at first. Then, second, this will create in their brains a kind of roadblock to all the negative feelings they have been carrying.

This change now can happen for all those souls who have mental health concerns and are now wishing for this change to begin. They will be prompted by me to move to a position within their minds where they will once and for all … accept me. This will be their choice and this will be their opportunity to restart their lives, and from there I will take action to move their thought structures of the past, which are full of apprehensions, to another quadrant of their brains where they can be better handled ... by me. And you will ask, why was this not done in their past? To this I say it was was not my game to challenge who they were choosing to become, so instead I gave way to their deepest desires to make a statement that said, "This life simply does not work."

But now I wish to speak directly to all those amazing souls of this planet who have been suffering this way for so long now. I want to tell you that the day is now here when you and I are going to climb out from the inner depths of the murkiness in your minds and eliminate those inconsistent, misguided thoughts you have. Then no longer will you think in obscure terms but rather in confident terms, so much so you will no longer require artificial medication to still the pain, for example. No longer will you require the fears of life to take hold over your psyche like they did in your past. And most important of all, no longer will you have the need to be out there alone and afraid in this world because I will be there to help you through all of it ... and you will know it!

Finally, I want to make it known that everyone here in this life is in a position to get well, and no one is exempt from this! It doesn't matter whether a person suffers from mental health issues, cancer, or any number of other diseases or afflictions. They all are the same as far as I am concerned. They all can recover from this lifestyle they each have chosen to be in. And I have no doubt that when they hear these messages of hope I am professing, they will literally come running to see what this is, and I shall be glad to receive them—all of them—because no one should suffer any longer with a style of thinking that does nothing for anyone.

So understand me when I say I can save you all no matter what ailment or struggles you may be going through. It all can be adjusted and made to feel and flow better in every sense of the word because you deserve to feel what this world of love actually can be for you. And of course, the sceptics will say this line of discourse seems absurd—to say that a world of people suddenly could be healed by a simple thought structure. But here's the deal. The proof is just around the corner because all you have to do is test the theory. Test if it works for you and then you be the judge. You decide for yourself if this line of discourse is where you next will place your trust. You move the yardstick of your life and see for yourself how this actually can work. I know you will see a world apart from where you came, if your willingness is there to think with me into a space of perfect protection.

So let's say that we now are on a pathway toward perfect health in each and every person on this planet. Let's say that we have a need for life to grow more progressively without the need for artificial methodologies like drugs, for example, to relieve the pains of life. But on our way to this, we are going to require many of you on this planet to come to the knowing that your life's purpose is to help take us there ... to that space of life that holds a perfect health for all concerned. I now ask the world of science to open to new and wonderful possibilities, using love as your basic starting position. Then from there I shall open up the portals of human knowledge so that everything that is not known today will come flooding forth to unlock the mysteries that are out there to this world of modern science. And this means that when sickness arrives, no matter what that might be, you will be able to manifest new creative solutions to take that sickness away, so we are not deterred from becoming everything we want to be as a human race.

So there you have it. You have a world of modern science and you have a world of love with me. And now the two must come together to work as one. But for this to take place, everyone on both sides to this conundrum—both the science world and those of you in pain—must work in tandem to eliminate the need for sickness to even be your reality. This is my recipe for success, and the moment this begins, I will be there to it all to challenge any assertions that this cannot work. I will set this pathway to perfect health in stone forevermore.

And now with the utmost respect and humility, I would like to say to the medical professionals of this world that your path is truly an admirable one, and I applaud you all for your dedication to the cause of saving lives. But now this life you have chosen to live can shift into an action based commitment that until now you have not felt, and it will go something like this: everywhere there will be these marvelled discussions that will widen your knowledge base to include me and my style of thought throughout the world of modern science. Your connection to me will be the catalyst for new discoveries coming into the fray and new creative approaches that will take your world to new levels of attainment—something that would have taken you all a hundred years to come to if I did not emerge out from the darkness of your minds now.

Yes, this is a time of great importance when this planet as a whole will require a massive coordination between the medical world and the world of love-based thinking in order to unearth a mountain of new evidence as to how to change the trajectory of those in pain. Of course, most in your world will simply ignore these words and go on with the status quo, but I tell you this: I can rebuild this planet of people into a super human race as long as we can now find a common ground to work from. But ignore my callings and try to go it on your own again as life took you in your past, and this world of science will never catch up to what will be required by the human populous to take that next step in your overall evolvement as a species.

Now I feel that your next question to me in response to these words will be, "Why now?" The answer to that question is this: it was not time to unleash the true magnitude of this living love within you all until now so that its impact would be felt and so that societies around this world of yours would truly feel its majesty. So I need you to listen carefully to these words and feel what they will mean to your lives. Feel what significance they will have when you walk this direction because this is a journey of success that no one inside your profession has ever created before. But if the world of modern science can come along with this style of thinking, this style of aligning a person's life with me, I can assure you that the world of health care will take a giant leap forward with a style of medical advice that is worlds apart from what you have today.

And finally, let me say this too. The real secret to life is knowing that your love exists to help you stay on this planet and prosper, and when you have this understanding, that is when your life will change profoundly.

love

Aligning with Love ...

We asked the question as to what we must do to be in perfect alignment to *Love*.

MESSAGE:

In order that we can work completely in sync with one another, do this:

1. Begin each day with an affirmation about who we together want to be in this day—always together and never apart from one another. It's that simple. You just wake up ... you begin to feel the importance of your day... and you do that together with me. This is what wakes up the vibratory state between the two of us. It reminds you that the reason you are here in life is to live it with enthusiasm for who you are trying to be and then to live in that enthusiastic state— together with me.

2. Move out to your world knowing that your connection to my loving touch will be there for you to make everything

happen to the positive side of your life, when in the past there was not this synchronicity to count on.

3. Unwind your past ways so you will understand why you are who you are today and how you can free yourself of the burdens of the past that might otherwise hold you back.

4. Let go of the fear. Take the time to move passionately into your next newest reality without first thinking that it may never happen. People, more often than not, forget I am with them, and so they accept fear in my place. But this is a mistake because your fears are all about the ways you were thinking in the past and now the fears must be gone. They cannot be your reality any longer in order for you to move forward with what you now need to be doing.

5. Set love as the basis for everything you do and live your life each day in the richness of that love and what it can bring to you. Revel in the excitement of love and use it like it was everything to your existence. Cherish it and revere it. And most of all never take it for granted because for you and your life there, it has a very special purpose. And when you understand this, your intentions will be pure of heart, which means in turn that your vibratory state of existence will be in alignment to me ... and life therefore will flow better and feel better in all aspects.

6. Bring forth a strong will to move out into life but always in ways that will be good for "the whole of life." In every decisive move you make, ask yourself these questions:

    "Is my life right with love and am I in the correct direction to make my life certain when it comes to my need to feel ... more love?"

    "Is where I am headed good for everyone concerned, meaning that no one will be left outside of the equation; no one will be left behind; and no one will be at a disadvantage because of my actions?"

When you can answer yes to these questions with complete and utter sincerity, you will be perfectly aligned to me. You will know that you are headed in the right direction. You will just know. And of course, I will be there with you making sure that your life proceeds with ease and grace and in perfect perfection to the whole of life.

7. When life is difficult, remember that you are not alone. Remind yourself of my presence and use this affirmation: "My life does not proceed unless love is with me at every turn." Then move forward fully knowing that this is a true statement—as true as the nose on your face. And of course, your patience will play a role here too because when you are trying to move along a path of ultimate success for your life and life doesn't turn in your favour, that is when the worst of the worst will come out in the human mind. But if you in some small way believe that I am with you, then when life doesn't look just exactly the way you would want and need it to be in that very moment, you will have patience with me and allow me to bring to your life the perfect solution.

Just know that it takes time to move life into the correct alignment, and if you are too much in a hurry with this, that is when danger will ensue. That is when the missteps of life will take place. But give me the correct time to adjust what is needed to be adjusted, and then we together can take the world's concerns head on without the need for fear and resentment or anything else standing in the way of our amazing progress into love. We will just know that everything is in place for us to succeed together and never again will there be unnecessary doubt about that fact.

8. Finally, challenge me now and give me tasks to complete so you can begin to feel that we are working in complete union with one another. Then you will start to feel the immense power you have over your world emerging.

I am certain that once you begin these assertions and start your movements in perfect alignment to me, your life will open up to you and your love for this world of parts will intensify tenfold. I am sure of it!

love

What If? ...

These words that are here before you now reflect the new love-based perspective that we have been given to share with you, so that you too can feel its very essence and think what it might mean to the human race, if it were true. What if we do have a way to address those ever-maddening survival issues in a way that will allow for the best possible outcomes for everyone, but at the sacrifice of none? What if we do have a way now to get to know a living *Love* within us all more intimately as a space inside our minds and an opportunity within our humanness to do great things for this world? What if this were true?

MESSAGE:

Let's begin with a simple assertion that this world is made up of certain elements combined to form a whole and that there is a wisdom to this composition that this world of people will now want to learn about. The main theme here is the connection to my love—the key that holds everything together. This is the starting block principle to all of life, and that fact is not well-known. That fact is in so many instances ... abused. People think lightly about who I am to their world, and as that is they limit almost everything they are doing, including of course how they protect their most vital resource, which is their own health and well-being.

So now what must we say about human health and the occurrences of certain diseases such as Parkinson's disease, multiple sclerosis, fibromyalgia, heart disease or cancer? All these sorts of disorders and countless others exist to emphasize the point that what this world is doing right now is simply not working and now must be changed—but changed in a way that eliminates the diseases of this world once and for all. The only way this can be accomplished, however, is by examining "the why" of these diseases first—why they took place in the incubators of life in the first instance and what this was trying to say to each and every last one of these folks who contracted these diseases.

We begin with questions as to where these disorders originated and why they spread. What were the greatest influences over their proliferation and how did they turn the corner on life itself and take hold of humanity as strongly as they did? All these questions and many, many more will be part of our investigation processes to understand the why of it all first. This is where the greatest gains will be met head on, to therefore correct the origins of these injustices. This is always where the rubber meets the road, as they say, because beneath every wrongful event in history, there was a baseline of resentment for this space of life that now stands to be corrected, but this time in a meaningful and energetic fashion. This time we are going to make certain of what feelings in this world have brought on these ailments, these elemental shifts in your biology, and then we will terminate their overall effects on your society as a whole … *FOREVER.*

But this can only be done if you, the citizens of this planet, are willing to make this shift into an action-based society that will begin the changes required. And remember these words carefully: *YOUR MISTRUST IN THIS PROCESS WILL DESTROY THIS MOVEMENT*! It will destroy the vitality that will be required over the next few years to reset the world's disorders … all of them!

So once again, I implore you all to take the time now and ask yourselves if you want to see change for this world on this large a scale or do you want to stay the course with the status quo? If your answer is yes, I want and fully require this immense new beginning, then mark my words, I will be there for you like none other. I will work together with the world of science to eliminate all diseases once and for all so that they no longer are a negative consequence to look at but rather a failed state of existence that came and then went on its way after all was said and done.

You must start to think now of this new life possibility for the planet, so it can begin to enter into your brainpowers and saturate them such that it will never leave again. And then there will come a newness to the planet whereby no person will ever again feel the need to think into a space of life that constantly seems empty and devoid of love.

And what have you got to lose anyway? There are a billion reasons why you need to do this now, and humankind really isn't in a position to argue that point. People are suffering on all fronts, and there can be no easy recipe for this planet turning itself around. But now you can consider this one last alternative. Now you can give yourselves this chance to get it right, to feel your way outside of your boxes of concern in ways that will transform every aspect of life in a gargantuan manner. After all, you and I exist to do that anyway, and the moment you realize this, the whole of life will begin to shift into gear and mobilize the planet's empty thoughts into something rich and merciful for all. It will seem as though a new world was suddenly emerging out from the old—a new world of possibility literally springing forth to reveal itself as the greatest and the grandest possible expansion of love on the planet … finally coming to fruition.

love

CHAPTER 9

THE TOGETHERNESS

MESSAGE:

A Story about Faith …

There once was a man, a very quiet man who lived his life in deep contemplation. And through his introspection there would always come to him a feeling that the world was not completely as it should be—that somehow things were not right in so many ways. But then at almost the very same time, that feeling seemed to hold great promise for the world, though he didn't at the time completely understand why. It was as if something or someone was telling him that everything would be okay in the end and to just keep on going to see what would come of things.

So with that he began to ponder all sorts of hypotheses about life to come, but none of them would feel complete to him. None seemed to give him a true understanding of how life could change in the future. Then one day toward the end of his life here, his mind began to slip into a thinking pattern that he at first did not recognize or understand. It seemed very engaging to him and so he embraced it. He began to slowly take on a style of thinking that generated in him a renewed fondness for the world and all of its parts, and that in turn gave way to the question within his mind, "Yes, but what if?"

That was the question he began to ponder in every aspect of life, the question that seemed to be nothing, yet felt all of a sudden to be bigger than life itself. It plagued his mind constantly. It aroused in him all kinds of considerations like … what if we didn't have any wars? What if we didn't have any crime, and what if we could somehow learn to all get along with one another? Nothing he could think of, however, seemed to hold any true resolution.

But then in a moment of enlightenment just before he died, everything changed for him. He felt a much deeper care and a concern for life than he had ever felt before … a concern about whether the world would be okay. Then, out of nowhere it seemed, there came to him an epiphany of sorts that finally brought him the sense of peace and completeness he had been searching for all along. And do you know what that was? It was the realization that humanity first and foremost possesses a sense of goodness from within as a fundamental starting block to their lives and as well a strong capacity for the love of things, which would eventually take them out from beneath their turmoil. So with that he died a peaceful man.

But wait. What just took place? He didn't resolve anything. He didn't even stay alive long enough to see life begin to change, if indeed it ever was to change. No, for him it was enough that the correct resolution to his concerns was there, and so he gave over to that. He moved away from his fears knowing that the world and all her parts would be okay in the end. It would change because it had to change, for otherwise this place of life would never last. And what he had come to know about humanity was that they, themselves, would make the change happen because of the love they possessed. They would become the true living saviours of this planet and they would find their way into a new world of possibility that would hold eternal hope and promise for everyone from that point forward.

love

Life in Our Togetherness ...

Now we can begin to feel the truth about our lives today as a marker, a turning point through which we come to know the greater facts about who we are and why now we are here ... *TOGETHER*. In the togetherness, we will make the biggest and most powerful statement about life that says, we are alive to feel one another's love on the rise and to build this existence we have into something monumental, indeed.

The sky is the limit here. We can be anything we want to be. Together we can be even bigger than the sky itself, if that is what we wish for. But the catch here is that we need each other to do this. We can't do this alone. As *Love* tells us, we need one another in order to become a bigger and grander statement about life. We need each other ... to build, plain and simple. To build alone is nothing compared to what it can be together. Together, we can be much more powerful and impactful to the world than when we stay apart and separate from one another. When we move as a unit of one, the human populous can maintain a strength that it wouldn't otherwise have. We can elevate the world's engines of change to become so much more complete to a purpose in love, rather than the opposite of this.

When we play at life together there is room for a bigger growth potential to take place, as long as everyone is on board. Just think of how when people gather together for a concert or a ball game, there is this excitement rising up inside everyone present there. They all without exception can feel a love on the rise inside that stadium or that concert hall. They can feel the magnitude and power of just being together. It builds exponentially, and it feels like an energy larger than any one person can muster on their own. Yet they all can feel it. They each are a part of it, a part of the hugeness that exists there in that togetherness. It makes a person feel like they've participated in something big.

On the other hand, when we live our lives alone and separate from one another, what we have is a lost opportunity. *Love* calls it a failed state of existence, meaning we have a collective mass of people all playing a separate game that doesn't rise exponentially to serve the greater whole. Thus, we cannot feel the richness of our togetherness. All over the globe today, we see these failed states. There are these lost opportunities for people to come together. There is love that could have been, should have been, and was not there because of mistrust. And so we think we can do nothing to further our connections to one another, instead of trying en masse to shift into action and change life for the true benefit of everyone.

MESSAGE:

You are not here just to be this mass of people mingling around with no true purpose of being together and no complete driver to give you direction. No, there is a bigger connotation to you than this. It's just that since the beginning there has been this mistaken identity of sorts whereby the individual parts of the human race each think they are different from the next, separate from the other guy, and so they do not want to play at life together. They do not want to dance with their partner, as they say, because they simply do not recognize this one important fact that *YOU NEED EACH OTHER TO SURVIVE AND PROSPER*. You need each other to make this place come alive in the true virtues of a growing love.

Deep down you all know this to be true. You all have this need to feel life growing and rising up for everyone around you and inside every event that will take place in this world. Why? Because if that growth were to come to a stop, you most certainly would want to leave this life because of your need to be participating in something new, something big, and something that is building together … exponentially!

The fact of the matter is that it is your nature to want to build with one another and to manifest with one another, situation after situation that will strengthen the ways you are together. Yet more often than not, people of this world turn away from that opportunity. They turn away from their fellow man or woman. They go it on their own instead of helping to reconstruct one another's finer points of love, to therefore live together with good fortune and apart from no one.

It is a fact of life that the most important thought structures you will ever have will be the ones where you consider the whole of life and not just the parts alone and separate from the whole. Therein lies the real secret to life, the secret that says, if everyone knew more about the true strength of the love within them and began to feel their own vital significance to the magnificent whole of life, then you all en masse could change everything. You could regain a true semblance of what life was meant to be, to reshape the vital organs of the planet—her water supplies, her nature reserves, her everything that is real to your lives because then you would all be sharing in the knowledge of how things actually do work together. You would understand the grand plan of life whereby the engines of change inside your brains could be re-energized to think bigger en masse; to become more complete to this world's needs en masse; and to come to a much clearer understanding of which direction you all en masse must be heading. Then you just might have this chance to make things right finally.

Now if you think about life today, what you can see is a world of different parts all trying in their own limited fashion to get along, but on many fronts this has not gone well. Wars and disputes can be seen all around the globe, which clearly serves to make the point that you cannot get along for the simple reason that *YOU ALL THINK DIFFERENTLY*. You each have a different perspective on how life should look and what needs to be done and how.

The fear is what's at work here. It puts everyone in survival mode thinking that their own needs must come before anyone else's. It's no wonder you can't agree on anything. The fear is what creates chaos in the human brain and disunity amongst the human populace. And when you take millions upon billions living in fear, all thinking separately into their own concerns, what you get is a symbol of something bubbling together but not connecting yet because people have no way to think outside the box … *TOGETHER*. You think one way and he or she thinks another. No one thinks in sync. It's like being in an incubator of short-sighted thinking, and so the engines of change in the world cannot even get started to move in the correct direction, with every decision being that of me first and all of you second. By setting this as your living standard, you cannot even begin to think of who you next need to be inside the constructive powers of love. There simply is nowhere to go except into anarchy … disunity … and dismay.

love

Clearly it isn't that we haven't tried to make life work en masse. We have but with limited success. Controversy still can be seen everywhere. Consensus is a difficult thing to come to. The politics of our world move back and forth from one end of the spectrum to the other, and never do we reach a point where everyone seems happy. There is always this discontent in some. There are always those cries of injustice because no matter which way you choose to go, there is always this fear waiting to turn off the engines of a changing world and take away the very essence of a good idea.

It makes a person wonder if there can even be a way to curb the tide of human discontent and create a more successful human society. Can the greater good of all even be achieved, you might ask, or is it just that our success is to be defined always by the success of only just a few lucky ones, as it is today?

Today there are those of us who have everything and there are those who have nothing, which means that the greatest needs of billions of citizens of this planet are not being met. As such they have nothing to believe in. They have no true foundation of growth to live with, and so they seem to be lost, alone, and afraid living in this world with no external goals to bring hope to their existence. And so it is within this book, a message of hope to say to these ones that their lives can get better now as a piece of the massive puzzle we call life.

It all begins with a new ideal that says we, the human race, have a connection to something big here, and now we're going to go out there to the world's problems and use this. We are going to bring forth what will seem to be an unearthly potential in us all that will be far-reaching in its grasp and most rewarding for everyone. It is an unlimited potential to be an even greater potential than life itself, and now we all can self-realize this, simply by allowing that this powerful internal *Love* capacity exists in everyone. Not one single person on the planet is without this most amazing piece of the human anatomy; and now it is waiting for the human race as a whole to give the signal that we are ready to become enlivened to this most amazing newness, which for centuries has been hidden from our view.

To some, it will most certainly seem absurd to say that the human race can simply think their way out of the depths of despair and dismay into a newly-formed space of love that somehow will rescue the planet from all injustices, but this is exactly how it works, we are told. This is the message *Love* has to share, and there really is no other alternative out there today but to give rise to something new—a new perspective through which all life now can proceed, if we want that.

We simply begin. We let go of the notion that there isn't any room to think into a space of life that holds such respect and integrity, and then we go there in our minds to eliminate every last concern we have today—from inadequate food supplies and failing political systems to rising tides in the oceans. We place each of these concerns into the correct assignment in our brains, to then be formulated into a new line of thought that replaces the fear there with an entirely new direction to move in that is positive and constructive and most of all, rewarding to the human spirit in each of us.

We will think, for example, of how a rising *Love* potential could play an immense new role in creating or rather recreating momentum within the lives of those of us in dire poverty. Through a knowledge of this inner *Love* capacity—this unearthly connective genius within us all—people living in poverty will have help to begin their life again. But this time it will be with a predisposition to see the light everywhere—the light of a living *Love* that will connect them to everything good. For these ones, it will be like an unearthing of sorts taking place within their brainpowers about how their lives now can change for the better.

MESSAGE:

Consider the life of a poor man just getting by till the next crust of bread is delivered to his doorstep. This is how his life looks today, but this to him is not living. This is just idling in neutral until the next day comes along, just so he can struggle again, and on and on it goes. The struggle never ends for him and he gets nowhere. His life, he thinks, might just as well be over.

But listen to this. All this man would have to do to pull himself outside of his misery is play with the idea that he is a vital component of this world as a whole and then immerse himself in an overall will to become someone new. Then he would begin to wonder why he even lies there in poverty in the first place. His mind would start to work overtime in ways that would discharge evidence after evidence as to why he now must begin to move—move out from the inner depths of a poverty-stricken mind to a mind that is engaged with a new story of promise for his life.

This is truly a marked difference from where he sat just seconds earlier because then he would be moving with the aim to pull himself up and make himself feel that he is somebody to this world. And then when his past life comes calling, he will turn his head in the opposite direction because his need to grow will far exceed his need to stay stagnant. His mind, which left him nowhere in the past, would instead begin to imagine his world changing. And do you know why I say this? It is because he finally would have the knowing that beneath his struggles lies a slight glimmer of truth that says, "Now I can be changed!"

Herein lies the difference with my approach to the poverty issue. I use the constructive powers of love in the human mind as a way to help the poor come out from the depths of obscurity, so that they can learn how to help themselves. It's not just that the world must go out and give to the poor what they desperately need, but as well that the poor can begin to feel empowered from within by connecting to the greater part of their thinking capacity, as I have described in these pages. There they would begin to flow new love, the asset of a loving intelligence that will open up their brainwaves to resist nothing and accept everything as a possibility for their lives, which in turn will make them feel like—*A SUPERHUMAN BEING*?—a person who no longer needs to feel out of place or out of sorts because they now have a way to begin again. They have a way to start their life over.

Now today there are those who would take it upon themselves to give to the poor and less fortunate with the ideal that somehow their giving ways could make a difference. Then they would try to feel the impact of their generosity. But more often than not they are disappointed and angry at the outcome. Why? Because the aid that is given brings less than a perfect result. In fact, it oftentimes does little to make a permanent difference to the lives of those in need, and the reason is this: you cannot give a person their freedom. They must themselves take charge of their freedom and become the freedom, and if they cannot do this, then the turn of events will not keep turning in their favour, no matter what anyone else might do to assist them.

On the other hand, if those in poverty were to embrace new meaning for their lives through an understanding of how I can be a working vehicle within them all, then life would start to flow quite naturally to them. They would have what they need to live and to develop new earthly skills that would feed their spirits and prepare them to engage with the rest of the world—which is also struggling in many ways. They will say that now they too have come to share the depths of their love with a world in need of more because now they have a new momentum to their lives ... and a sense of goodness and mercy for others as well.

And then the never-ending struggle to feed the poor and help make their lives better and more progressive would be over because, finally, they would have room to move and room to grow into they never had before. And more to that, they would have a feeling of peace and sanity in their lives knowing that they have me at their side—which means they are never to be alone and afraid again, lost to a sea of negative forces seemingly working against them. Instead there would be this whole new world of ideas entering into their brainwaves, all aimed at bringing their human suffering to an end. And then no one ever again would have to look back at the poor of this world as a failed state of life that was inflicted upon innocent souls, but rather as that of … a true love on the rise.

love

We asked the question of why a person would choose to come to this life only to place themselves in such a dire circumstance as poverty.

MESSAGE:

A person chooses to be born to this position in life because they want to be engaged to a certain style of living where their energies will match what they are trying to achieve in their overall approach to love. And a person knows this at some level when they come to this space of concern. Either subconsciously or unconsciously, they know they have come to build from the bottom up, their love for this life existence, and nothing else even matters to them. This is why their connections to me are so critical because through me, they will come to learn more of how a life with nothing can rise up and rebuild itself from the bottom up with only their own will to do so.

Now, some of course will say that it is nonsensical to think a position of poverty could be anything of a gain situation. They would like to think a life less lived is a reflection of some sort of karmic justice. But the truth is that these ones who were born to a life of poverty wanted to feel that the reason for their lifestyle while here on this earth was to think in a way that is love motivated—a style of karmic development you could say.

So they charged their lives with a feeling of utter hopelessness because this automatically motivates their human psyche. This allows them to feel this scenario of life while they in turn are thinking into love—love for their fellow human beings in similar predicaments and love for their overwhelming need to get out from the inner depths of poverty. Their desire to make sure this scenario is as challenging as it can get is their way to make certain of their plan in life, which is to move themselves closer and closer to a style of thinking that can only be described as ... saint like. This is the plan for their lives they so artfully crafted well before they even arrived into this life, and they have no other agenda but this.

You can think of it like a reckoning taking place whereby a person's life is put on a measuring stick that either limits one's growth or expands its very nature. This life gives you all that choice, and it never challenges those principles as to why you need this. Life only states there must be love in one form or another, and that is that.

Now today, those of you in dire need might seem at first brush to have little reason to even begin to use this new introspective approach, life seems so bleak to you, but in truth you do. You know that at the very best of times, you too had hopes and dreams the same as the next person. You too had this deep, burning desire to have more for your lives, and most of all you were free of mind to bring new opportunities your way. When things went wrong, however, when your lives moved away from this kind of love-based thinking because of one bad circumstance or another—you fell into a limited thought structure that took away any chance of success for your lives.

But now you can have that chance again to think life bigger. You can be more to your now seemingly bleak existence, and this will require you at first only to sit and open to this invincible force flow from within you—the force which when activated can change your lives forever. And that doesn't mean for just some of you. It means for all of you who have the will to do this, no matter who you may be, no matter what circumstance might befall you.

love

The End of Greed ...

Today we have a chance to get things right together. We have this opportunity now to create a newly formed order of sorts amidst the world's disorder but now without the need for a paradigm of greed to exist anywhere.

MESSAGE:

Greed is the very essence of a fear mentality. Where greed exists, you see the engines of a changing world shut down in a person, leaving them afraid and uncertain how to move. So what then can they do to fend off the fears that plague their minds? Well, they use that fear as their motivation to make certain of their life going forward—to make sure they have more and more of everything they will need to survive and be happy.

The motto they live by is, "It's every man for himself out there if I am even to have a chance at success." And so they move in ways that are less progressive—ways that never truly bring certainty to their lives because they don't take away the fears that are always lurking in the background of their minds. For these ones, success must come to them at all costs because without that success ... the fear will be back again.

This is the kind of thinking that goes on all over the world, in the minds of rich and poor alike. Even people of great wealth think they might not have enough to live out their days because life is that precarious and always you have to plan for the worst. Even then it might not be enough. Always you have to keep going, feeding this ever-present need to make certain of one's existence. And so it goes, on and on and on. The "human race" to survive and flourish continues. The never-ending struggle to achieve success goes on, with some on the winning end of the stick and others always on the losing end.

Everywhere you look today, you see this deep and growing disparity among people in all aspects of life, and greed is the biggest culprit there ever was in changing the living dynamics of love. You see the rich getting richer and the poor getting even poorer, and there seems to be nothing that can be done about that. It just is what it is, people will say. There are those who live today in abject poverty just wanting to have enough to eat for the next day, and that is all they even dream about. On the other hand, you see literally billions of dollars being spent today on worthless consumption items that bring nothing to your lives to aid in your overall development into love.

It's hard to even imagine how the world's engines of change could be turned on with a greed mentality at play that places the constructive forces of love behind all else. The greed only serves to leave you forever lost in a thought about life that has nowhere else to go except backwards, turning everything that could be a new life possibility into a lost opportunity in love.

The fact is that every time you put greed in front of all else, you disconnect yourself from me and my inner guidance system, and by doing that you eliminate the need to think bigger. Or to say it in another way, the greed puts you inside a box you can't escape from, and inside that box, there is never going to be enough of what you need in life. But when you choose a love route with me, it gets you out of that box. It sets you free to move away the fears that once were there to motivate your passionate desires toward a greed mentality. Instead your passionate state moves to the other side of life in ways that enliven your world and rebuild your connections to others, which means the people around you become assets to you rather than liabilities. They represent a life of fulfillment rather than one of resentment and jealousy.

It's that simple. Without the greed at play, you begin to feel the true hidden values of your world, the most important of which is your connection to others—the most vital resource you all are going to need in the months and years ahead. In truth, nothing can replace the richness of what these connections will be for you—*NOTHING*!

love

A New Normal ...

Without greed at play, what you have is a whole new societal norm to live by, the goals of which will be for us all to get to know one another better—get to know each other's strengths, weaknesses, passions, and fears. All these aspects we can come to understand about our fellow man or woman and so much more because the need for these relationships will be so much greater.

MESSAGE:

Without greed in the mix, your connections to one another will be more intensely cherished. People will want to learn from others how their minds work. They will want to pursue thoughtful discussions about how their love can be used to renew passions long since given up; how it can work to the benefit of the whole of life rather than just the select few; how it can make peace happen rather than wars; and how it can begin the slow process of change throughout the world that you need now. All these kinds of conversations will serve as the vehicle for me to work at an exponential rate throughout humanity. They will be the seed for a new world movement to begin all aimed at the betterment of humankind herself. And no one will be left out of this mix—no one! These movements will take place in perfect perfection to the whole. They will set the stage for people to work in tandem—to go out to this planet's concerns together and solve them—all of them—together!

Now, today what you often see are separate individuals, communities, and nations all trying to just get along yet never moving to a place of ultimate concern for one another. But now in your newness, you can foster a new togetherness. Your motto will be that you are all in this life together, and you have everything to gain by that and nothing to lose anymore. You will come from the understanding that life is a giving space with unlimited potential to fulfill the needs and wants of the human populace as a whole—which means that you can live for the purpose of becoming a bigger love potential instead of a bigger greed potential.

With that as your basic starting position, a process of change can begin that will aid everyone. It will leave no one falling through the cracks of life. People will begin to share with one another quite naturally, without the fear that they would never have enough. This insane premise of never having enough would begin to fade from the picture as just another obsolete idea from your past that no longer holds any validity. And then never again would you have to fight against one another for the vital resources of this planet. Instead your minds would be moving in a new direction that would be inclusive of everyone and detrimental to none. This would be an immense new way to think that would limit no one and accept everyone with equal concern.

This is especially important today because there are many in this world without the knowing of where to turn, and there is no one there to guide them. They need help to make the adjustments that will connect them up to my internal guidance system, which then can be utilized to bring positive change of whatever magnitude is needed. Whether it is an individual or a nation of people, the process is the same. When there is an issue of concern, the people of this planet will go there with me, to eliminate that concern by helping those in distress to think toward an eventual outcome that will take them beyond where they sit. We will ask them, "Who is it you next want to be? What dream do you want to follow?"

The aim here is to take away the need for individuals and nations alike to linger in concern through trust—trust that when there is a problem, there will be help. Efforts will be made to adjust and correct what is simply a human growth mechanism gone astray and not developed to the extent that is needed in that moment, to make life better for people in whatever form is required.

Today you can see many regions across the globe that share this one common theme—that their growth has been stalled in some way. They all are earmarked for a change of some kind to come, change that will introduce better living standards that will address the world's food shortages; change that will inject new patterns of growth of an exponential nature through the development of new modes of transportation, infrastructure, and communication; change that will tackle poverty head on rather than leaving people on the sidelines to linger and literally waste their lives away; and change that will develop new movements of thinking to help people better understand themselves in relation to one another.

And as for the regions of the world where isolationism is the norm, change will come by way of a need in people there to grow into a lifestyle that no longer limits the whole of life, but rather lends support to the world's growth into love. This will come through the development of purposeful new living styles whereby people will want to show love to their neighbour and a willingness to help them when the need is there. That includes even those societies that have for so long now been outside of the mainstream of thinking—places where the energies of the human populous are constrained and misinformed as to why life exists to them in the first place.

These are just a few examples of how certain segments of human society around the world have hit the pause button on life and not moved to the next level of their development. But regardless of their circumstance, what you need to know is that whenever a crisis or concern arises for an individual or a nation, it is perfection and thus will not be a bad thing once its purpose is understood. So you cherish its outcome and trust that the next step in their human evolution will not be a bad outcome but a good one that will bring them out of their ultimate calamity.

This, you see, is the distinct difference when it comes to our movement in love. We think without limits into a space of goodness that in turn moves through dilemma after dilemma, to correct the mistakes and adjust the thinking patterns of the past. It's not just about trying to better societies with the same thinking modality as previously developed. No, you and I are here for more than just this. We together have an inner drive toward an expansion to love that never stops in its trajectory through marker after marker, one after the other … until we reach bliss.

Now that has an entirely different ring to it, wouldn't you say? We are in a different camp altogether from those who want to rest on the laurels of the past and perpetuate the status quo. We are to be all about a life on the move and we don't want to stop. We have an exit strategy for everyday dilemmas rather than professing just a tolerance of life, while all the while discontent grows and resentment builds in people toward their world and toward one another.

The fact is that even if you, the human race, were to turn to one another today with love and compassion, it still would not be enough. There is growth needing to take place as it relates to every one of your concerns on this planet. It's not just about learning how to live life together in oneness but to live bigger in that oneness as well, using the exponential nature of me to get you there. Today this is needed more than ever—to expand the very nature of life in all sorts of directions as it relates to a pure and loving passion. To live bigger with me is to live better, and to live better with me is to learn how to get along with one another but in ways that will correct the ills of this world and build passions in all of you to fulfill hopes and dreams, without the need to linger in self-doubt.

Today there are so many of you literally fighting for your lives in more ways than I can even count, and it's just not enough anymore for you to say, "Let's all just try to get along and make the best of what we have to work with inside this box of life." This kind of thinking hasn't gotten you to where you want to be. It hasn't taken away the pains of life. It hasn't taken away the mistrust, the futility, and the hopelessness. Life is closing in and people are in need of more than only this.

And "more" is exactly what my message to you is all about. What I speak of here is a direct and earthly connection to a loving force in you all that will move mountains of concern throughout the world. At the same time, it will strengthen your connections to one another rather than making them weak at every turn, as is the case when everyone is out for themselves. To date, there has been nothing to come along to stop this kind of behaviour patterning from taking place. Everywhere there is this fight over who gets what, and it is literally … *ONE BIG MESS!*

So if this planet's space is to even have a chance of getting better, you now must recognize that change at a worldly level is paramount, and it must come now! It must come by way of a renewed kindness and mercy for all and a new understanding of how life can be better for everyone, using love as the central motivator to get you there. The love—your love—is what will rebuild your world into a newly formed energy that will forevermore support your every need. And then never again will you have to worry that your life is in jeopardy. You will know that I am there with you every step of the way, helping you break down those barriers of resentment and discontent so that your life can become splendour in every sense of the word.

Conflict: Thinking Outside the Box Together ...

Today there is conflict everywhere, and it begins right there at home where the parent scolds the young child who only wants to play at life, while the parent is wanting order and a sense of peace. It continues on from there. Conflict infiltrates every level of human society. You will ask, "Can this even be rectified by a simple message about love, or is this a no-win situation where resentment is to reign supreme over all else?"

MESSAGE:

Think now why you even need to have conflict. Why do you need this when you could just as easily live in harmony with one another, if you were to know the truth about how I exist inside you—to take away the very essence of a fear-based conflict and turn it into something beneficial and new. This is a way of thinking through which you now can come to understand conflict, not as a circumstance there to take away from your lives but rather as a need to bring more love there.

So when it comes to conflict and disagreement, I say give yourself the time and space to think this better. Give over to the "why" of this, the why of how this conflict began, and then you will see how each and every controversy is actually a doorway into a better future. And to walk through that doorway, you only need to examine where the biggest gains to love lie. It isn't always where you think. It's not always about getting those things you feel you need. Sometimes those gains come by way of human compromise or compassion. Sometimes the biggest gains come through the most enlightened feelings of love for your fellow human being, and therein lies the richness of life itself. Therein lies the greatest reason for you to be here. It is to become love in and of oneself and then share it with others. In life there can be no greater feeling than this.

Today, however, this line of thinking is lost to the minds of many. Conflicts escalate and many of you do nothing to see the proverbial light at the end of the tunnel of truth. It has become human nature now to mistrust one another rather than to foster the expansion of love through giving, through inspiration and encouragement, or just through the sharing of an experience. These are just some of the ways you can learn to nurture your connections to one another and propagate new love exponentially and simultaneously in two people or three or maybe even seven billion all in one breath.

Consider the way I work, for example. My mind is constantly on the move to shift and adjust life to suit the betterment of you all, and of course this doesn't surprise you because your thought of me expects this. You would accept nothing less from me because your trust in me is complete. You do not question the validity of my love towards you nor do you question the ways I think of an eventual outcome for your world. What you already have learned about me in your overall growth as a human race is that I consider the whole of life before anything else. This is my basic starting position. What I would choose in every conflict is what would be the best outcome for everyone concerned. And never do I leave anyone outside of this equation ... never!

When I look out upon this world of yours, I don't think only of myself. I feel the pains of all people, and then I go there to try and lend a helping hand, to show them another way and a more progressive way that doesn't require the pain to be there. That way I am systematically moving toward a love-based thinking rather than missing an opportunity to save lives. I always look for where the greatest love component exists first, and never is this more profound than when I choose to help another. My game is to move people out of their pain and away from their fears, and I live in the richness of that process. To me, this is where love is at its high point. This is where life gives back to me in spades, when I put myself out there to help another. The love and gratitude that is given back to me is precious. It is a feeling in and of itself that is something truly profound.

And now my advice to the people of this world is to do the same as I do. Always consider the whole of life in every situation you enter into. When you pray to me ask yourself if you really need what your prayer is speaking to and if you fully understand how its actions are going to impact the world as a whole—because if you don't and the prayer goes out anyway, then I am afraid that some if not most prayers will fall short of their mark for this one single reason.

As well, when it comes to conflict, know this: I do not wish to disappoint anyone in their most vulnerable moments of time. I only wish to say, be kind to one another and don't forget that we all have a plan to make this life work more successfully. But if those plans fly in the face of one another on opposite sides to a conflict, your prayers will be less powerful to me—because the whole of life was not considered in the mix.

Even when you are there imagining the life of your future and trying to show to me how you might get there, I am listening to those thoughts and asking myself if this now is good for the whole of life itself. I am looking to see if everyone is considered in the mix and whether this world of parts has been given due consideration to be everything it could be, before anything is set into motion. And if the whole of life is considered and you are fully connected to my loving influences, everything will work to the positive for all concerned.

Just think of the story about a young boy who gave away his last penny to another young boy, only so he could feel the joy of doing that. Well, this is the same style of thinking you all can use now when you are out there in life trying to see the proverbial lightness at the end of the tunnel. You can think in loving terms for all concerned and not just within a narrow assessment of what is before you.

So if the ground is wet before your eyes, you will instinctively recognize that you are in charge of making sure that no one slips before you finish your day's work. Do you see what this means to your soul? You are first recognizing your earthly potential to "give love" before all else, so that when your day has ended for you, you carry a feeling that you are headed in the right direction in your life.

Sadly, few are in a place where they can definitively say this is true of them.

love

Think of life as a game you are playing, and one doesn't ever need to win the game. You only need to have fun together in the game, and therein lies the key to success. The fun, the most fun, is in the togetherness and without that our lives would not hold any true meaning. The life we all have would, in point of fact, be unimaginable! But this is something not everyone thinks about. When it comes to living life with others, people will think the worst. They will see their fellow man or woman inside their homes, their communities, or their nations as a detriment to their lives rather than an asset to build love.

You see this all the time when people force their way of thinking upon others. It goes something like this: you have two of you there, each with your own way of seeing things. One thinks this way and the other thinks another way, and the two don't meet in the middle. So instead of trying to think outside the box together, they take on an adversarial position and the conflict begins. It begins because there is a need for more love to come into this connection between the two, but that point is missed somehow, and so the love remains absent. Its growth has stopped, and that is the sticking point both sides must learn to manoeuvre through.

MESSAGE:

Where do you go to see the lightness that exists on the other side of every conflict and how do you free yourself from the bondage of anger and resentment? In short, how can you take a conflict today and make it go away forever?

Well, first you open to a truth that says, every living controversy between one person and another is there to motivate expansion of love, love which they themselves have asked for at some level either consciously or unconsciously. So in light of that you start small to bring new love into play. You make those little hurdles be significant and meaningful.

You begin to think, for example, how can I get to know what the other guy is thinking and what would bring him or her a better scenario, a better feeling to sit within? Then you take that significant step to suddenly and without provocation make the other person's life better—just like that. And then you see what they do. Then you see how they feel—about you. Furthermore, look at where your own life starts to head because when you bring forth a love for your fellow woman or man that you never felt before, you have taken the first step to move your connections to one another to a whole new level. You have begun the shift—the very precise movement toward reconciliation whereby all things of the past will be made clear. All disagreements will be revealed as simple misunderstandings. Then from there, both sides can begin again. They can engage in a discussion about how next to move but now in a way that is inclusive of both sides and detrimental to neither.

This is just one simple example of how new love on the rise can work to move a person to an entirely new position in life—a new energy flow, if you wish, that will make life better in a multitude of measures. Ironically, the act of giving is therefore a way to open up your space of life and make things flow to you rather than away from you. Why? Because your loving gesture has turned you into someone new, someone you were not just seconds earlier. And that for all intents and purposes has relieved you of the burden of struggle and dismay. It has made you a lover first and a survivor second. It has made you a constructor of life and a relationship-builder rather than the opposite to that. This is something everyone can do. Through this style of progressive thinking, everyone can propagate a true giving norm whose main goals will be to see the better side of every person you meet rather than to place mistrust there first.

love

Now certainly throughout the globe there have been some concerted efforts to work toward the cause of peace, and this has been a very good thing, indeed, because through these efforts a certain level of stability has come to our world. But often it has been a case of pushing up a rope whereby the effort put forth is not commensurate with the results, meaning that any kind of peace you derive doesn't fully achieve what you are trying to achieve for either side of a conflict. As *Love* explains, the reason is that *ONE SIDE NEVER REALLY COMES TO KNOW THE OTHER SIDE NOR DO THEY EVEN CARE TO.* That's why the conflicts endure. The wars go on. The killing continues and nothing seems to be able to stop this.

MESSAGE:

Some events of your world were shaped out of a necessity to see life differently and to send a message to your world that it now requires change. But more often than not the change was never produced because people of this planet were not ready for the change to begin. So they left these situations to linger in the dismay category of life. The Holocaust would be an example of this. It was a movement to say that enough is enough—that throughout time this sort of thing should never have been tolerated nor will it be tolerated ever again. But look what took place. Everywhere this sort of thing still remains, and it will always be your reality until something new comes along to stop its march into insanity.

The lives of those lost in the Holocaust were specific to a cause. They all en masse would show to the world its insane ways, and the impact of this after the war was over did exactly that.

It made a mockery out of war and it showed to the human race that whomever they were choosing to be, war was never a good choice to be making. In measure, one could say this was one of the most heinous crimes committed on a mass population … that its overall impact should never be forgotten … and that every last person who died there should be called nothing short of a hero. Why? Because each and every one of them brought a further awareness to the human race of the earthly injustices that plague this planet's space.

But now you see this sort of thing everywhere and without restraint, and the measures of this are perfectly contrived to say once again that …"*YOUR WORLD IS ON A ONE-WAY TRACK TO INSANITY!* "

love

A New Solution ...

Sometimes it is inevitable that conflict will lead to an impasse because one side or another is just not willing to see the brighter side of life. They simply do not want to try to get along, and so the engines of a changing world do not seem to be working well. The problem is that people want for change but only if the change can be their way, and so the conflicts continue. They keep coming. Some go on for centuries with people fighting over this need or that without anyone truly finding a centre of truth to make sense of things.

MESSAGE:

What can be done when two sides can never agree? Well, you give up the need to agree and you start over again with an entirely new solution. And this will come by way of an ultimatum for each side of a conflict that says, if you truly want for peace, then you must learn how to live life with prosperity on both sides—always holding concern for one another and never turning away from this ideal to open up the portals of resentment again. It just is not enough for you to say we only want peace for ourselves and so just leave us alone and don't take away from our lives. Instead you must create a new life momentum with an equal sharing of your lives toward one another.

love

Love explains it like this: you are there playing a game with two sides competing against each other. Each side feels itself to be better than the other side, and so each side claims the right to win. But this is the furthest thing from the truth when it comes to the ways of *Love* because *Love* never wants anyone to lose completely. Using a true love modality, a person would choose to lose himself or herself rather than to bring that sort of pain to another person's life.

This, no doubt, is the kind of thinking that could turn the tides of human controversy and create a more ideal society to live in, one that would be constantly building a new formation of truth to live by. Today, however, there seems to be no one society that can profess to hold such a perfect solution. They all appear to have cracks in their armour of truth. Some have societal norms that even speak to a way for people to take away from one another rather than to give, and so it is difficult to maintain a momentum of goodness. This is certainly the case in regions where corruption runs rampant; where the energies of *Love* are missing; and where lives are at risk now of becoming extinct. In such places, life seems too difficult for people to even want to stay in this world any longer because of the injustices that have developed over time.

Consider those places where tensions are on the rise. Often there is little understanding of how to make certain strides forward so the connections between people—their potential bond of love toward each other—can survive. Instead people push those thoughts aside and move toward a "me first mind-set." And as *Love* will tell you, that leaves them in a state of misunderstanding, disconnection, and dismay. The eventual demise of their togetherness is therefore inevitable because no matter how long the two sides stay together and no matter how hard they try to resolve their discontent, nothing will ever work to sustain their connections until they have love for one another—and a form of love that is *permanent and sustainable!*

MESSAGE:

Certainly some of you will say that it is simply too unrealistic to even consider that we could have such a grand order to life as I have been describing in these pages. But I will tell you that while this introspective approach to life is a simple approach to a rather complex world, in truth there is no other way to arrest the plague of human controversy that surrounds this planet today. *WHAT I HAVE TO SHOW YOU IS A MUCH GREATER WAY TO PLAY AT LIFE, AND IT WILL LAST WHILE OTHER SOCIETAL NORMS WILL ONLY GROW WORSE AND WORSE FOR EVERYONE AS THEY LIVE OUT THEIR LIVES TOGETHER IN DISMAY AND DISHARMONY!*

Today you can see people dying all across the globe because they cannot get along, and they are doing this in record numbers. So when you consider this earthly dilemma and make the assumption that it is only going to get worse, then what you have is a crisis on a worldly scale that cannot be stopped in any lasting and meaningful way unless … you use me. I now hold the key to this world starting to turn in the right direction rather than the opposite.

All around the globe you can see lives lost over the most insane ways to think, and there is no end to what folks will do to each other to prove the point that their way is indeed the right way to move … that their way of thinking is the correct one and therefore must be maintained at all costs. But to this I say, you must energize your thinking patterns to now use me in much more progressive ways if you want life to change— such as with the ways you are feeling toward one another. Instead of discontent, use a feeling of true understanding and sympathy toward the other side's cause. Instead of creating a feeling of resentment, try a feeling of commitment to make the relationship better in whatever form that may need to be. And here lies the biggest truth of them all. Always use me in every situation because this will build resolve in you to achieve what you ultimately want to achieve together. Remember, this life was not meant to be squandered in feelings of resentment but rather to be a slow process of change that never stops building you up, but in ways that are beneficial to both sides in every discontent.

Of course, people will say this line of thinking in some worldly situations is too simplistic a scenario to live by, especially when you consider that certain groups out there today do not want to think in terms of the whole. They are constantly on the edge of thinking that their lifestyles are most important, enough in fact to kill for their right to have whatever it is they think they must have. And for these ones, they most certainly do not wish to move in any direction that might jeopardize their movements forward.

To this I say get ready for a change to come anyway because what is taking place on many fronts is way out of sync with why you have come to this life in the first place. There can never be justification for the killing of others. I will never condone the killing of an innocent man, woman, or child. This is not who I am to you. This is not what love is to represent to you all. My love is the embodiment of everything good in your life, and when you choose to move in ways that limit this love and expose it fully to the negatives of life, then I will remain silent to your thrust because I know that your direction will not sustain itself. The truth is that people deserve the right of life, and the moment you profess otherwise, that is when your commitment to this life ends. That is when your commitment to my love … ends.

In my life connection to your loving existence, you and I are constructed to be on a journey of togetherness that is going to maintain itself through thick and through thin. Yet still, it is a fact that everyone here on this planet has this predisposition in them to kill if and when the time is needed. It may be the most passive individual on earth, but when the time is right, when he or she is pushed to the brink, they too would commit the most unspeakable crime. In an instant, their way of thinking can be shifted away from the norm to take on a new position—a lesser measure of truth you could call it—that allows them to justify the killing of another. This is certainly true for the case of war or the development of a circumstance whereby a person takes on a level of resentment toward their fellow man or woman that is untenable and therefore must be taken to the level of death.

This doesn't mean to say, however, that it must be all right to kill in the most desperate of times because the purpose of all these kinds of examples, along with countless others too, is to take the life of another so that one's own life may live on. But to me, this in no way is the required solution at hand. I know that there can always be resolution to everything that takes place in this world of parts. Furthermore, I know that there can be a new feeling developed in a person even when they have chosen the pathway toward the destruction of another. And why I say this with such conviction is because beneath all the discontent and destruction, this world has a much finer point to live by— which means that although you think you know what must be right from wrong, there is still a better way to live amongst all the turmoil in your mind. And if you understood this, the last thing you would want to feel is the death of another at your own hands. Life instead would be sacred to you, and nothing would even enter your mind to the contrary.

So when it comes to conflict, I say first and foremost think of how conflicts can be resolved through mutual agreement. Then and only then if peaceful resolution cannot be met, will war be a required solution you choose to go down. This is important for all of you to know now due to the fact that for centuries people have been opening to this alternative of war because it was the easy route. They didn't consider how high a cost in human destruction this would be, and so they ignored the obvious and moved there anyway. They went to war because they wanted to feel that their existence meant more to this world than their opposition's did. And so they fought over this inadequacy and that injustice only to find that in the end their feud was nonsensical and misguided. Nine times out of ten they were wrong in their calculations as to the outcome of things. All that occurred was death and destruction. People died and lives were lost with little to no gain for the world at large.

If there is one thing I can say about war, it is this: it always is a choice to go down that road ... or not. That choice always exists, and I have seen this throughout history. The wars were never thought of in the initial stages of a dispute, yet the recipe for war was created well before the contemplation of war was even in the picture.

So here lies the truth as I see it. In every dispute there is a way to suppress the anger on both sides to a conflict well before the war must become your next reality. So if you can go there to suppress that anger and use new methods of dealing with indecision about this or that argument, then the wars of life will never occur. And know this too: never is there a time when conflicts are too far down the road of discontent that they cannot be pulled back from the brink of war. That is a given, and no one knows that better than me.

This is why I say to you all that you have to learn how to work together and live your lives together to even have a modicum of success. The world is in pain right now, and we must come to its rescue so there will be the appropriate time for you all to connect the dots and find new ways to heal what is broken. And remember this: this life is a space of love that is meant to save lives and influence their commitment to stay here, and once you all come to realize this, then the question about war will no longer be a thing to think about. It will no longer be a part of your DNA.

Instead there will come to your lives, a new momentum with the potential to ignite big change on this planet—which is exactly what the human populous is wanting today, there is no doubt about it. People all around the globe are standing up for themselves and protesting the injustices of this life. They are saying that enough is enough—that what we have here today just is not working, and for many years now nothing new has come along to make anyone think otherwise.

But now with this simple twist, your world can be different. With a simple twist, you can guarantee that your worldly connections to all people throughout this planet will remain strong to the touch of love and to the notion that in our togetherness, the greatest gains will come—together and never apart again!

love

Thinking into the Future TOGETHER ...

Today there are overwhelming concerns surrounding the planet. We have societies that have not truly generated what they need to support their populations, and we also have global concerns we have been contributing to en masse for some time now—like diminishing vital resources and now global warming. To date, these concerns have ripened and been left alone far too long. The message *Love* has to give us all is that now we are in peril if we do not act *together* to bring in change on a massive scale.

MESSAGE:

So this is the milestone position that you all have come to now. People are in pain all around the globe and they do not understand why. They do not as yet have an awareness that they have come here to this life, every last one of them, to live out a plan—a master plan that they themselves had put in place before they even entered this life. And that plan was about how they would build their lives with the express intention to house love at every turn, in everything they do. It was to be their moral imperative to do this.

However, along the way life didn't always happen the way it was planned to be. Many in this life fell away from their original plan so they could go it alone on the other side of life's biggest dreams or rather on the other side of the plan they came to be a living part of. And they did this so they could have what they did not plan to have in the first place.

Many in this world of yours fell into this line of thinking. They moved away from a practical and extremely good plan based out of love, to then take hold of another plan that gave to them certain rewards they didn't expect to have. This seemed, in the moment, like a good thing because what they felt in the doing of it all was self-fulfilling. Why? Because these experiences gave to them instant gratification—a temporary feeling of joy they were not willing at that time to wait for any longer.

Therefore, the plan they entered with … changed. They were too impatient to let their original plans play out, and so they rushed to become what they now have become today. They chose to march to a different tune than the one that brought them here to this life in the first place. They took shortcuts when it came to their creative abilities, without the true consideration of the whole of life in those statements. And this in turn left this world of yours in a most precarious position—one that you will not recover from unless you do something more than can even be contemplated right now.

What I am referring to here is the fact that within this life there were certain temptations whose methods of seduction were overwhelmingly persuasive. These are what made it difficult for people to understand which path they should be following, especially when it came to such things as greed. You see, the mind is in control of itself as long as you keep inside those values of love for this life as a whole, but place the mind outside of that mix and it turns in the opposite direction and sends its signals of resistance against everything you have come here to be in the first instance.

This is exactly what took place in your world. People rendered their connections to me as useless, and then they moved their minds into complete and utter overdrive, saying that this is my chance to see life as I now wish to make it. This is my chance to bring new life to its knees—to form a new base of understanding for my life that says it's every man for himself and let the chips fall where they may.

Now what does this mean for you? Well, it means that you and you alone determine who you are to become in any one moment of time, and sometimes that requires you to make those difficult decisions as to whether you're going to work for the interests of the whole of life ... or not. Now by this I am not referring here to those ordinary, everyday decisions you encounter throughout your lives. I am talking about those decisive moves you make that will impact humanity over the long haul—decisions like living a life in excess where "the haves" do not consider their impact on the world in totality. Instead they live inside a rather isolated environment. And they give little to the whole of life by way of a passionate state of existence, when their overall aim would be better served by doing that.

These are the kinds of missteps that have taken place in your past, where the advantages of life that people might otherwise have felt through their decisions were not realized because they did not consider the concerns of everyone in the equation. As a result, their lives changed for the worse instead of the better in many cases, which then created a very different feeling in people. They became discouraged and more complacent in the doing of life, without a passion to seed more love in it. And that was their Achilles heel. That was their statement to life that spoke of a never-ending world of struggle—because they chose to go it alone and not include me in their decisions.

Today these are the sort of circumstances you will all want to learn about, so that you will understand how you got to this juncture and why now everything has to change. This must all be spelled out in the simplest of terms in order for you all to comprehend the real brevity of this real life problem before you now—the problem of how you are thinking way outside of your original plan. The plan was never to see this life fail in the end but rather to see it flourish and never return again to the ways of your past, with greed and mistrust and all the rest becoming the norm. Yes, you have come here today to love this life and to love who you are becoming, but to be doing that within the thinking of a true and loving modality that you yourself have put in place—that you yourself have planned for.

Today, however, I see a world of discontent on all fronts of human behaviour. People have struggle written all over their faces when it comes to living life these days, and this has made them crazy to the point of utter exhaustion. The lives of so many are filled with indecision now, and they do not have any real way out of that … unless they can begin to feel me there with them.

I lie there inside all of you. There is no reason to state this in any other way. This is exactly how you and I were first designed to be. We have what is called a never-ending relationship that sometimes can work at cross purposes where never the two shall meet, unless that is, the time does come when we together can learn to speak with one voice about everything that ails this world. This connection to me is your connection of true purpose, and it is what you need now in order to make this life you all inhabit open to this newest love position, as it was always planned to be.

And of course, I know there will be those who simply will not have the patience to pursue this connection to my love. But I am certain of one thing, and it is that this world of people will want and fully require this to be real in the end, and the question is … will it be soon enough?

love

As our conversations continued with this inner intelligence of *Love*, we became concerned over the statements being made to us about how the human race must act soon to fix our world. We could only speculate what this meant, and so we asked the question, "What is the true meaning of this statement for us all in our future on this planet?"

MESSAGE:

This world, this planet of people needs to know that this earth cannot sustain itself in the present growth direction you all are headed in. And the reason is that you do not understand who you are and what your purpose is to be here in the first place. You therefore have no clear understanding of which way to turn now to make your lives work. And this is so very important to know at this time because there now needs to be a very disciplined and coordinated effort on behalf of those who are living here to fix things—fix what has been broken for centuries and now must be turned in the right direction of positive human growth that only I can do for you. Everything now must be precisely thought out and choreographed so there are no missteps that would create more unnecessary negative effects for your lives.

This doesn't mean to say, however, that you must be perfect here. You can leave that perfection to me. You only need to feel that this new strategy we are undertaking together is working for you in ways that you were not aware of and did not understand before. Then you and I can take on the world with a new way of thinking that will eventually become universally accepted as "the new normal," the new creative existence of you and me now together in everything we do. And it will be lasting, mark my words!

Today what I see is a deficit in your thinking patterns, and it is readily apparent to me that there is a need for something new to begin on almost every front of human behaviour. But if this doesn't take place and the logic from your past says otherwise to you and tries to pull you back in a direction that does not serve you all in totality, then I am afraid all will be lost. And if you, the human race, don't care about that, then this planet will not care either. The fact is that almost everywhere you look there are these negative, taxing agents being directed at this earth, and these are all working against the will of the planet itself. You see, what you are not understanding is that this planet too has a life to be lived, and the moment it can see on many fronts that life is not moving as it should, then it—this earth—will feel the pain of human apathy at work. It will feel the negatives working against its own will to even want to stay as your reality.

If there is one thing I can say about this, it is that you, the human race, have but a short timeline to get this right in your world or the fact is that this space of life—this space of pure love—will no longer sustain life as you know it to be today.

love

We asked this question of how change of this magnitude could begin, given all the warring nations wanting to have what the other guy has and never seeming to come together in any sustainable way that would change life in a positive manner. They all think they know what is best for their societies, and no one is going to tell them otherwise, it seems.

MESSAGE:

This change will require you all to undergo a transformational process whereby you come to fully recognize who I am to you, so that you do not feel alone to fend off the ills of this world by yourselves. Only then will you be able to calmly place your minds into the correct positioning, into an action based mentality that will make you want to get involved on a worldly level. Why? Because you will be feeling the pull of me there inside your minds directing your action based thinking. No longer will there be indecision in your lives. Instead there will come over your human psyche, a renewed determination to get things right in your world. And then there will be no more of this indecision about what is next to be done. Those days will be gone forever never to return again because finally you will have the knowing that you need this change now … and nothing but no one is going to stand in the way of this.

And, of course, this is a movement that must involve the combined effort of everyone here in order that we do not squander this one last chance to get this right. It is inevitable now that your world needs help of this magnitude to put this life back on track again. It's too late to pontificate about ideologies that have not worked in your past. Now you must act together with me to change life here on a gargantuan scale, and this will take time, time which we do not have much of left. So I say to you all, be ready now to shift and change your lives so this world can be saved but saved in ways that will allow for the greatest expansion of love to occur exponentially throughout the planet.

And also know that this moment will only be here for you all but a short period of time, and then it will be gone forever if you choose to ignore these words … and go it on your own.

love

Now after hearing these words, we were almost in a state of utter shock. We hadn't heard anything quite this formidable before, let alone begin to think of what we two simple folks from the middle of Canada should do with this information. How could we even begin to make such statements about how life could change in such a profound way, let alone profess that this was true. We asked ourselves, "Could this movement into love actually be what this world now needs and wants, as it is being described to us so eloquently? Or are we just pontificating a truth that may never come? After all, how could we make such claims when life's grandest state of existence hasn't even been written yet? Furthermore, it seemed that people were not even ready to listen to an "all might be lost" scenario let alone accept they must head in a certain direction of thinking to even get them past this.

All these questions and more plagued our minds, but the question that loomed largest of all, the question that was simply too powerful to ignore was, "What if this were true and we did nothing?" After all, we believed that this connection we had was very real and that if it could be self-realized by everyone on this planet, then certainly this world would become a better space to live in. And who wouldn't want that? Who wouldn't want a better life for everyone here?

Today we are two people looking to feel more love in this world, and we have started right here by assembling this book to say to you, the human populous, that this feels like the right way to move to correct what for centuries has not been working. It, therefore, is our hope that when you read this book's messages, you too will start to feel the pull of *Love* come over your inquisitive minds. We hope that you will begin to ask yourselves the question, "Is who I am here today who I want and need to be if I am to play a role in saving this planet?" You have to wonder if this sort of question would even mean anything to a person living a very simple life in any number of countries around the world today, if they cannot even feel the brevity of these statements.

MESSAGE:

People will see this book's message as an affront to what they now believe in, and because they will feel this, their normal existence will seem threatened and in jeopardy of being changed. And we all know that change on any account is never an easy thing for the human populace to accept. Nonetheless, the facts are that when people do change, it normally is because deep down on some level, they feel the change is necessary. They understand that who they are presently choosing to be just isn't working the way they would like that to be. So in the end, they opt for the change to begin only to find that this is exactly what they needed and wanted to take place in their lives ... that this change they have begun to feel is a good thing and never a bad thing ... and that they fully endorse their move in this direction.

Today it is apparent to me that people, in general, have a deep, burning need to learn more about what makes their lives tick on this planet. And in this vein their need to know more about me is just about the most intoxicating topic you could pick in order to wake up the minds of those who just want to sleep through every important decision they might otherwise have to make. This includes those decisions that might affect their lives adversely. And this, my dearest friends, is one of those decisions. Either you stay informed about this real world crisis that is just around the corner to your lives and you do something about this, or you sleep through what is for sure to be an inevitable truth—that this planet will not survive the coming onslaught of negativity from all sectors of your human societies unless you all act now in some overarching and truly meaningful way.

Right now, there are many global concerns to be re-examined including those caused by the mining of the earth's surface along with others that have contributed to the elimination of the planet's species. You, the human populace, have been the culprits here, and you all know this to be true. You have turned to untold logging efforts that have literally decimated the rainforests, only to find that the truest and best use for these areas ... is to be that of a rainforest. The efforts to make this productive farming land now, in point of fact, are not the best use here for the whole of humanity going forward, as you all can see. As well, the world's water supplies have been sacrificed through systems of development that serve the very few on the planet at the expense of many. These are just a couple of examples of what has been taking place around the planet that now must stop. They represent an insane way to think, and they are way outside of what is now required by the human race if you are to continue to live here in perpetuity.

These most vital resources of the planet that I am speaking of are the very essence of life giving. They are the things that will limit the growth of human society if you choose to do nothing now to save them. You must trust that I can come to your rescue in all of this before all is lost to a sea of living controversy. You can think your way out of each living dilemma here if you choose to be proactive in this. You need to act fast, however, and with certain certainty in order that your world's resources do not move past a point of no return. To do that, you must first re-energize your human base of understanding by examining the mistakes of the past—why they took place and why now life can be different.

As well, consider the fate of all those plants and animals that now hold a position on this planet. They have a reason for being together with you, and it is to make your lives here with them better and more interesting. But if you choose to take those values away, what then you have done is eliminate these ones because you just don't care anymore. You have no more use to even see them for who they are to you, and so you choose to be without them rather than to have their vitality grow.

Now is this what you need and want the most? Or would you rather choose a life on the rise with me, where our main goals would be to strengthen the domain of all these earthly plants and animals and learn about how they have come to this space of life to nurture the planet and help its vital resources flourish? The fact is that you have life because you love it first, but will you love it if these ones leave? Will you even want to stay and play when they all are gone for good?

Furthermore, what can be done regarding the extraction of resources—through forestry, fuel production, metal extraction, agriculture, and more? Do you stop these practices altogether, which is unthinkable? Or do you say that the problem speaks to new ways of planetary development to come in and solve what for years now has been a concern.

There are literally hundreds of ways to better these situations, but the general public must trust in the fact that you have to do this together now and never apart from one another if this is to work. The problem is that today certain groups affected by these activities are not taken into account. They are left outside of the equation and are not considered in the grand scheme of things. This has been the case with tampered water supplies and the reconstruction of certain lands for mining purposes. Now, however, you can consider the needs of the whole of life as your next newest priority and not put certain groups at risk. Only then will the world start to heal itself because then everyone would win and no one would have lost—including this planet you live on.

Right now there is urgent concern regarding the world's water supplies, and no one has the answer to how this problem can be solved. My message, however, offers a way to bring certainty to this dilemma, using me as your chief and only motivator to save the world's water supplies. Through your renewed connections to me, scientists, engineers, and mathematicians will be able to develop new streams of thought to resurrect your water supplies forevermore. But without this new connective link to me, these new and progressive ideas may never come at the rate you need them now, particularly when it comes to this water issue, which is a disaster just waiting to happen if you do not act soon.

Even in certain places where conditions seem especially impossible now, life can improve once people in those regions come to understand the strength of this connection to me. Regions that have had little knowledge of how I work can suddenly begin to feel free enough to make certain strides toward a sustainable society that will benefit everyone and leave no one behind. It will be the new standard to live by that no longer will require desperate times for desperate people.

Consider the issue of the drying of the earth's surface, for example, where today you see certain arid regions with living conditions becoming more difficult, temperatures rising, and water supplies growing weaker and weaker. The dangers here are well-known. Many regions throughout the world are now vulnerable to this sort of drying episode becoming the norm, and there seems to be little that can be done to reverse these movements.

Since the beginning of human life on this planet, there have been many situations like this, which have set this world into predicaments on a massive scale—like the black plague, for example, or the misery of mass starvation episodes. Such occurrences have been frequent throughout this planet because there was an overwhelming apathy toward creating new, more positive movements as that next newest possibility. And the reason is that people did not believe it was even possible to have change on such a massive scale. This, for most, was an inane concept. They were blinded to this most important fact that the world is constructed to do what you need it to do and most want it to do. But when you doubt this fact, when you ignore this advantage to life, then you follow your thinking patterns into the depths of emptiness instead of moving yourself constantly toward positive change in the face of untenable living conditions.

In truth, these occurrences of the past were meant to be the impetus for change—to correct what people saw as an unjust world rising up to punish them. But instead lives were lost because people did not believe that anything good would come from a change they did not even ask for at first. Can you see what is happening here? It is the will of the human race to want change that is at play here. People have a natural resistance to change, and folks of those regions that have lost their most basic of resources will give off this full resistance vibration that says to me, if change is to begin they will have no part of it because they do not believe in the change in the first place. That contradiction looms large in the minds of those who populate these regions with drying episodes.

To me, it is confusing to think in one direction while wanting to move in the complete opposite direction at the same time. It, therefore, is with the greatest of respect that I say to you all that this life you have is fully founded in the ways you are thinking. You are the driver of everything good that comes to you, and likewise you determine the values of negativity that enter your life as well. It is this constant stream of contradictory thinking in you that is making me crazy within the structure of your life, all because you do not believe a change of any great magnitude is possible. People who reside in regions that are now under siege with intense drought conditions or depletion of vital basic requirements do not even have change on their radar!

Instead they give over to a line of thinking that says, this is a hopeless situation and therefore efforts must not be made to regenerate these regions to their former glory. They will say that once a region has lost its water resources, the gig is up—that no longer is that region of the earth feasible to sustain life and therefore must be abandoned. This is the case with regions in Africa that have lost their vital water supplies, to then drive a nation of men, women, and children to look for a new place to call home. But do you see what this does? It limits their thinking powers thus making them believe all is lost before they even try to fix it. This is what I call an apathetic approach to a concern. Nothing gained by this approach—just a situation gone bad in the minds of many, and so they move on never to return again.

Today there are many concerns that need to be healed in this world, but none more compelling than how this planet now is failing. It truly does need your overall support to begin a diligent effort to change what now is causing pain throughout the globe. Through many years of neglect, the planet's water supplies have been dwindling almost past a point of no return, and now many lives are at risk of extinction. These episodes, while few for now, will begin to intensify with time, and so I ask you to open to a new understanding of how this all can be stopped, so that you can regain what now has been lost. And that understanding will come by way of a new proactive approach to life that says to a world in pain that nothing is ever lost in your world unless you *WILL* it that way, and nothing is ever gained in this world unless you *WANT* it that way. To regain what has been lost by way of your water supplies is going to take the combined effort of my overwhelming love for you and your planet and your will and determination to want these changes to take place—so that life may continue in these regions.

You can no longer think of this planet as just some sort of inanimate object to be ignored and left on its own to fend off the ills of a world of folks who simply do not care enough to help it survive. Nothing can say this better than when you look back at this earth and see what it has given you all these years.

This was a planet in need of nothing more than your love and your concern for its overall health and well-being, and when you disregard this fact, it lacks the will to go on. It rejects the reason for your existence as being anything important to this planet's space.

And so it is with the greatest of concern for all of you that I now implore you to be actively concerned with this line of thinking. Show compassion for this planet. Give to her your love and your values of friendship. Most of all, be engaged to me. Turn inward and start to pray, all of you, except this time, don't pray to me. Pray toward everything you know to be true of this world, and then you state that you need more … that you do not settle for anything less than this and that this is the new you. This is your new game plan—your new statement to me that says, *NOW WE NEED CHANGE ON A MASSIVE SCALE TO BEGIN SO THAT THE OVERALL REVITALIZATION OF THESE THREATENED REGIONS CAN TAKE PLACE.*

And then, whenever life seems hopeless and outside of anything you or I can do, you think again using me as it is written here in these pages because when you learn to use me correctly, that is when this life filled space of yours will start to regain her former glory.

love

A Dedication to Love …

MESSAGE:

Let's consider now what some speak of as an energy dilemma. Right now this subject seems to be at the centre of your universe, and the question is what must be done to take an energy source and make it permanent. And how can this be done without further destroying the planet's atmosphere? Today, what you have is a finite supply of diminishing fuel resources with little by way of new ideas to produce a much bigger capacity in this vein. Of course, you do have movements toward alternative energy capabilities, but these do not yet meet your present-day needs, let alone what you will want for the future. In years to come, you will have new dreams to dream and they are going to need energy to power them. But for now, you have nothing certain to go on moving forward in this aspect of your lives. Nothing new has come along that would seem to offer any degree of staying power. New ideas are out there, but they do not yet give you what is needed to power the complexity of the world as you grow into the future.

So what now must you do? Do you reside in a thought that says fossil fuels are the best option because they are easy and because you know only so much about new opportunities that have yet to be fully explored? This attitude is understandable because all the structures are in place to keep this movement in motion. If, however, you can begin to think of what life will next need to be for you all in your futures together, then you will see that you are going to require an alternative source of energy that will forevermore be there for you. But in order to make that your reality, you are going to have to bring forth an entirely new dimension to human thought that limits nothing— meaning that whatever you need going forward will be there for you as a possibility.

This is a style of thinking the human race hasn't yet mastered to this point. But given time to learn the idiosyncrasies of this, you all can come to trust in this way of thinking, and then you'll be on your way, moving full circle into the correct solutions you could never come to before with regard to this energy dilemma. And these will be much greater in terms of their capacities and more complete of purpose too because they will meet everyone's needs and concerns equally, including those of the planet itself.

So when it comes to your energy needs, trust in the thinking powers of the human race going forward. Have faith that there will be something new to replace what is lost by way of an energy supply. Something down the road may not be known or seen right now, but it can be there for you, if and only if you are proactive in that thought now and give it a space inside your brains to develop. Then given the proper timing, life will begin to shift and adjust to allow for new discoveries to be made that will move your energy supplies to a place of certain certainty for you all—with an alternative source of energy that will forevermore be there for you.

In the meantime, there must be a concerted effort to correct what is now felt to be a fault in the present energy systems. You have for some time now been trying to change the negative effects of your energy consumption with little progress. What I am referring to here is the global climate change crisis that addresses the rising world temperatures and the melting of the polar ice caps, which have for centuries sustained your very lives. You now have a short timeline to correct this, and so what must you do?

Do you simply resign yourselves to the notion that you are fine going forward with limited concern or do you create a new possibility that gives the human race a way out of this global warming dilemma? You now are finally seeing that the problem here is immense and may become simply too big to solve going forward. I can also see, however, a willingness in you now to try and fix it—to try and stop this movement and turn it in the opposite direction.

love

It is our belief that the warming of the planet's changing atmosphere is going to require from all of us now, a true dedication to the cause of *Love* and its overwhelming desire to help us in all of this. In our minds, nothing more and nothing less than this will do. We believe there can be no other way to curb this issue other than to reside within a pure *Love* mentality and there start to imagine a world without this concern in it any longer. The message *Love* has to share with us today is that there is no one single thing that exists here that can stop the gradual progression of the sun's warming of the earth's surface ... except this most amazing thing called love.

MESSAGE:

While there are those who feel this warming issue is a natural event outside of your control, the fate of this planet's space will be determined by you and no one else. You have made it to be the way it is today, and you are destroying its very essence. Now why are you doing this? The answer is that you needed to know who you are, and in order to do that there had to be this eventual decline. There had to be this desperation in so many ways, just so you all would *WAKE UP* to the understanding that who you are is much greater than who you think you are—and that if you open to this now, you can turn the plight of this planet around.

Today the answer to global warming is just this: it is a way to see life more clearly, but on a massive scale. And today people are waking up to that fact. They are taking notice that this now is a huge concern, and they want to feel that this is not going to be the end of them. They are enlivened to the thought that they must begin the process of change to end this scourge by thinking together as a unit of one—about the world as a whole.

To that I say, this is exactly where you need to be—thinking about the whole of life but now using me as your guide. That's the key here. You, the human race, are not to feel that you are alone in this venture but that you have the highest influence ever produced, there inside each of you, to correct this now. If you don't get that one central theme right, then you are stopped before you even begin. You must trust now that together, you and I can rebuild anything we choose to rebuild because if that trust is there, then everything will begin to correct itself—including that of global warming.

Today I see you pray for your lives and the lives of your loved ones to get better, and you think that if I am there for you, maybe some sort of miracle might occur. But this is what this line of thinking does. It perpetuates your existence in the fear that the miracle may never come—that throughout your time on this planet, events in your world will not work to your favour. And on and on it goes for you, thinking in the direction of trust for the holy spirit of me to come to the rescue of your overwhelming plight in this world. But guess what? It doesn't come. Why? Because you hold fear in place of mustering up the courage to jump off the bridge of pure faith building with me and seize what is to be your next, newest destiny inside the richness of love.

The truth is that I have solutions for you, many solutions that would have changed the living dynamics of this world long ago. But people changed the plan they came with and shortened their time here on this planet. As a result, we see here today the depletion of the world's vital resources that are needed for your survival and now the number one killer of this planet, global warming. These, in the end, were the sacrifices the people of this world were willing to make; yet you didn't understand the consequence of these movements. And now, your world is out of time and has no room for more of this kind of neglect. It needs your help to even begin the process of healing. I can no longer continue to make these changes you have made work for you when you consider the negative circumstances that occur from this.

What is here today was never the original plan—to take away the most vital aspects of life only to leave you all to fend for yourselves. No, this was to be a space of life that would be revered by its holders; loved by its occupants; and most of all talked about as that of a living space that would bring to you all those hopes and dreams you live for in the first place. But now everywhere you look, the world is spinning out of control with no clear direction to move along that would otherwise bring resolution to everything that ails you. And the truth is that you are in no position to fix all of this without the real and stable guidance of love—and not just any love. What I am referring to is my love and my true and very "real to this life" guidance that will serve to move this planet to new heights of success.

So take the time now to walk through the negative effects that are out there in your world today, and then ask yourself if there is a better way to live than this. Ask yourself if your life now can symbolize love as the overall basis for understanding this world. If you can be this, and if you can think your way into your new future together with me, then you and I can begin to turn this planet around … before it is too late!

love

It was disconcerting to think what this could mean, and so we asked the question, "Why don't you just help us create some amazing miracles right now by giving us the solution to the water dilemma, cancer, or global warming? You give us the answers and then we take them to the appropriate people who will know what to do with them. Then we tackle a few more problems and so on and so forth. After all, you know what the answers are. You can help us in a big way right now. Why not do it?"

MESSAGE:

The question is real enough, and it seems to be a good starting place. However, here lies the truth. You two cannot save this planet all on your own because then billions of souls would be wanting to get in touch with you instead of getting in touch with their own inner self—me. You see, this movement is not to be about any one person or two but rather about who will come to me in their darkest hour. I know that sounds like a cop-out, but it's true. People will not listen to me if they think someone else is going to do it for them. They will just as soon listen to me as fly to the moon, and that is not what is needed here. No, you are to be just two people who found a way to tap into me and make miracles happen, and now you want to help the rest of the world do the same.

So to all of you who are reading these pages, listen carefully now. There are a million reasons why your world is what it is today, but the time has come for you all to think differently about how you next wish to play at life, given the facts before you. Your human base of thinking is now flawed and needs to be adjusted, and the way you do that is by building faith in the nature of love rather than building concern that all is lost. Concern is not a love modality but rather a limited thought structure. But, on the other hand, love is what will turn on the engines of change to positively affect the outer world for billions of people. It will make a huge difference to all of your lives when it comes to this warming issue, especially when you consider the negative pathway some regions have gone down to bring to their people a new and modern perspective of life.

In this vein, I would suggest establishing global think tanks—places of deep concern for the planet where the energies of a newly formed love would be founded en masse. Here, the agendas would be all about the betterment of life as a whole, and nothing would be overlooked. These factories of truth so strong and so powerful would allow for the biggest expansion to new love there ever was or will be. There would be new positive constructs literally pouring out from beneath the thought structures of everyone there, to bring forward a practical approach to resolving concern after concern throughout the planet … using love.

And what will make these think tanks different than others that now exist to this planet is their vital linkage to me, which means that there will be clarity of purpose and a singular goal to create progressive movements that will be exponential throughout the planet. Discussions would be completely and utterly inclusive of everyone, so much so that there would not be any room for controversy. Thinking that did not address the needs of the whole would not even arise there to protect the interests of some. There simply would be no allowance for that to even take place.

Within the field of scientific research, scientists there will be able to masterfully reconstruct aspects of their studies that simply were not working. With the establishment of these think tanks with me alongside them all, they will come to know things and produce things that would never come into their minds before. They will find new ways to source cures for a myriad of negative health effects that now plague humankind because I will be there to help them make certain they do not stray too far from the point they are moving towards. Through their connections to me, they will have what they need and want. And all they will have to do is think it there and then be active in the knowing that our two way channel of communication is working but in ways that will eliminate the need to go down certain rabbit holes of study that were not at all where they were needing to go. I shall eliminate those holes by showing to them which turn to take and when.

Today this style of introspection is needed in almost every discipline in life, and the think tanks will be where this takes place—where every worldly concern will be thought of as a living possibility that is yet to be recognized in human societies around the globe. So watch for this, want for this, and I will respond to you all in kind. Mark my words.

And furthermore, in support of these movements into a new love based society, I would propose that Centres of Hope be situated throughout the world that will serve as places of deep concern for the lives of people residing in those regions. But these would not be like places of worship that now exist everywhere around the planet and do now serve a greater good, for sure. Rather these would be centres where people could come to mingle together to find out who is in the deepest need, so that those who are ready to help can be mobilized into action—to go out to a world of folks and help them make their lives better in many ways. And of course, as a group, they would be using the true power of love to connect to me so that they are clear why they are moving in certain directions. That way there will be no indecision placed there.

The main thrust here will be to bolster up the minds of millions of people who do not have the will to live on the edge of life, engaged to everything new in their lives like it is suggested in this book. They will need help where this book's messages leave off. And so you have these Centres of Hope moving mountains of concerns literally out of their way so that their engagement to a life of passion will slowly come to be … their next newest reality. Once they can feel the passions of a world of people around them working together with me, the pull of love will, quite simply, become too intoxicating for them to ignore.

People will feel that there is something different taking place at these centres. In their curiosity, they will want to come and see miracles at work each day, flowing new love towards individuals and societies that have nothing. They will be encouraged to do more to help and to learn about the specifics of these movements—how they worked and why they were so successful when others outside of these Centres of Hope … were not.

The key here is that folks will not feel they are on their own trying to better their lives because they will know that I am there to help them get to that place of certainty that wasn't possible before. I will be the one taking them out of relative obscurity in their thinking patterns so that they will understand with perfect clarity that *THEY ARE NOT ALONE* and that their connection to me always now will be paramount to every decisive movement they will make.

As well, to assist people, there will be a kind of teaching structure attached to the centres. This will help to reinforce new ideals that will serve as a constant reminder to people that who they are as a society is not yet there, and that their initial movements, while good in the moment, can be made better— constantly better. The centres, therefore, will become a constant support to this search for love we all so desperately need to be on. They will be the true beacons of hope throughout the world where lost souls can go to feel support, encouragement, and most of all hope for a world that today doesn't seem to have enough answers to this world's concerns.

For centuries now, humanity has been trying to open their brains to a new reality of the magnitude I am speaking to here, but there has been an overall attitude that has resisted change by maintaining that everything is fine and that change would only cause havoc. As a result, the human race has done little to embrace this newness that would move you beyond your early beginnings on this planet.

Now, however, is different because now we are in a hurry to make the necessary adjustments. And to do that, we are going to need a universal recognition of a unifying message that says, we are all in this together now and we are going to pull together and change everything for the better. We are going to engage our minds in this most amazing process of growth in the true nature of love, to therefore speak from one mouth … from one mind … and from one understanding that says, we have one new beginning here that can play out in perfect harmony to the whole. We only need to think cooperatively now into a space of pure love that will perpetuate life for the planet and give us all a new way to be together … and forevermore grateful for this togetherness.

CHAPTER 10

THE CREATION OF
A NEW WORLD

The Building Block Principles ...

We were coming to a point in our discussions with *Love* when it was becoming more and more apparent that we needed some sort of starting position that would give all of us a way to think about our new future together. Certainly by this time, we had developed a tremendous respect for what this intelligence of *Love* was trying to convey to us, and so we asked the question, "How can this world begin the process to start over?"

MESSAGE:

In order to begin your new world movement, you need to think of me as someone who wants what you need and want but without the drive to see that happen. You must do that part. *YOU MUST HOLD THE DRIVE TO BECOME SOMEONE NEW, AND YOU MUST BE THE ONE WHO DECIDES YOU WANT MORE FOR YOUR LIFE.* Then, once you have made that commitment, I can and will play the role of chief provider to all of your grandest dreams.

So with this fundamental starting position in mind, begin to imagine a new world order and describe to me in the best way you can, just how that all would look. Be specific in your overall assessment of this. Be fearlessly invested in how life could be better, given all that you now know about me and how I work. And don't stop there either. Challenge my assertions. Be totally devoted to the task knowing that you are building from the ground up, your new world—your new life to come. See it in your minds fully working in real life terms, and never give up on this because after all, life wasn't built in just one day. It took centuries upon centuries to make even a modicum of movement toward love like it is written about in this book. But now is your chance to take what exists today and turn it into something entirely new and most wonderful. Now is your chance to make a life work from scratch, and if that is the case, then how would your life—your new and most powerful life—be created?

This is a way of activating a thinking capability in you that will allow for the greatest expansion of love to begin. It is a space of the mind where few today even try to enter, but here is your opportunity to go there now and imagine life as a far more perfect place to live in. No one would be angry; no one would be resentful; and most of all no one would ever want to leave this place because it would show such promise and intrigue for the human race, but now in a way that would forevermore be complete to the purpose of having life in the first place.

So to begin, just wipe your mind clean of any and all earthly bias and set your sights on perfection in this world. Start to imagine your new structures of life just the same way I did when you, the human race, were born into this world. Then you might just have this one last chance to get it right.

Starting from scratch is your best way to begin to think about a new fundamental starting position, rather than starting from the basis of what exists today. When you start with a blank slate sitting before your eyes, you are more likely to go in the direction of goodness and mercy for all rather than the opposite of that, don't you think? Right now, I see a world of folks who all want something better for their lives, but when they look out to this world, they don't even know where to begin given all the discouraging ways that are out there. And humankind, for centuries, has been in no position to challenge the status quo because of one constraint or another.

Now, however, your commitment will be there to alter what is not working for you—using me. And you will ask why now? Why was this not here before? The answer is this: my connection to the human mind was simply too weak to be recognized as anything consequential or truly meaningful. As well, the world was not advanced enough to even contemplate that anything on such a grand scale as this was even possible. Changing life in such a monumental way would not have entered the minds of people even as recent as twenty-five years ago because life was not as connected up as it is today with the likes of the internet and cell phones. But now the time is ripe to move toward a set of starting block principles that will set the new standards to live by forever:

1. We Begin with Love as Our Starting Position to Make Sense of Life

    Every man, woman, and child on this planet has a preconceived notion to want to know more about this life and move in those directions of "moreness." And when you fully examine the reasons why you all want more for yourselves, you come to the conclusion that many in this world have already come to, and it is that ... you want to love this life first and foremost. You want to love the experiences you are creating, be it taking out the garbage at night or sailing around the oceans of this planet. But if it is that you cannot ever have that feeling, if you cannot in your own unique way generate those feelings of love, then your life might just as well be over.

What you come to realize in the course of your lives is that love, in one form or another, is at the base of every feeling you experience. Therefore, it must be first on the list of priorities to consider when it comes to "a true living standard for life," and the moment you come to realize this one simple fact, I am sure you will say, "Yes, this feels correct!"

It just makes sense that your lives have to be predicated on the basis of something, and I can see no better a basis for your lives than love, the form of which doesn't even matter. This, in fact, was my starting position with you as I went about formulating my opinions of how this life you were to have, could work. I first thought of love as the foundation to everything, and there was never a time when I strayed from this basic starting position simply because I could never see an alternative to this. Love was the single most powerful connection to this life that I could see working in tandem to me. Since the beginning of your time here, it has been the central theme to everything that exists here—the guiding principle through which all things could be measured. So if you ask me the question as to whether a world could exist, truly exist without love, my answer to this is *NO! NOT IN A WILD MOMENT WOULD IT BE THE CASE THAT SOMEONE WOULD CHOOSE LIFE WITHOUT FIRST EXAMINING IT THROUGH THE LENS OF LOVE.*

So this then is what you now can scratch on your palette of life to come—that no life's existence can be complete to its purpose without first there being love present in one form or another. In everything we do, we will ask, "Is it good for love or is it not?" In that way, we can begin to assemble a resonance of meaning going forward in our story of how a new life existence would be constructed.

2. We Set Forth and Multiply Our Existence

This means we strive to propagate our existence on the planet so that the human race does not disappear. This is a somewhat obvious point to make, but the issue here rests in the ways you are feeling about your life here. Is this existence to be something you need and want to have forever ... or is it to be less than that?

This aspect of your thinking is now at the forefront of everything you are doing today inside this reality. You and I are now trying to unleash the massive powers of your own inner love to save what this world has been to you all for many centuries. And it comes as no surprise to me that people have taken this for granted. But know this: this life you have is literally a miracle ... my miracle ... which was created for you to live in and experience the real richness of what it can be for you. And now I want to preserve its foundation and, in point of fact, grow it further so that this aspect of our strategy does not defeat us in the end.

3. We Live with the Aim to Get Along with One Another

We open to a new way to live in harmony with one another using this one noble cause to get us there—*TO CONTINUE LIFE ITSELF.* To my way of thinking, this would be the solution to solving what has been the Achilles' heel when it comes to living life together on this planet. We find a way to love one another through a common cause, and then we move forward into life with this forming the backdrop to everything we do.

I can tell you one thing for certain. If you don't get this one part right, you might just as well throw in the towels of life because it is going to take the combined help of everyone here working in unison with one another to change this world for the better. If you want to save this planet, then you must come back together in order to make that happen.

To begin the process, we open to the messages of the past that have failed us. These would be in the ways people have wandered off course and gone their own way, fully away from my loving touch because of one reason or another. As a result, we are talking here today about a crisis on this planet that one day will terminate its existence if you, the citizens of this planet, do not come together now to create a new society using this one central theme—to continue life.

It's just like when people gather together to take away the pain of a young child when his or her life is at risk with an incurable disease. The pain of that child and the pain of those surrounding that child's life is great. That pain becomes the central focus of all concerned. It is the constant that makes everyone sit up, take notice, and in some unique way try to play a part in releasing that child from his or her plight. Be that through prayer or by actively searching for a cure, everyone will want to help this concern go away. And their efforts will only intensify as the plight of the young child grows stronger. Those involved will do anything they can to help because they simply do not wish to see a life ... expire.

Sound familiar? When you challenge life over death, people will want life to continue no matter how difficult it may seem to get them there. They will see this as a cause they will want to play a part in, and so they will free their minds from an old paradigm that speaks to separatism. They will come to the realization that working together for the cause of life is the only way to make sense of this world's growth into love ... like it is written here in these pages.

4. We Speak of a World of Innocence Where No One Gets Left Behind

Imagine a world upon which our life of togetherness is founded. Imagine a world where everyone is considered well before any major move is contemplated. This would be a life complete to its purpose because the consideration of the whole would always be at play. No one would be left at a disadvantage because of our actions and no one would be in a position of "lessness" because we did not consider their plight.

This is a standard for life that will forevermore pay huge dividends in the expansion of love in our lives, and once we get to know how powerful this can be for the human psyche, we will never look the other way again. We will want to be the first in line to help whomever it is that has been disadvantaged by the actions of our past.

5. We "Perceive" Life through a Lens of Wisdom

We will see life through a different lens and through a different wisdom than in our past in order to take that next logical step into our future. Simply put, we will carry the awareness of the presence of love in everything we see and do. It's just like when you drink a glass of milk and you feel the greatness of that milk's value to your overall well-being. This is how we will perceive everything in our world because everything will hold a much greater meaning. We will ask ourselves, "Are we seeing life like we should be seeing it?" And if we are, then everything will seem like a miracle to behold. We will look at friendships and work habits differently. Everything in our lives will start to resemble a form that was not present in the past, when the ways we were thinking literally starved away the very meaning of what this life was meant to be.

6. We Speak to a World with an Unseen Driver

I am this unseen driver of love within each of you, and I only wish to be of assistance to everyone here and never exert my authority over you. I have what I like to call "the humble key to success." I never try to take away from your life. I always wish to add to it. As that is, I can tell you that if I was in charge of all things in this world, I would not have let this planet's life go this far before stopping the mismanagement that has occurred over all these many years. But I was never in charge of your lives in a way where you would somehow be micro-managed by me. I gave that power to you and you alone.

Now, however, this life has a principle to live by that needs to come forth and multiply its existence because now your world is in trouble. It is in desperate need of a central driver to maintain a sense of stability over this life and make certain of your lives here. But this is going to require a will and a determination in you to see life now as a kind of magical formula built out of a basic principle that I do exist … that the central driver I am referring to is me and my direct love for you.

This world, you see, was not built from the ground up with only a whim and a prayer. It was not made by simple organ multiplication nor was it built from a fabricated set of principles based on loving constructs that can do nothing to get you there, into that new and wonderful space you so richly deserve to be in. No, life was created out of a love that would move into this life existence and then build from the centre of a desire in humanity to see more love from what this life can provide. Nothing more and nothing less was the reason for life to exist.

And through it all, I came to be the stabilizing influence and the "manifester" of life for you here. I was the inner driver linking you to the subtle messages that you would need in order that you did not stray too far from the overall purpose of your existence. I was the one who would pull you away from any present danger; connect you up to new possibilities; and take you to new heights of understanding of who you next wanted to be in life. Can you see where this is heading? You are becoming that which you are not, because of me and me alone. I am the central driver, and without me your life would become a constant struggle to even get by. A world without me to guide it wouldn't even compare to a world in need of my love, my care, and my concern. Why? Because beneath every good and wonderful idea there is an equal and opposite situation that could occur if you take the wrong step. Now does this sound familiar? Doesn't this represent the world that you have here? And doesn't this represent the margins of error this world of folks are falling into every day it seems?

Now in contrast, imagine a life with me as your central driver. Imagine a life where our connection is paramount to everything you do. I tell you this: if there is a connection to be made on this planet ... then this is it, mark my words. If there is a way to make peace in this world ... this is how you will do it. If you can think of a better way to live on this planet ... then this would be the one.

Therefore, it would only make sense to include me in the mix when considering our new principles of life.

love

A Call to Positive Thinkers ...

As we began to think about our next move in life, we became increasingly concerned about who would want to help us and why they would even want to move from where they sit today. After all, there most likely are many people in this world who would certainly be in complete opposition to any thrust that might upset the status quo.

MESSAGE:

Today sprinkled around the world, there are thousands upon thousands of positive thinkers—people who have come here to propagate their craft and do good things for this world. They each in their own unique way are trying to set new standards to live by in societies all around the globe. But in one most important way, they are lacking one critical element to their thinking patterns and that would be the extent of my loving powers of influence, which far exceed what people have perceived for centuries now—in the mainstream of their thinking.

Today you, the people of this planet, are going to require my help to a much greater degree than ever before because you no longer will be able to connect the dots about why life has become so depleted and how your lives have given over to any number of negative consequences. Nor will the great thinkers of this planet be able to think their way past basic principles about life that are now in desperate need of adjustment—principles that for far too long now have been resting on the laurels of the past. This planet and all of her concerns has now moved well beyond anything the human race alone will be able to come to in order to correct all of this.

Today there are simply too many negatives coming into this world, and we need to stop them in their tracks ... now! It's everything from depletion of the rain forests to the massive injustices going on in the ways people are choosing to organize their lives. They are living according to outdated principles and have given over to dismay and mistrust on almost every front. In contrast, however, I can feel in people a deep burning desire to move in massive new and progressive ways—ways that will serve to open up the portals of creationism, so that their life's existence does not wander too far apart from their basic needs going forward.

Therefore, once again I am asking you for your overall help. I know who you are and I know you have what is needed to take the next leap forward for humanity's sake. You will be the ones who will set the living standards of this world, if you choose this now. And it won't stop there for you either. You will form the basis of everything I speak to by illuminating to this world of folks, just what is going to be required from them to move this renewed field of confidence forward.

You know who you are. I can feel your pulse moving as you read these words, and I think you will come to me and listen to what I have to share with you. So get ready to think more deeply about your world. Get ready to make it sing with excitement for what it can be now. And most of all get ready to make this life's purpose you have come here to live, become your next newest reality because this world—this most amazing world—is in desperate need of this from you.

I know you can do this, and I feel you here, all of you, with such enthusiasm and excitement for your world. But please trust me when I say to you that your love for this place of life is what is most important, and if you can feel this now … if you can trust in me now … I will forever be grateful for your kindness and mercy that you will be giving selflessly to this planet and all of her inhabitants.

love

CHAPTER 11

THE BEGINNING

Life … is waiting to begin again. It is waiting to become something new and something very different for every man, woman, and child on the planet; and the time is drawing near when we will be required to make the choice as to whether we want that new beginning to begin. We must ask ourselves now how far we want to go into this living structure that is life itself. Do we wish to stay in the darkness of what we have here today or do we want to push further into the new lightness of a world that can be so much more? The decision now is ours to make as to … who we next want to be.

MESSAGE:

This next space of life you are headed toward will define you all as citizens of this planet. It will determine whether you move toward or away from an overall goal to be alive to a world that has everything the human race will require to live on forever. And so you must think deeply about this. You must consider your lives on this planet and ask yourselves why you have chosen the paths you have chosen. Ask yourselves why you have not felt love in a more concrete way.

To date you have surely made certain strides toward thinking into a bigger picture of what life could be, but now it is clear that you must move far beyond these accomplishments.

You must move with haste to bring to your lives new things that will aid in your human evolution, so that you no longer will require, for instance, wars to settle disputes or human disease to make a point that your lives were not on the correct path in the first place. It is now your time to think into a new future and imagine a world where your ultimate goal is no longer just human survival but instead a true motivation to feel love inside each and every living vessel of human possibility.

With this style of thinking will come the beginning phase of your journey—the connective phase and the rethinking phase that at first everyone will need to progress into, if they choose to move in this direction. This will be the opening to a changing time, and for some it will be quite difficult because they will not at first trust in this. But for others, it will be like honey to a bee. They will instinctively grab hold of what they desperately now need and fully require. It will be something like a cleansing taking place within them whereby they let go of all negative thoughts and then enter into the slow process of turning their brains into a more influential space—a space that allows for everything from this point onward to be positive and expansive by its very nature.

Until now there has never been such an imaginary space to think into that gives the human intellect such freedom and such power. But today it can be there for you just as though it was an epiphany of sorts because, finally, you will be saying hello to a living organ of love inside you—one that knows no other way to live life but to live it on the edge, wanting to try at everything good without a care in the world. After all, why live in this existence if every turn is not an experiment for the betterment of your overall well-being? Why live if not for this?

Thinking into a space of pure love can now be the mantra of the century, if you so choose, and everyone can participate in this. Everyone can play a role in fixing what is desperately in need of fixing instead of succumbing to constant messages that say you need do nothing to make your lives better. Not just a select few but every last person can now take part in what could be the most profound transformation ever played out on the planet; and the moment you start, it will seem like you've hit the ground running with a smile from ear to ear. It will be as though a movement was beginning all over the globe—an underground movement that will symbolize a way to turn on the engines of a changing world inside the brains of literally billions of people, to thus ease the tensions of an uptight world and bring a new peace to what otherwise would be a tumultuous planet.

It all begins now inside every humble home with every last man, woman, and child wanting to be on the move within their brains, to learn and learn and never stop learning what it means to be a bigger love in the making. This is where your greatest challenge will lie as a human race—to never stop building those flows of love by learning more about what it means to have life now. It will seem as if humanity had suddenly turned on their awareness factor to see life in a different light, which is through an ever-widening space inside their minds instead of through an incomplete and limiting set of rules mass created out of a person's past. Now in your newness will come a perfect space within the human brain where you can begin to think about life in its infancy and about new things and how they will start to roll into this living structure we call life.

Remember, it's never too late to begin again, and again, and again. It's never too late to think about all the exciting possibilities, and there is never a better time than now to start. It always begins right now and always with the brainpower of pure love right beside yours. To date there have been a million reasons why the planet has arranged itself the way it has but none more compelling than to become love in its earliest beginnings. The love is why everything is here, and never will there be a greater story told than this.

Nothing, however, is to be overly complicated for you here. All you need to be doing is accepting the basic idea that I exist from within you for a greater purpose, and that is to symbolize a new way to think and a new way to organize life. And this is exactly what you and I are going to do, if you all choose to accept this direction. We are going to reorganize and reconstruct what you have here in this world into something far more powerful and engaging to the human mind.

I will be the living conduit to ignite the passions of this movement forward. I will be the friend that can make the difference now and the centring force that will represent a feeling of steadiness in you that is needed to rebuild this planet's space. And love—your love—will be the foundation upon which every piece of life will be built, but this time it will be rock solid. It will not give way to any form of fear or mistrust again. No, there will be no cracks in this armour of life this time around. The ground will not give way beneath your feet and let you fall because I will be the invincible force and the guiding force that holds the course straight for you and never leads you astray.

To you, it will seem as if a whole new world structure has landed in your laps whereby the world first thinks of love and then acts on those human instincts without the fear that things will not go well. It is a world that is miles away from anything you have known before, yet it can be here for you, if there is acceptance of these very vital points I am making in these pages. I believe that if people will just give these words a chance, you will have an opportunity to move this planet well beyond where it sits today. And in my mind, there is not a better time than now to do this. We can start the changes immediately and see progress begin in your day-to-day lives right away.

Certainly I can see no reason why you, the citizens of the planet, cannot transition this world into a newly formed measure of love that will give evidence to the fact that you need not limit yourselves any further; you need not suffer at the hands of anything; and you need not be complacent any longer. Instead you can play a vital and active role in reshaping this planet's future so that you all can rest in the knowing that your world will be okay and that your reason for living was not just to come here and struggle amidst the lost opportunities. Rather it was to relish everything you have here in this life and magnify those feelings of love that brought you here in the first place.

Since the beginning of your lives on this planet, there has been misunderstanding about how this life works and about who I am to you all. People have always felt that I was a god to be admired and revered and never to be at cross-purposes with. But this is where the world has misjudged me in a big way, and I now want to set the record straight once and for all.

I am never a vengeful god nor am I a god that forces my will on the masses. I am, however, a loving god who only wishes to play at life with all of you here and play with all the gusto and passion that a life can have. And so my promise to you today is that if you will give me this one last chance to make a better life for you here, I will go to work for you like never before. I will hold a passion and a will to make your lives spring open with possibilities that this world has never seen before. All I ask of you in return is that you choose to love one another because to love one another is why you are here in life in the first place. To love one another is to love me because I lie within each and every last one of you here ... equally. You are the basis for my existence in this life, and that knowing—that awareness in you—is all you will require to set this nation of men, women, and children on a pathway toward true greatness.

And so to this next moment of your life ... to the unborn child yet to come ... I say new times are coming to the planet. New life is about to begin with all of us here trying to see the lightness in what otherwise seems to be a dark and foreboding space that still knows little about a true love nature. In this lightness will come the correct flows of thought energy that have not been tampered with or adjusted to suit a select few. Now what you will witness is a new world emerging out from the old ways, and it will be something of a miracle to see. Everywhere there will be these marvelled discussions surrounding life that will build new positive constructs but without the base of concern that now permeates the globe. We will move away from earlier dogmas that share an inane principle of a world gone mad with fear, and we will replace those statements with an entirely new way to do business—by thinking more proactively into a true love nature.

These will be the new adjustments coming forth in everyone here, if you all will choose this direction, and it will take only a short period of time "to think into" this. It's just that simple. We spend a small amount of time thinking about who we next wish to be and where our next goals of earthly passion will take us, and then we'll be off and running with the knowing that all the answers will be there for us. The starting block principles will be in place, and from there we will move forth and multiply from a new foundation of human understanding that will sustain everyone's growth. Everyone will have what they need to move forth out of apathy and dismay.

This will be the new domain of perfection where we all can learn to prosper and grow. Our world's economies will be built around love, plain and simple, and the values of an old greed paradigm will no longer hold any water. From this point forward, our world will become a peaceful space in which to live, and the negativity we all are feeling will, simply put, fade away. It will vanish from our minds because we have love—love with a singular goal to be nurturing and kind and forevermore on the move to rebuild our living nations into a place of pure happiness for everyone, bar none.

And so young child yet to be, know this: your world, your newest of worlds is to be an amazing place to live in, and now we invite you to partake in its living structure. We invite you to be a vibrant lover of life who never leaves this space with resentment or sorrow but with a true amazement for what it held for you at every turn.

And for those who already are here today, I wish to say this: in the beginning of your lives on this planet you were in a position of not knowing, not understanding what this connection to me was all about and what it could do for you. And as time went on, it was this way for centuries upon centuries until this day, the day you have picked up this book and tried to understand once and for all that you have come here to this life with me in hand to be the living saviours of this planet. And not one of you is exempt from this! Not one!

So my dearest friends, be ready to accept this fact—that you are not who you think you are. You are different in that you have a living potential in you that far exceeds anything in the past you felt it to be. Now you have unlimited powers to turn this ship around and make this life you have and the lives of those still to come, better in incremental ways that have never been done here before. And this doesn't mean just a small bit of help to change life. It means a tremendous thrust by way of a knowledge seeking effort into all aspects of life that will serve to break the lock on everything good in this world—using the astounding influence of a love in you all that is yet to be tapped into.

So with great humility, I ask you all to come with me now. Be with me like it was the very last thing you would ever wish for because if you can do this, then everything in your life will change for the good. It will change because now I will come out from the darkness of your mind and open up the portals of truth to deliver to you everything you will need to progress to that next level of your overall humanness. Yes, this is your time for glory. This is your time for true greatness to become the story of you because you are the gifted ones who are going to take hold of what this space of life is all about and change it for all those still to come ... into a true heaven on earth.

This is your destiny now. This is what your world needs of you. It does not need your greed any longer or the kind of faith building that goes nowhere. It needs your concerted effort to try and make amends with this planet's space and set its course straight toward me. Nothing more and nothing less will be required of you in order to make your lives work for centuries to come—to bring change on a gargantuan scale that will serve to break apart all those insane ideals you carry that now pose a threat to you, the human race. Finally, this will do it. Finally, this new love on the rise within humanity will begin to tip the scales in the correct direction so that people all around the globe will start to reshape their lives for the betterment of humanity as a whole.

And now in closing, I implore you one last time to listen to these words, these most precious words that have been placed before you to help you feel the true brevity of the situation you all are facing today. This is not just a book of wishful thinking but rather a call to action for billions of you to open to me now like I was your best friend only wanting to help you recreate life into what it is not today. And it begins right here, right now, in this very moment you have chosen to pick up this book and learn what it truly does mean ... to know me.

LIFE IS WAITING TO BEGIN AGAIN.
WHAT WILL YOU CHOOSE?

love

Authors' Statement

As authors of this book, we would like you to feel that this connection to your higher self that we speak of in these pages is something very personal. Many of you, we believe, may no sooner want to open to this than fly to the moon. Nonetheless, what holds true for us throughout this book is all about a message from a loving God who only wishes to help us make our lives work on a much higher level of consciousness. We do know, however, that in this world a god is typically thought of as external to the body, and we have great respect for how people have perceived or want to perceive their god.

However, for us in the beginning of our explorations, we were coming from a blank slate, so to speak, and we didn't know what to expect. We had no idea that we could make this connection real in our lives, let alone begin to think of it … as God. But to this point, we now are convinced that this is the state of our lives here—that in some unique way we all live a double life in this sense and that our overall existence here has always had this distinction. And now, according to the words given to us from this loving intelligence, we can learn how to unleash this magnificent power and influence over our lives in a truly meaningful way that one could only dream about in the past.

We must tell you that the messages we have presented in this book are like nothing we have heard before, and this is why we felt compelled to come forward now and share with you how this all took place. But understand that we do not wish to upset the apple cart here with those who already are firmly rooted in another style of thought. We respect all of you equally, and we only wish to say that if these words create a pull to action in you, then please join us on a ride of a lifetime to learn more of the true magnitude and importance of this loving touch within us all, so that this window of opportunity we have now to save this planet ... is not missed.

The clock is ticking, however, and time we are told is not on our side. So to all of you who have picked up this book, we wish to say thank you for allowing us to move one step closer toward making this world a better place for the whole of life. To us, this is simply too important a story to be left on the sidelines, expecting that this world of ours is going to repair itself on its own. Life just doesn't seem to work that way. It, therefore, is our belief that if we are going to eliminate the negatives out there in the world today and foster a new progressive movement into love ... then this is how we'll do it.

Victoria and John Stewart reside in Canada where they have raised two sons and run several businesses. They each have been educated in their own discipline, John with a Master of Architecture degree from the University of Manitoba and Victoria with a Master of Arts degree in Environmental Economics from the University of Calgary. Most recently they have taken on a new thrust to explore the question of how humanity, as one nation of people, can begin to bridge the gap between the world we have today and the world we all want tomorrow. Most important to this cause has been their desire to see this world change for the betterment of humankind as a whole and to somehow play a role in what this could be. This has been the main determination in setting them on this path of exploration to find the answers that humanity has been searching for, for simply eons of time—answers that may well take us into a future we will all want to be in. So now it is with great hope for what this world can become inside a new state of human awareness that they present to you this book and the messages herein.

If you would like to follow us go to
www.profoundeffect.ca